Catholicism and Modernity

Also by James Hitchcock
   The Decline and Fall of Radical Catholicism
   The Recovery of the Sacred
   What Is Secular Humanism?

Catholicism and Modernity

CONFRONTATION OR CAPITULATION?

James Hitchcock

SERVANT BOOKS
Ann Arbor, Michigan

Hardcover edition originally published as
A Crossroad Book by The Seabury Press, New York.

This edition published by Servant Books, Box 8617, Ann Arbor, Michigan 48107.

83   84   85   86   87   88   10   9   8   7   6   5   4   3   2   1

ISBN 0-89283-179-0

Printed in the United States of America

Library of Congress Cataloging in Publication Data
Hitchcock, James.   Catholicism and modernity.
Bibliography: p. 248
1. Catholic Church — History — 1965-present
2. Catholic Church — Doctrinal and controversial works.   I. Title.
BX1390.H5   282'09'047   79-90   ISBN 0-89283-179-0

Grateful acknowledgment is made to the following publishers for permission to use the
material listed:
America Press, Inc., for excerpts from *The Documents of Vatican II*, edited by Walter M.
    Abbott, S.J. © 1966 by The American Press.
Harper & Row, Publishers, Inc., for specified excerpts from *Fellow Teachers* by Philip Rieff,
    copyright © 1972, 1973 by Philip Rieff; and for specified excerpts from *The Triumph of the
    Therapeutic* by Philip Rieff, copyright © 1966 by Philip Rieff. Used by permission of
    Harper & Row, Publishers, Inc.
J. B. Lippincott Company, for excerpts from *The Nuns* by Marcelle Bernstein. Copyright ©
    1976 by Marcelle Bernstein. Reprinted by permission.
Paulist Press, for excerpts from *Religion and Alienation* by Gregory Baum. Copyright © 1975
    by The Missionary Society of St. Paul the Apostle in the State of New York.
St. Mary's College Press, for excerpts from *God Present as Mystery* by James Ebner.
    Copyright 1976 by St. Mary's College Press.
The Thomas More Association, for excerpts from "Color It Black" by Kieran Quinn, in *On
    the Run: Spirituality for the 70s*, edited by Michael McCauley. Copyright © 1974 by the
    Thomas More Association.

For Helen

Contents

1 The Flight from Eternity 1
2 The Loss of History 15
3 The Imperial Self 31
4 The Sensation of Movement 58
5 The Illusion of Pluralism 74
6 The Triumph of Bureaucracy 96
7 The Road to Utopia 126
8 The Kingdom of Politics 150
9 The Coming World Religion 180
10 The Future of Roman Catholicism 216

Notes 233
Bibliography 248

CHAPTER 1

The Flight from Eternity

O NE of the great human mysteries of modern times is the amazingly swift process by which the Roman Catholic Church, apparently one of the most solid, self-confident, and enduring institutions in the history of the world, was plunged into an identity crisis of cosmic proportions. The crisis still goes on, with no satisfactory outcome yet in sight.

The media have, inevitably, bestowed great attention on this occurrence, which has proven simultaneously fascinating, titillating, gratifying, agonizing, humorous, tragic, depressing or instructive, depending on the mood of the onlooker. Such attention has been at best a mixed blessing.

Standard sociological theories have been put forward by way of explanation, all of them valid to greater or less degree. Most are a variation, in one way or another, on the thesis that, having deliberately insulated itself from modern culture for so long, the Church could not easily survive the opening of windows which the Second Vatican Council authorized. "Liberals" and "conservatives" are in large measure agreed on this fact; they disagree as to whether or not the windows should have been opened, and how far.

Such an explanation falls a good deal short of finality, however, because it fails to comprehend the exact nature of the crisis through which the Church is passing. It is a truism to say that long-cherished beliefs have been called into question, or that new and threatening ideas have entered the sacred portals. What, however, has been the exact nature of this challenge?

The answer to that question is perhaps best approached by noticing how the crisis developed and its exact locus. Immediately it becomes necessary to dispose of one common myth, that the crisis was somehow a democratic uprising from the pew, forcing the hierarchy of the Church to reconsider its doctrines. Anyone with even the most elementary acquaintance with sociological principles realizes at once how such an event could scarcely have occurred in the kind of society which was the Catholic Church of 1960.[1]

Instead the roots of the crisis must be located among the elite of the Church, including some lay people of advanced educational attainments, but mainly with the Church's official leadership, the anointed guardians of its laws and traditions—the clergy. It was a crisis which quickly spread beyond the priesthood as such and into the ranks of nuns, brothers, and seminarians. Only from these very strategic centers did it begin to permeate the Church at large.

The clerical crisis (using the term *clerical* as a convenient designation for both priests and religious) is very familiar in general outline, and this familiarity has tended to obscure a complete understanding. Church professionals, before the Council was barely over, began to show themselves restive under the kinds of discipline they were made to endure—anachronistic and confining clothing, petty and outmoded rules of conduct, pious practices left over from another age, authoritarian and frequently arbitrary superiors. Finally this restiveness reached the heart of the matter—the vow of chastity or the promise of celibacy and the very notion of lifelong, unbreakable commitment.

For a time the priesthood seemed almost fated to disappear, as thousands of men who had supposedly committed themselves for life gave up their offices and, usually, took wives. Nuns, who were if anything popularly regarded as even more exalted and sacrosanct than priests, appropriately went through an even more dramatic crisis, one which shows no sign of resolving itself short of the eventual disappearance of many existing communities of women. It was this dramatic story, shocking to anyone of authentically Catholic upbringing and literally unimaginable to many people, which served as the major catalyst, the central and very powerful negative symbol by which the laity too were drawn into the maelstrom of uncertainty. People who by habit and lack of education would have remained largely oblivious to new ideas could not ignore the dramatic evidence of the clerical identity crisis which reached into almost every parish and school.

Why, however, should rules and practices which were if anything less rigid than they had probably ever been in the history of the Church (certainly less rigid than in the nineteenth century), and of which few people complained prior to 1962, have suddenly become so irksome to so many? Why did the clerical crisis rapidly extend beyond the externals of religious life and lead to a questioning of that life at its very foundations? The Second Vatican Council is hardly an adequate explanation, since in this as in all things the Council offered judicious and moderate charters for the renewal of clerical and religious life, documents which seem in fact quite conservative by the standards of the 1970s.

The key to understanding this phenomenon lies in appreciating the fact that the mythical "modern man," still less perennial human nature, does not reject discipline and sacrifice, sometimes even of a quite arduous kind, completely and totally. In fact opportunities for such a life are frequently welcomed, especially by people who are disdainful of the traditional cloister.

The restiveness of the postconciliar Catholic religious cannot be understood merely in terms of the alleged "absurdity" or "inhumanity" of the consecrated life. Rather such a life, in all its manifestations, came to seem absurd, inhuman, and finally insupportable because so many of those immersed in it had ceased to believe, in any vital way, in its central rationale, the central purpose for which its disciplines were devised. Human beings find almost anything endurable, and can endure privations even with joy, if the underlying purpose for the self-denial is meaningful to them. It was the absence of this which plunged the Church's elite, specially formed corps of leaders into their postconciliar malaise.

The Second Vatican Council said of those in religious life that:

> . . . they have given answer to a divine call to live for God alone not only by dying to sin (cf. Rom. 6:11) but also by renouncing the world.

And of the Priesthood it said that:

> The ministerial priest, by the sacred power he enjoys, molds and rules the priestly people. Acting in the person of Christ, he brings about the Eucharistic Sacrifice, and offers it to God in the name of all the people.

The Council then went on to extol the appropriateness of celibacy to priests:

> By it they renounce the companionship of marriage for the sake of the kingdom of heaven (cf. Mt. 19:12); they devote themselves to the Lord with an undivided love which is profoundly proper to the new covenant; they bear witness to the state which the resurrection will bring about in the world to come (cf. Lk. 20:36); and they gain extremely appropriate help for exercising that perfect and unremitting love by which they can become all things to all men through their priestly ministration. May they deeply sense how gratefully this state deserves to be undertaken . . .[2]

It is not inaccurate to say that before the ink was even dry on the conciliar documents many priests and religious found these concepts troublesome and finally intolerable.

The Second Vatican Council was popularly understood, even by many well-informed people, as essentially a process by which the Church opened itself to "the world," and thereby chose to relegate the supernatural dimensions of life to the background. (Practically no advanced Catholic is now willing to write the word *supernatural* except in quotation marks, since its very existence has been rendered suspect.) Even the slightest familiarity with the nature of historical Catholicism reveals how improbable such a course would have been, and in fact the Council followed the time-honored Catholic path of emphasizing "both . . . and," the "vertical" and the "horizontal." The Council's openness to the world is well known. Less widely publicized are its equally characteristic statements:

> The People of God has no lasting city here below, but looks forward to one which is to come.

> Although the mystery of death utterly beggars the imagination, the Church has been taught by divine revelation, and herself firmly teaches, that man has been created by God for a blissful purpose beyond the reach of earthly misery.

> The Church truly knows that only God, whom she serves, meets the deepest longings of the human heart, which is never fully satisfied by what this world has to offer.

> Everyone should be persuaded that human life and the task of transmitting it are not realities bound up with this world alone. Hence they cannot be measured or perceived only in terms of it, but always have a bearing on the eternal destiny of men.[3]

Three of these passages are from the Council's allegedly most "revolutionary" document, *Gaudium et Spes*.

The Second Vatican Council, quite predictably, affirmed the classic Catholic notion of human life on earth as in tension between the natural and the supernatural, the eternal and the temporal, the material and the spiritual. There was even a reference to the Augustinian notion of citizenship in two cities.[4] The affirmation was not merely a mandatory nod towards tradition, however, for the history of the Church demonstrates abundantly that it is precisely in this tension that the most creative developments are generated; it has provided the energy by which the Church periodically renews itself. Alternatively, the loss of either side of this tension has often been the cause of heresy and debilitation.

The major thrust of much postconciliar "renewal" was precisely to relax this tension, however. The meaning of renewal was generally presented in terms of relaxation—the Church, which formerly "made" its members do many unpleasant things, was now giving them permission to live simple worldly lives. Thus disproportionate attention was paid to such things as the abolition of mandatory Friday abstinence or the simplification of the rules of convent life. Little effort was made to transmit, at the popular level, the authentic meaning of renewal in the Council's own terms.

Various factors conspired to abort genuine renewal: its systematic misrepresentation in the popular media, which influenced the clerical elite probably as much as the people in the pews; the fact that certain of the ideas of conciliar theology (cited above) are uncongenial and even incomprehensible to modern culture; sociological situations within clerical and religious life itself; and the influence of certain theologies, rightly or wrongly understood, which falsified what the Council had intended.

Not only did the number of converts to Rome decline precipitously after the Council, but the very phenomenon of conversion as classically understood—stretching all the way from St. Paul to the Second World War, and especially notable among intellectuals since the time of Romanticism—ceased to have any meaning. The classic conversion stories—Augustine, Newman, Maritain—all involved the sense by the convert that he was being summoned, even against his will; that what was chiefly required of him was a submission to which personal desires became irrelevant; that he must accept a way of life which was liberating at the deepest level but requiring sacrifices in its initial stages.

After the Council the characteristic story—recounted by the hundreds in the popular media—became that of deconversion. "How I Learned That What the Church Taught Me Wasn't True. How I Found Out I Didn't Have to Do Any of That Stuff. How I Was Duped and Misled. How I Regained Solidarity with the Human Race after My Sojourn in the Priesthood."

Rectories, convents, and monasteries were within a few years' time revealed to be filled with people who desired nothing so much as to lead ordinary lives as their culture understood the ordinary, who were weary of holding the world on their shoulders, who were shedding the burdens of specialness. First religious life, then the wider life of the Church, came to be characterized by a tired giving up, communal sighs of relief, the exuberance which comes from the relaxing of long-held tensions. There was an almost obsessive return to normalcy. A few highly publicized former religious did pursue, at least for a time, vocations which were perhaps more demanding, even more heroic, than the ones they had left. There is no reason to suppose, however, that the great majority of them sought anything other than a comfortable lay life.

A former Franciscan writes of his own vocational crisis:

> It appeared to me that the believer was caught in a schizoid existence, a double life, membership in two worlds, a secular and a religious one. . . .
>
> I began to ask whether or not a spiritual world existed. Perhaps the supernatural was a myth. . . . To me Christianity has meaning only insofar as it casts light upon my experience of life. . . .
>
> Monasticism appears to be an insidious heresy which negates the major consequences of the incarnation, namely, that the Christian finds salvation where he is and he is in the world. We are called to effect the kingdom of God in the world, not to create another one. . . .
>
> The pursuit of spirituality, apparently, requires us to take time out during the day and do something specifically religious, like make a retreat, attend devotions. . . . Incredibly, we've sold this monumental nonsense to generations of believers. It's time to stop. Fortunately, there is a new vision of Christianity on the horizon, one that will direct the believer's energies toward understanding through life in this world.
>
> . . . I think the direct pursuit of God is an illusion and a fairly common one. Of course, the human animal can believe and be convinced of absolutely anything. . . . I've abandoned all the old roadmaps to holiness, discarded the elaborate prescriptions for spirituality. My main business now is living, plain and simple. . . . My task, I see now, is one of becoming more human, not more spiritual. . . .[5]

Priesthood in the Church had always been regarded as an awesome responsibility, but insupportable only to those who did not fully believe Christ's promise that His yoke would be sweet and His burden light. Once, however, the central "other-worldly" meaning of the religious life had been obscured, once there was no longer an overwhelming core mystery which bathed all in its brightness, the conditions of that life came to seem almost wholly negative, the desire to shed its burdens virtually obsessive.

It was not merely the inconveniences of religious life—the possibly uncomfortable clothes, celibacy, obedience to rules—which understandably rankled. It was in fact the whole special character of the religious identity. The religious habit was discarded not simply because it was out of date or unfunctional but because of its symbolism, its marking the wearer as an ambassador of God to the world, a responsibility the wearer no longer wished to discharge. So also the decision by many vowed celibates to enter into marriage was not simply a concession to personal desire but a symbolic statement of immense importance. As one priest-psychologist noted:

Being apart—even being alone—have been celebrated as strengths of the priestly class in their work of standing somewhere between God and man. That is one of the reasons it has always generated a certain DeGaulle-like mystique, intimidating [*sic*] a private dimension of the priest's life through which he turns away from men in order to be more completely with God. Celibacy has always fascinated people because, although it may seem odd, it has also seemed challenging.[6]

Numerous priests and religious announced, during the postconciliar crisis, that they no longer wished to play a special role, that the burdens of living up to what the Church expected of them were now intolerable. Humanly such feelings were quite understandable. Yet unnoticed was an implication of the most profound theological significance—no longer was the religious vocation treated as a call from God that might or might not coincide with the individual's own wishes. The possibility that God might will certain people to assume tasks they would rather shirk was implicitly denied. The entire Judaeo-Christian understanding of the ways in which God deals with man was being silently rejected.

The political philosopher Eric Voegelin noted that within a mass church there are likely to be many "who do not have the spiritual stamina for the heroic adventure of soul that is Christianity." Instead of faith in its fullness they substitute "experiential alternatives, sufficiently close to the experience of faith that only a discerning eye would see the difference. . . ." And as a result, "the spiritual strength of the soul which in Christianity was devoted to sanctification of life could now be diverted into the more appealing, more tangible, and, above all, so much easier creation of the terrestrial paradise."[7] It was something very like this, something the character of modern Western culture rendered almost inevitable in the absence of rigorous safeguards, which swept over the Catholic Church following the Second Vatican Council.

It is tempting to judge, given the eerily swift collapse of so many religious communities and lay movements, as well as the personal religious unravelling of countless individuals, that the apparent strengths of preconciliar Catholicism were in fact illusory, that the seemingly solid piety of those days was deeply flawed. Such need not be the case, however, and it is inherently improbable that so many evidently dedicated and deeply pious individuals were living a kind of falsehood. Given the reality of human freedom, the Catholic Church has never had difficulty understanding the possibility of dramatic reversals in spiritual condition, either for good or for bad. As St. Teresa of Avila warned,

I tell you, daughters, I have known people of a very high degree of spirituality who have reached this state, and whom, not withstanding, the devil, with great subtlety and craft, has won back to himself. For this purpose he will marshal all the powers of hell, for, as I have often said, if he wins a single soul in this way he will win a whole multitude.[8]

It is revealing of the completeness of the intellectual revolution that has occurred that, although for many centuries this idea would have seemed commonplace and undeniable to anyone seeking to lead a truly Christian life, it is now likely to arouse either anger or amused condescension.

When some Catholics began insisting, after about 1965, that "there are no absolutes," they were usually referring to the laws of morality. Yet there was a perhaps unintended pun involved, because it was finally the denial of the Absolute, or more accurately the flight from it, which was the essence of the Catholic crisis. There could be, obviously, no questioning of the reality of God. Yet there was a notably diminished interest in God for His own sake, a willingness to think about God only insofar as He could be considered an immanent component of human existence. God, considered in and of Himself, was like a blinding light which blotted out every feature of the human landscape and on which human eyes could not gaze for long. To escape from that overwhelming presence, to diffuse that light into softened beams which did not hurt the eyes, became the aim of much of what passed for renewal. Sophisticated Christians of the 1960s insisted that they could no longer believe in a God "up there." But more was involved in this disclaimer than the mere rejection of a crude physical concept. The rejection of a God up there often meant the turning of one's back on the transcendent God altogether, a decision to deal with divinity only as it was mediated through the manageable channels of worldly existence.

Many Catholics of the postconciliar era were like concert-goers who had struggled for years, dutifully and piously, to penetrate the inner mysteries of Beethoven and Stravinsky, only to be told, finally, that their music was outdated and that Henry Mancini was indeed the truest representative of artistic profundity. The message, announced publicly by the very conductors and critics who had tried to instill a love for Beethoven, might at first be greeted with incredulity and resistance, but soon the sighs of relief, the comfortable settling back, could be heard from all over the concert hall.

Relatively few Catholics ever had the theological sophistication to appreciate deeply the central mysteries of their faith. But in its liturgy, its catechisms, its popular devotions, the Church conveyed to people a strong sense of a transcendent and absolute God, an awareness of mystery, a realization that they were a part of a great cosmic process which shaped and gave meaning to their lives at every point. Much of that awareness was lost after the Council, partly because the attempt to purify popular piety often killed it, partly because of the misguided attempt to impose, in the Council's name, an ascetic which was wholly immanent.

It was fitting, however, and probably inevitable, that the loss of contact with the transcendent realms, the headlong flight from the Absolute, should originate with those who had stormed the portals of heaven, sought the more perfect life, wrestled with the angel, before giving up in weariness.

The danger now is that having settled for a comfortably this-worldly religion, the religiously tone-deaf, as it were, will come to dominate the life of the Church. By a religious Gresham's Law it has proved easier to "sell" ersatz liturgies, theologies, and spiritualities with strong contemporary flavor than to initiate people into the profoundest mysteries of their faith. The force of earlier training is now the principal sustenance of a deeper kind of Catholicism, and in the nature of things this force is bound to diminish if it is not deliberately, and by set policy, reinforced.

Traditional Catholicism is variously patronized, derided, condemned, or ignored by self-consciously modern Christians, on the equally various grounds that it is outdated, narrow, inhuman, or incredible. Yet behind these sundry forms of rejection lies an unacknowledged fact: a firmly transcendental religion, a deeply held belief in the eternal God, is a constant threat to the humanistic Catholicism so skillfully fashioned in the past twenty years. To take seriously the Absolute, to endeavor sincerely to see all of life under the aspect of eternity, is to impose great inconveniences on the comfortable arrangements which advanced modern Christians have made with the world. Thus the priest or the nun is tolerable in his or her role as "minister," that is, as a professional specialist applying skills to the facilitation of community life. But the priest or the nun as representative of the sacred, as ambassador of God, cannot be tolerated. For the same reason not only are classic conversion stories no longer told, but those converts who entered the Church because they experienced the call of the absolute and unwavering God are sometimes the objects of hostility.

The "relevance" of Catholicism has always lain in its power, not its contemporaneity, that is, in its ability to communicate to the individual a sense of God's majesty and unchanging will, along with the concomitant promise of eternal life. It is this which is now, under the misnomer of "triumphalism," rejected by so many Churchmen who enjoy strategic influence. The Church's crisis is not primarily intellectual, as it is often stated, not primarily the question whether its doctrines are any longer credible. During the supposedly intellectually barren period between Modernism and the Second Vatican Council, the Church did not cease to attract or keep highly respectable individuals from the artistic and intellectual worlds—Maritain, Gilson, Claudel, Peguy, Waugh, Greene, Rouault, Mauriac, Marcel, and Chesterton, a few among the many, along with others like Bergson and Simone Weil who were attracted but never formally converted. There is no even remotely comparable record of distinguished adherents to liberal Protestantism, despite the most strenuous efforts to make Christianity intellectually respectable and up-to-date. The crisis of the Church is not primarily intellectual and probably never was. It is personal and spiritual, a crisis of fundamental self-understanding and will. It proceeds from the failure of nerve, not the perplexities of the intellect.

A characteristic strategy of the religious modernizers has been to assert that certain traditional beliefs had been overemphasized at the expense of certain others, a charge often enough true. In the process of "correcting" the mis-emphasis, however, the accepted belief was often disposed of completely, merely by virtue of ceasing to speak of it. In contemporary Catholicism perhaps no doctrine has suffered this fate more completely than the belief in life after death. Few indeed have denied it, or would do so. Many, however, have simply begun to act and speak as though it were not true; for practical purposes it has ceased to matter.

Yet historical Christianity makes quite clear that eternal life is not simply something added on at the end, a bonus given to faithful workers, but is central to belief in Jesus Christ. Thus on both theological and psychological levels the presence or absence of this belief cannot help but profoundly color all aspects of human existence. Belief in life after death is a threat to a determinedly this-worldly religion.

Thus the influential theologian Gregory Baum asks, "Why should a social thinker hold that death is the universal fact that has meaning apart from the social context in which it occurs?" In his opinion, death is dreadful only in an achievement-oriented society, and belief in personal immortality is unnecessary. He therefore concludes:

> . . . we claim that the church's teaching on eternal life is a revealed utopia. The message of the kingdom . . . proposes a vision of the future in which people live in justice and peace, conjoined in friendship and the common worship of the divine mystery.[9]

Langdon Gilkey, a Protestant theologian who gives avuncular advice to Roman Catholics, similarly proposes that:

> The goal of Christian faith, then, is not to transcend this life into another, by a sharing in the divine life that abrogates or absorbs natural life; for the perfection of nature is the sole value.

Quite logically, Gilkey therefore sees clerical celibacy as of doubtful value.[10]

Despite talk of a "pluralistic" Church, with many alternative theologies, those who have fully embraced a liberalized Christianity cannot in fact tolerate a staunchly other-worldly Catholicism because it calls into question the basic terms of their own revised faith. Traditional Catholics, for the same reason, cannot tolerate much of what calls itself renewal; but they never claimed to be pluralists. Thus a seminary professor says that:

> I cannot grasp how "man is rooted in a community of God's love" or what the "primal experience of being grasped by God" is about. "The transcendent openness to the indwelling Trinity" are only words to me. . . . I would never dare use this language in the pulpit or in talking to theology students.[11]

A staff member of the National Catholic Education Association, perusing a modern volume of lives of the saints, complains that they "often behaved in bizarre ways" and ends by urging that their examples not be followed. "For right now, if we must have models, let them be saints who are happy, healthy, and hopeful."[12]

Nowhere perhaps does the modern Catholic draw a stricter line between acceptable and unacceptable religion than over the matter of joy and hope (the title, in fact, of the Second Vatican Council's declaration on *The Church in the Modern World*). Yet in the process the nature of these things for the Christian is badly misunderstood. The "gloomy" saints of the Church's rich history demonstrate the true nature of Christian joy and hope and the fact that, ultimately, these are not dependent on happiness as the world understands happiness, nor are they necessarily manifested in ways which the world will immediately recognize. For Christians life has meaning beyond earthly disappointments. The perspective of eternity, if taken seriously, makes all the difference.

What is at stake here is not this world *versus* the next, human good *versus* the divine will, a mentality which sees the world as merely a vale of tears and nothing more. That way of seeing was indeed a kind of heresy, and one which the Second Vatican Council strove to overcome. True humanism is also being undermined by a shallow and too consciously "relevant" faith. Many Christians are deliberately choosing to live life on the surface, within a manageable range of religious experiences.

An exponent of the "new theology" explains:

> If we are attentive, we discover our graced moments. We say good-bye to grandmother—and suddenly we are somehow overwhelmed by the good-

ness of the universe. We sit on a rock watching the waves, impressed by something unending. . . . In our depths, then, we have hints of some ultimate, ungraspable and unnamed. Such experience leads us to faith but does not coerce us to say Yes. From the community's store of symbols we get the name "God" to indicate the experience.[13]

In the process of combatting the excessive rationalism and love of system which was characteristic of much older Catholic theology, an approach like this succeeds merely in trivializing the sacred mysteries, dissolving them in a bland stew palatable to any devotee of popular psychology. The Christian faith is made "relevant" at the cost of what it really has to say to the world. Its function is reduced to that of merely giving reinforcement to attitudes and ideas which certain segments of the population currently find meaningful. In doing this it is short-changing people even at the purely human level. (It is worth noticing that perhaps the great majority of influential modern poets, novelists, and philosophers of life would have to be dismissed as "gloomy" in accord with this particular version of Christian joy.)

The new "relevant" Christianity has won its place in contemporary culture through its promise to be unobtrusive and untroublesome so far as the demands of enlightened worldliness are concerned. The price it has paid for this acceptance has been the loss of its own power and authority, its capacity to inspire and to mediate God's life to man. For many people the fruits of a misconceived "renewal" would probably not be greatly different from those described by an editor of a Catholic publishing house:

I don't pray anymore. I've given it up for Lent. Also for Advent, and Pentecost.

My prayer life is a room with no furniture in it. Even the wallpaper is gone. I don't go there.

In church, when I attend . . . I sit now waiting for something to happen, but nothing ever does. Who are these people around me? . . .

Occasionally I'm asked to say grace before meals. . . . What words can I use? How can I maintain, without lying, that God has a hand in the meal? . . .

Somewhere, it seems, in the last decade or so, all the lines went dead. Words became deflated, flat. Hands once raised in gestures of benediction fell flaccid and powerless. . . .[14]

A black priest, describing the "fantastic leakage" out of the Church of previous black converts, says that "it wasn't so much racism that turned them off, it was change. They joined the Church because it seemed a stable, timeless rock in a swirling sea. Suddenly the old traditions, including the Latin liturgy, vanished. The anchor was gone."[15]

Accepting the inevitable strictures against a religion which is merely an escape from life, it is nonetheless true that the image of the Church as a "stable, timeless rock in a swirling sea" would have seemed perfectly appropriate to all the generations of Catholics down to the 1960s. The meaningfulness of faith is intimately related to a permanent sense, on some level of being, of man's ineradicable alienation and dissatisfaction in the midst of life. It is also intimately related to the belief that fundamental choices have to be made, and made every day, which affect one's eternal destiny. The early Catholic novels of Graham Greene, for example, or virtually the entire corpus of François Mauriac's work are now literally incomprehensible to many Catholics, because for them there is no real possibility of damnation; the very term has no meaning.

In seeking to make faith relevant and comfortable, within the confines of contemporary Western culture, many reformers have robbed it of even the possibility of grandeur. Recent reforms—in catechetics, in moral theology, in religious life, above all in liturgy—seem designed to prevent the very possibility of such a thing. The Catholic imagination is now thoroughly impoverished and expresses itself only in banalities. One of its greatest failures is precisely its inability to imagine the prospect of eternal life. Converts have been attracted to the Church not because they found there a warm human community (often they did not) but because they believed that what the Church taught was true, that it had the words of eternal life. Thus in making Catholicism more relevant on one level, these reformers succeeded in robbing it of its true relevance on a deeper level. The Church loses credibility not because it insists on teaching "outmoded" doctrines but because it lacks the courage to continue teaching what it knows to be true.

The justification for this state of affairs is often to say that faith in traditional doctrines had already badly eroded before *aggiornamento* and that the Church had been expounding teachings which many people no longer believed. There was, however, little measurable evidence of this before the Council, and as the "new theology" began to find its way into catechisms and Sunday sermons the shock and bewilderment of many Catholics seemed to demonstrate something less than a sense of welcome acceptance. The revolution in belief, to the extent that it has occurred, was an emanation from an elite center, the use of authority to undermine authority.

The 1960s may have been a secular time, but the 1970s proved to be a religious tropical jungle, overflowing with every kind of exotic sect. No belief—astrology, witchcraft, faith-healing, reincarnation—was too old-fashioned, too supernaturalistic, too unscientific to be taken seriously by sometimes quite sophisticated people. Having primly vowed not to cater to "outmoded" religious needs, Catholic spiritual teachers left the field largely open to charlatans and eccentric enthusiasts. The mainstream of Christian spirituality was blocked up at precisely the moment when it might have offered refreshment to many thirsty souls.

Until the time of the Council the tide seemed to be running in favor of the hierarchical, ritualistic, dogmatic churches. Roman Catholicism and High Church Anglicanism seemed to be almost the only faiths which thoughtful nonbelievers could take seriously. (Besides the numerous intellectual converts to Rome, Canterbury attracted men like Eliot, Auden, and C. S. Lewis.) In recent years, however, it has been the religions which can broadly be called "enthusiastic" (not necessarily in a pejorative sense) which have retained vitality and attractiveness. It is a judgment on the architects of renewal that none of them even dimly foresaw the emergence of the charismatic movement as the single greatest religious phenomenon of the postconciliar era. That movement, with all the uncritical allegiances and hostile criticisms which it inspires, is, in terms of the familiar colloquialism, the only game in town. It is a standing rebuke to the process of Catholic renewal because it alone has seemed able to speak to the spiritual needs of large numbers of people at a time when a good part of the Church's leadership seems determined not even to acknowledge that such needs exist. Much attention has been paid recently to the needs of the elderly, for example. Yet how many of those now involved in that ministry are able with full conviction to remind such people of Christ's promise of eternal life to those who believe in Him? In practice the Last Anointing has been so reinterpreted for use with the sick that the Church is in danger of losing any ritual appropriate to preparing people for death. For many of the clergy who watch at deathbeds it must now be the case that death is merely the doorway to the Great Unknown.

The Catholic crisis has been dissipation in the literal sense—the center has disintegrated, and the parts fly off in all directions.

CHAPTER 2

The Loss of History

A phenomenological investigation of the Roman Catholic Church would inevitably yield the conclusion that, throughout its history, the Church has demonstrated extraordinarily high regard for the authority of tradition. Indeed, among the institutions of the modern Western world, there has probably been none so respectful of the past, and of its own organic development. The Second Vatican Council strongly reaffirmed this:

> Among those various ministries which, as tradition witnesses, were exercised in the Church from the earliest times, the chief place belongs to the office of those who, appointed to the episcopate in a sequence running back to the beginning, are the ones who pass on the apostolic seed.

> Consequently, it is not from sacred Scripture alone that the Church draws her certainty about everything which has been revealed. Therefore both sacred tradition and sacred Scripture are to be accepted and venerated with the same sense of devotion and reverence.[1]

In the postconciliar period the dimming of the sense of eternity, of the Church as mediator between two worlds, was paralleled by a drifting away from many of these traditions—in doctrine, in liturgy, in morality, in structure because they were irreformably predicated upon belief in the Church as a supernatural institution. Reformers who began with the intention of remaining respectful of the past soon found this impossible, given their belief in the essentially temporal mission of the Church; the traditions could scarcely bear such reinterpretation without violence to their fabric. Conversely, the lessening of the authority of the traditions also meant that the eternal dimension of the Church became less and less intelligible, since the very language through which it could be expressed was lacking.[2]

The greatest impetus to the loosening of the authority of tradition came, paradoxically, from the desire to purify it. Such a desire recurs through the history of the Church, and can lead either to authentic renewal—which the Council strongly encouraged—or serve as a prelude to abandoning tradition completely. The subtle psychological processes which stimulate the yearning for purity are always difficult to evaluate, but in the postconciliar period it is now clear that for many people this yearning for a "purified" Catholicism, or a "purified" form of religious life, was the expression primarily of personal restlessness. Within a few years, some Church members went from being docile and conventional to become evidently superior Catholics—on fire with God, eager to give themselves entirely to Christ's service, impatient with any religion which was comfortable and routine. They ended merely as good citizens of the Secular City, their earlier religious enthusiasms viewed as ridiculous or even unsavory.

The search for purity in religion was primarily a search for roots, a going back to the fonts from which the Church draws its waters. Thus there occurred, with the Council's blessing, an intensified interest in the Scriptures, the desire for a simpler liturgy which would be close in spirit to that of the early Church, and the search for modes of theological expression not totally dependent on medieval Scholasticism. Reform was being undertaken in the true sense—recalling the Church to closer and stricter fidelity to its original revelation.

There was grave difficulty, however, to the degree that reformers forgot how the Church also develops organically from its New Testament roots. It is an essentially Protestant idea to be willing, in effect, to cancel out all the intervening centuries of Church history in order to recapture a pristine Christianity unsullied by time. Once this sense of development was lost, the results were likely to be disastrous to the orderly historical life of the Church. For example, firmly established doctrines are cavalierly dismissed because they took explicit form "only" in the thirteenth or the third centuries.

The process of getting back to the roots has had results in modern Protestantism which the original Protestants would have found shocking and unacceptable. The traditions of the Church, allegedly devised merely by men, were first criticized in the name of the absolute authority of Scripture, which was taken to represent the authentic teaching of Jesus. It was belatedly discovered, however, that these despised traditions were a necessary protection for Scripture itself and for God's word to men. The more ardently the reformer seeks a "pure" Christianity distant in the past, the more that phenomenon eludes him. The closer he tries to come to the historical Jesus, unmediated by any Church, the further that Jesus seems to recede into myth and legend. The supreme irony of modern Protestantism has been the fact that a movement which began with stern condemnations of all man-made teachings in religion now ends in the ability with positive eagerness to embrace and assimilate every kind of contemporary human wisdom, no matter what the cost in terms of fidelity to Scripture. Christ himself comes to modern man through the Church, so that a rejection of Church tradition ends with Christ also as an expendable inheritance.

In liturgy the desire to cut through the accretions of centuries of cultural development, in postconciliar Catholicism, has often led to the devising of liturgies which have few echoes of even the day before yesterday, much less of twenty centuries ago. Contemporaneity alone rules; all traditions are rejected except those recently devised. In doctrine a dissatisfaction with Scholastic formulas of relatively "recent" vintage (often seven centuries or more) has been followed by a rejection of much of patristic theology and the early ecumenical councils. The Council's exhortation to religious communities to rediscover the authentic visions of their founders has produced bizarre expressions of "renewal" such as the following:

> We must not be hung up on this brides-of-Christ nonsense; we've got to have a broader vision. Though I don't go to bed with men, I have close relationships with men for whom I have a very deep love and strong feelings. But that could change—though it wouldn't necessarily be a formal church marriage if it ever happened.
>
> The chastity business is a bore to me really. It's not something I see any virtue in doing.[3]

If there was one thing virtually all such founders would have agreed on, it would certainly have been consecrated chastity. The alleged vision of the original founders has, in innumerable instances, proven to bear a remarkably convenient resemblance to what "modern man" also happens to find relevant.

One of the great positive fruits of renewal has been a reawakened interest in Scripture on the part of Catholics, especially in the New Testament. Yet this too has had unforeseen ramifications, because Catholics have been encouraged to ground their faith on the Bible at precisely the moment some theologians are finding the Bible a very shaky foundation.

> In any event, the texts which the early Church has bequeathed to us can no longer be regarded purely and simply as *the* World of God. . . . They are, first and foremost, a collection of human words, expressing the vital experience some men had of Jesus. . . . We must interpret these texts, therefore, as we do any human words. . . .
>
> . . . Scientific reading has forever broken the taboo of the "sacred text" (and therefore the untouchable text). . . .[4]

If not all scholars would be quite so blunt, it is nonetheless true that biblical scholarship has generally had the effect of making almost every passage of the New Testament ambiguous and problematical, often because the demands of current theological controversy inspire repeated rereadings and reinterpretations of familiar passages and each reinterpretation, speculative though it may be, is then offered as scientifically authoritative. Because of the paucity of available sources, biblical scholarship can scarcely avoid being highly speculative, and therefore a reflection of the scholar's own theological presuppositions.

The process of purifying the traditions necessarily involved scholarship, a new objectivity, a willingness to look at cherished traditions without preconceptions. One of the hallmarks of the postconciliar age is said to be its historical-mindedness, its taking the Church seriously as a historical institution. But it must be said that as yet *aggiornamento* has inspired little in the way of impressive history. Although it has certainly given impetus to new historical investigations, these frequently focused on topics of contemporary controversial interest—papal infallibility, contraception, the status of women, the Virgin Mary, Modernism, etc.—and clearly show the desire of the authors to make a timely point. The treatment of Modernism, a kind of litmus test of "advanced" opinion in the Church, especially shows this bias,[5] and a standard history of modern theology, by a Dominican, polemicizes openly on almost every page.[6] A well-known Austrian historian liberally sprinkles his account of the modern Church with accusations of "magic" and "fanaticism" and concludes that "the Church has shown itself untrustworthy in its teaching and its practice."[7]

Every scholar knows that objectivity is a fragile thing, possible perhaps only with regard to subjects which do not engage the scholar's own personality. Religion is not one of these. Theories and revisions of theories succeed each other with almost predictable regularity, one scholarly epoch pronouncing as untenable what another takes as undeniable. The intellectual fashions of each age, even such ephemeral things as moods, have immense influence on shifts of opinion.

It can be argued that religious scholarship has always been ecclesiastically oriented, either positively or negatively. The scholar is inclined, by predisposition, either to assume the truth of the Church's teachings and to interpret evidence to support them or to assume that the Church is unfaithful and must be corrected. Neither stance need involve conscious dishonesty, or misuse of evidence. In the postconciliar era, for a variety of reasons, Catholic scholars have increasingly tended to take a critical stance towards their traditions (in the process, incidentally, sometimes falling into very uncritical attitudes towards certain other traditions). Gregory Baum has stated with considerable frankness that,

Believing intellectuals *gladly* admit that religion contains destructive and anti-humane trends and hence ever remains in need of transformation. . . . Christian intellectuals, therefore, are *quite ready* to discern in their religious consciousness various inauthentic trends. . . . [Emphasis added.][8]

Although an intellectual's loss of faith in his own traditions may be an anguished experience, it is just as often an experience which seems personally liberating. Rather than being forced by honesty and respect for truth to follow a path he would rather avoid, the intellectual often discovers in his researches exactly the justification he needs to follow a new path towards which he is already personally inclined. This seems to have been the case, for example, with most of the Catholic Modernists of the early twentieth century. Scholarly conclusions are sometimes quite aprioristic, arguing for example that because "modern man" knows that miracles cannot occur, the miracle accounts in the New Testament cannot be taken as historically factual.

The Catholic idea of intellectual growth has always meant deeper penetration of inexhaustible mysteries, not breaking free of those mysteries. The Church has maintained an organic concept of doctrinal development, in that sometimes quite bold new theories can be entertained to the degree that they are not contradictory of past formulations. The scholar or theologian has been defined as a participant in the full life of the Church, taking nourishment from that life, not an outsider subjecting the traditions to a sterile and "objective" scrutiny. But the concept of the Catholic intellectual's function changed drastically within a few years' time, as many people came to think of themselves as precisely capable of evaluating and judging the Church's traditions from some superior stance—Scripture, scholarship, or the demands of modern culture.

It must be acknowledged that every age tends to distort the Christian traditions in terms of its own culture and that there is, consequently, no wholly pure period to which the believer can look (although some ages are certainly purer than others). Thus the need for reform is perpetually present, and the traditions can never simply be accepted uncritically.

However, at no time in the past did churchmen, no matter how corrupted their understanding may have become in certain ways, fail to acknowledge the existence of some authority superior to their own judgment, whether Scripture, tradition, the general councils, or papacy. Every age maintained in principle the ability to correct itself in terms of authentic doctrine. The postconciliar period is the first in the long history of the Church when certain influential people have claimed liberation from all the authorities of the past. Thus this age is also the first in the history of the Church to render itself in principle irreformable; it recognizes no source of correction outside itself.

A Jesuit historian has provided the charter for this new outlook:

Vatican II determined that religion should be changed by men, in order to meet the needs of men.

Catholicism as we know it is not simply adjusting to the present. It is being transformed into something different, even while it clings to the soft word *aggiornamento*.

What this means is that we are freed from the past. We are free to appropriate what we find helpful and to reject what we find harmful.

The only meaningful questions we can ask the past are ones which are somehow relevant to our own needs and interests.[9]

Apart from its misinterpretation of the Second Vatican Council (which the author admitted failed to embrace this philosophy explicitly), such an analysis also fundamentally misconceives the nature of the Church as a historical organism, indeed misconceives the nature of incarnational religion.

Since the Council, many Catholic thinkers have fallen into the habit of calling Christianity a historical religion in the sense of its being the product of historical developments, therefore culture-bound, therefore relativistic in its teachings. But a more important meaning of historical as it applies to Christianity is that it has been a truly existing faith, coming down through history, based on actual historical events rather than on myths and legends. Ironically, the renewed emphasis on Christianity as historical has occasioned a denial of that historicity, in that much of the Church's tradition, even much of the New Testament itself, is now regarded precisely as legendary. Jesus Christ has been turned into a misty and remote figure about whom little is really known.

The historicity of the Catholic faith has rather meant that it is a faith which commits itself to specific doctrines and symbols which develop through history. It is not religion-in-general. It is not mythological; therefore it cannot endlessly refashion itself to meet the needs of the human psyche. In the abstract a thoughtful Catholic might think that at numerous points in its history the Church ought to have developed differently than it did. Nonetheless the fact that it did develop in certain ways and not others is accepted as part of the very nature of the Church's historicity, in the same way that it is idle (and perhaps blasphemous) to speculate, as some medieval theologians did, on whether God might have become incarnate in some other way than in fact He did. At each point in its development the Church opens certain new doors, which may reveal hitherto unrecognized possibilities, but—equally important—firmly shuts others. Certain possibilities are controverted and, after a time, ruled incompatible with the Church's fundamental historical identity.

The unflinching present-mindedness of post-conciliar Catholicism suffers, in this as in many other ways, from poverty of imagination. It is unable to imagine any religious possibilities besides those which today's culture provides. The modern liberal mind has a horror of geographical arrogance—the claim by one culture to be superior to other simultaneous cultures—but perhaps for that very reason embraces unhesitatingly a temporal arrogance, in which the claims of past cultures are scarcely even listened to. The present alone is granted validity. When it is asserted that the only meaningful questions we can ask the past are those which arise from our present needs, the appropriate Catholic response (albeit one whose aptness is not limited to Catholics) is that an attention to the past in its own terms can alter our basic understanding of who we are and what our needs are. This has always been one of the Church's chief functions.

The willingness to jettison whatever in the Church's traditions does not seem suitable for the present is precisely to reject its historical character, to project its teachings back into the realm of the mythological. The Church ceases to be a living community stretching across the ages and becomes either an abstract idea or a mere present collection of vaguely like-minded individuals. (Both views of the Church are present in the easy and fashionable distinction of the "people of God" from the "institutional Church," a distinction which the Council specifically said was a false one.)[10] Discussions—in regard to schools, colleges, church membership, etc.—of what it means to be a Catholic often focus entirely on "the Gospel" or on personal moral values, without reference to the fact that a historical Church even exists.

Much of the loss of tradition after the Council came about stumblingly and inadvertently, because insufficient thought was given to how renewal might be achieved, insufficient attention paid to exactly what the Council had said, people (even in high places) were caught up in a euphoria which tended to make them careless. It is astonishing that in all the incalculably vast literature inspired by *aggiornamento* so little attention centers on the question, "What exactly do we wish to preserve from the past, how do we reconcile it with change, and what are the conditions which will make its preservation possible?" The historical and sociological naivete of Catholic reformers was almost complete. They suffered from an error common to first-generation reformers—since the traditions were deeply internalized in themselves, they took them for granted and concentrated most of their energies on innovation. They forgot that a new generation was rising which knew the traditions only vaguely if at all.

Part of the problem was an excessive confidence in formal instruction as the chief vehicle for passing on the faith. The sudden changes in liturgy, the suppression or dying out of old forms of piety, the weakening of lay movements the often radical changes in the character of religious life, meant that many very important channels for communicating a living faith were now blocked or diverted to other directions. Young people had to rely mainly on what they were taught in the classroom to gain any coherent notion of what it meant to be a Catholic. Parents found that they could not hand their own faith on to their children, because the conditions which had made that faith possible were rapidly changing. Indeed many adult Catholics were now told that they had never understood their faith properly and would have to go back to school. The living religious traditions of pious devotions and beliefs, devout families, ascetical regimens, etc., were within a brief time rendered dysfunctional, leaving only the dead traditions found in books.

Yet even this formal instruction, because of the prevalence of certain fashionable theological and pedagogical theories, often failed to communicate the heart of Catholic doctrine, even on the university level. So problematical had the core of the Catholic tradition become in many people's minds that it was deemed better to talk around it, never providing a solid doctrinal basis which the student might accept or reject at leisure. There were no longer any points of reference for belief, other than a vague fidelity to Jesus which itself often came to seem arbitrary, a mere holdover from the past.

Young Catholics of the postconciliar period drifted away from the Church in immense numbers, an unanticipated event of the "renewed" Church and one usually explained in terms of the Church's failure to change fast enough. But there is an even more obvious point—these young people grew up in a period when literally no one could offer them a strong and coherent account of what it meant to be a Catholic. That they were not simply rejecting "outmoded" doctrines is evidenced in the attraction of so many of the avant-garde young to sects and movements which are, if anything, even more "incredible" than those of the Catholic Church.

Few young people of the past fifteen years have had sustained contact, during their crucial formative years, with firmly orthodox, serene, self-confident adult Catholics of the kind that every parish and school used to provide in abundance. Parents who have tried to create such an atmosphere in their homes have often found their efforts undermined in the Catholic schools, many of them dominated by church professionals suffering from crises of faith and vocation. Practically all social loyalties require that the society have a past in which it can take pride, and which engages the imagination of the young even before they understand the group's explicit values. Not only were young Catholics of the postconciliar era not introduced to such a past (religion classes not uncommonly skipped from the New Testament to about 1960) but they were even given to understand that there was something shameful about it and that they were fortunate to have escaped from its clutches. Deeply pious parents often found that *aggiornamento* required them to reconcile themselves to watching their children drift off into agnosticism, and sometimes into anti-Catholicism.

T. S. Eliot proposed that one of the minimum functions of Christian education, which it could perform even for nonbelievers, was to enable people to "think in Christian categories."[11] This is one of the functions, however, which Catholic schools gave up, following the Council. A "relevant" religious education became one in which either Christian doctrines were understood in secular terms or secular ideas dressed up in theological clothing. The notion, which no previous generation of Catholics would have doubted for a moment, that to be a Christian means to see the world in a radically unique way came to smack of narrowness and fanaticism. Catholic doctrines often ceased to be believed because they ceased to be taught, or were taught in such a way that they could not possibly command belief.

The fashionable pedagogies of the 1960s eschewed "imposing" culture on students; there were no normative ideas which the school might insist that all students ought to be acquainted with, even if only to reject them. No ideas, no human creations, especially the classics from the past, were to be conceded any greater value than what an individual student, here and now, himself considered true or wise.

The deleterious effects of this in secular education are now coming to be widely recognized. (As usual, Catholic thinkers lag behind.) To expose young children to powerful symbols or ideas, though they may not understand them, can still be extremely effective, leaving deep impressions on their minds. As they grow older, the process of formal education may then be one of coming to penetrate intellectually what had previously been held in a merely intuitive way. The best Catholic education has generally proceeded by this method, but it was exactly this method which was widely abandoned after 1965. Young children were adjudged unready for the full rigors of doctrine, so its teaching tended to be endlessly postponed, failing to make its appearance even in the colleges. In 1976 an instructor at an elite Eastern women's college reported that even graduates of the most prestigious Catholic high schools lacked an intellectual understanding of their faith, and many felt a need for it.[12] A comprehensive survey of American Catholic adolescents the same year revealed that only 68% believed in a personal God, a percentage lower than among Protestants.[13] The following year a survey of young Catholic adults in the New York City area found a massive decline in church attendance, which was linked to loss of belief in the central mysteries of the faith and confusion as to what exactly the Church teaches. One respondent said, "Most priests I know would rather not get into any deep discussion about Faith. Maybe it is my misfortune knowing only those who seem not totally committed."[14]

A distinguished Jesuit scholar has identified the cause of many of the most serious mistakes made in the name of renewal:

> One of the problems in the present-day church, as in human society in general, has been that we have undertaken to change things without really knowing why they were the way they were. . . . When we have approached the liturgy, for example, we have often done so ingenuously, without an understanding of, or even a decent empathy for, the deep unconscious structures that the liturgy registers.

> Other institutions within the Church, the practice of devotion to Mary, clerical celibacy, the vows of religion, attitudes toward marriage, are also the results of very, very deep unconscious drives as well as of conscious rationalizations.[15]

However, if most of the loss of contact with living Catholic tradition has been the result of misconceived or badly implemented ideas, it is also true that some of those who have guided the directions of ecclesiastical change have set out deliberately to undermine the force of tradition, recognizing that such force, by its authority in the lives of Catholics, prevents the emergence of a faith which can be molded wholly to suit contemporary needs.

It would not be an exaggeration to say that for some of these people tradition has an entirely negative value. They consider it merely the collected debris of centuries which must be cleared away so that real Christianity, no longer compromised by its connection with the supernatural, can finally emerge. Here the arrogance of present-mindedness is most keenly apprehended, since the present takes on meaning precisely in proportion to the degree that modern Christians "liberate" themselves from the past. They demonstrate the purity of their own faith by the many ways in which it has ceased to resemble the faith of their ancestors.

This view of *aggiornamento* requires that a constant warfare be directed against those who still "cling" to old beliefs. The popularity of the word *cling* among reformers betrays their conviction that no one could hold to old beliefs out of principle; all traditionalism is merely insecurity. A barrage of ridicule, anger, or cajolery emanates from the pulpit, the press, the lecture platform, sometimes the diocesan offices, all aimed at those who refuse to change fast enough. Orthodoxy itself is placed on trial, and a moral premium is offered to Catholics who show themselves most open to every change. In a society which has lost its identity and its purpose, the ability to change, and to change often, is itself a sufficient purpose. The promised land lies beyond each new horizon. In a world where an attachment to tradition and stability are likely to cause anxieties, the only security lies in the ready acceptance of every innovation, the exorcising from oneself of every unshakable conviction. Basic religious meaning is found in an endless series of "breakthroughs," by which one after another of the Church's doctrines is discovered to be no longer binding. One remains a Catholic primarily because it provides a negative identity against which to react.

Many of the promises of renewal were ruined by the tendency, especially promoted by the media, to present every theological development in negative and destructive terms. Instead of doctrinal development there was doctrinal contestation. Instead of seeking to see how new insights might be reconciled authentically with traditional teaching, the latter was directly assaulted. Theological "progress" was measured largely in terms of how many of the old teachings, especailly those involving some practical rule of behavior, could be called into question. There was sometimes a fierce and thrilling joy to be gained from breaking old taboos, especially in worship and in morals. If the traditions could no longer inspire, then their abandonment would supply an inspiration of its own. (One of the most popular spiritual writers of the 1960s proclaimed that the Lord's Prayer "teaches error.")[16]

The inevitable result, willed and planned by some, was the murder of a living tradition, a process by which an ancient and nourishing body of religious teachings became a mere burden. More serious, perhaps, than the deliberate abandonment of tradition was the situation of those who had lost living contact with their past without realizing it, who had sought to maintain continuity with the past but to whom the past no longer spoke. Many, for example, sought to retain the attitude of Christian hope but without the dogmatic basis which alone rendered that hope more than merely sentimental, or continued searching for a "relevant" way of celebrating the Eucharist long after they had rejected the essentially ecclesial context of that Eucharist.

Daniel Berrigan, perhaps the most famous American Jesuit alive today, affirms his solidarity with his sixteenth-century spiritual forebears in terms of their living among the poor and attempting to practice real poverty.[17] Yet such community can be maintained only by a kind of censorship of the Jesuit tradition, tacitly omitting other aspects of the early Jesuits' lives—their complete loyalty to the papacy, their burning

desire to convert the heathens, their unwavering doctrinal orthodoxy—
that some modern Jesuits find much less attractive. Father Berrigan,
although claiming the Elizabethan Jesuit martyrs as models for his own
actions, concedes that "I can't conceive of myself as a Jesuit priest dying
on behalf of the Eucharist, dying to vindicate the truth of the Eucharist,
except in a very new way. . . . Today, in other words, the important
questions have an extraordinarily secularized kind of context. . . ."[18]
Insisting that "no break" has occurred with the tradition, he seems unaware of how profound a gulf in fact separates him from the religious
attitudes of men like Sts. Edmund Campion and Andrew Bobola.

Sometimes efforts to reconcile the modern and the traditional have
bizarre results. The Society of Mary, for example, was founded in
France following the persecutions of the Revolutionary era and as part of
a conscious attempt to recover the Christian values which the Revolution
had suppressed. In 1975, however, an American provincial of the order
could tell the press that the group had been "inspired" by the Revolution
and was "an attempt to express in religious life the same spirit that the
revolution created."[19] As a perceptive layman has written, "In the arrogance of the present, time gets flattened out procrusteanly, so that the
past can be instantly invaded by those pieties of the present that are
imagined to be eternal verities."[20]

Many contemporary Catholics are now part of a tradition only in the
sense of an eccentric tradition which has existed on the margins of the
Church and sometimes outside it. Knowingly or not, they are closer to
Loisy than to Newman, Lammenais than the Curé of Ars, Descartes than
Pascal, Montaigne than St. Teresa, Erasmus than Loyola, Wyclif than St.
Catherine of Siena, Abelard than St. Bernard, Pelagius than St. Augus-
tine. (Despite the heralded fruits of scholarship, educated modern
Catholics remain in ignorance of their traditions in negative ways also—
an inconveniently strict sexual morality can be blamed on the Jansenists,
without awareness of the fact that Catholic sexual teaching has been
remarkably consistent throughout history and owes little to Jansenism.)
They tend to prefer, among the martyrs to Nazi tyranny, the ambiguously secularizing Protestant Dietrich Bonhoeffer to the Franciscan
Maximilian Kolbe with his fervent Marian devotion. St. John Fisher must
seem like a stubborn old man who violated collegiality by supporting the
papacy against the consensus of the English bishops. The most popular of
all Catholic saints—Francis of Assisi—can only be used by turning him
into a merely kind person or an early-day ecologist. His fierce ascetical
practices, his hatred of sin, his almost exaggerated respect for the sacramental priesthood must all be overlooked.

If "holiness is wholeness" as the world understands that concept, then a high proportion of the saints must be dismissed as unbalanced, their theological and ascetical attitudes incomprehensible if not actually pernicious. If "making a better world" is indeed the chief purpose of Christian living, then few Christians of earlier times qualify to bear the name. Martyrdom, which past ages regarded as the culminating Christian witness, grows more and more dubious because so few Catholic beliefs seem worth dying for. Attempts to save that witness by positing that St. Thomas More, for example, died for "personal integrity" or to protest political tyranny, succeed merely in subtly falsifying what the martyrs themselves thought they were doing. A Jesuit journalist has pointed out that, given certain prevalent assumptions about renewal, America's newest saint becomes almost a negative example:

> [St. John Nepumocene Neumann] was no miracle-worker, no scholar, no grand spokesman for the Church in public affairs.
>
> He was one of the "brick-and-mortar" bishops treated today with kindly toleration. His intellectual accomplishments were reduced to editing a question-and-answer-learn-by-rote catechism. . . . His chief claim to fame includes the feverish building of churches, which he did in fulfillment of a vow.
>
> He was a zealous promoter of the Forty Hours—a devotion of which liturgists today . . . take a dim view.
>
> . . . [His] ecumenical sense was hardly in evidence. . . . What he thought of slavery is not recorded by his biographers. . . .
>
> . . . As for enlightened concern for the emancipation of the laity, the historical feud with the trustees which he inherited was certainly no basis for permitting largeness of view.[21]

A historian has aptly identified how the modern outlook often obscures rather than enhances understanding:

> None will dispute that in the twentieth century Christians no longer feel passionately about theological controversies concerning the Real Presence or liturgical opposition to the use of images. Christians in the sixteenth century, for very good reason, took these matters very seriously indeed, for they were of utmost importance. The modern ecumenical and "irenic" viewpoint, in the name of tolerance and charity, undermines the ability to understand the more contentious past.[22]

Loss of contact with the Catholic past is not merely a matter of the inevitable receding of what is ancient and distant, however—the formulas of the early ecumenical councils, medieval Scholasticism, or Reformation controversies. A former president of the Catholic Theological

Society of America, for instance, finds even Karl Rahner propounding doctrines which are "oppressively narrow," "ascetically quaint," and "marred by a residual ecclesiocentrism."[23] A Jesuit journalist relates that his generation of seminarians was nourished by Teilhard de Chardin, "though I'm sure none of us would think of reading him today."[24]

Self-consciously well-informed Catholics, confronted with the following statements, would knowingly and condescendingly dismiss them as "preconciliar."

> They are fully incorporated into the society of the Church who, possessing the Spirit of Christ, accept her entire system and all the means of salvation given to her, and through union with her visible structure are joined to Christ, who rules her through the Supreme Pontiff and the bishops.

> But the college or body of bishops has no authority unless it is simultaneously conceived of in terms of its head, the Roman Pontiff, Peter's successor, and without any lessening of his power of primacy over all, pastors as well as the general faithful. For in virtue of his office, that is, as Vicar of Christ and pastor of the whole Church, the Roman Pontiff has full, supreme, and universal power over the Church. And he can always exercise this power freely.

> Therefore his definitions, of themselves, and not from the consent of the Church, are justly styled irreformable, for they are pronounced with the assistance of the Holy Spirit, an assistance promised to him in blessed Peter. Therefore they need no approval of others, nor do they allow an appeal to any other judgment.

> With ready Christian obedience, laymen as well as all disciples of Christ should accept whatever their sacred pastors, as representatives of Christ, decree in their role as teachers and rulers in the Church.

> I feel in my heart and soul a love of those rules, precepts, and regulations, and obedience to all this human and ecclesiastical legislation, and I always keep a careful watch over myself where they are concerned. . . .

The first four statements, far from being preconciliar, are from the Council's allegedly "advanced" decree on the Church, *Lumen Gentium,* while the fifth is the inner thoughts of Pope John XXIII, written down less than two years before his death.[25]

Programs for the "renewal" of the Church have frequently been forced to ignore the conciliar decrees altogether, since they are replete with restatements of traditional doctrine, in favor of an amorphous "spirit of Vatican II" which can be made to mean anything anyone wants it to mean. In this situation there is a good deal of practicality in the rather ingenuous opinion of one American historian that he was better off not having had a profound Catholic education, since he could therefore accept the postconciliar changes with equanimity. For the same reason, he thought, religious communities of women could "renew" themselves most quickly because they possessed the inestimable advantage of a "shallow" theological background, which meant that "they had less cultural baggage to jettison."[26] When the traditions of the Church are viewed merely as encumbering baggage, this kind of ignorance is highly desirable. (There is, however, something odd about proposing as models of successful renewal communities many of whom seem destined for extinction.)

Many "renewed" Catholics are now in a situation where they can scarcely even understand what certain fundamental doctrines and practices of the Church might conceivably mean. They have rid their minds of the ability to think in genuinely Catholic terms. Many younger people, having never been exposed to any serious effort to do so, cannot imagine what intelligent defense could be made of traditional doctrines. There is now so complete a present-mindedness that these traditions are almost like the newly unearthed scriptures of a long-extinct faith.

The noted sociologist Daniel Bell diagnoses a fundamental aspect of modern culture which is now affecting the Catholic Church to a degree that would not have seemed possible fifteen years ago:

> Nihilism, then, is the end process of rationalism. It is man's self-conscious will to destroy his past and control his future. It is modernity in its *extreme*. Although at bottom it is a metaphysical condition, nihilism pervades all of society, and in the end must destroy itself.[27]

Within an unimaginably brief period of time, the attitude of many Catholics towards their past recapitulated modern Western cultural history. Beginning with an enthusiastic desire to "purify" the traditions, such people at first allowed themselves a rather cautious stance of "objectivity" towards the Church of which they were a part. This detachment, experienced in a characteristically modern way as implying "liberation," tended to give way in time to cynicism—regarding the "institutional" Church and its traditions as merely oppressive, almost as historic conspiracies against personal freedom. In this understanding, the essence of Church life becomes power relationships, and renewal ceases to have much to do with the things of the spirit (which are naive and distracting) and begins to focus on strategies whereby power can be redistributed. The demand for "empowerment" now raised by women's groups and various racial, ethnic, and cultural minorities within the Church, as well as by self-designated spokesmen for lay people's rights, priests' rights, deacons' rights, etc., often betray the absence of any real concern for the Church's inner nature and mission. It is power alone which seems real and worthwhile.

A sympathetic Lutheran observer has noted,

> The destruction of these traditions, whether of fundamentalist revivalism or
> of Marian devotion, whether by modernization or by insistence on chemi-
> cally pure Christianity, is also the destruction of the seedbeds of most of the
> genuine Christian vitality and authentic Christian faith that still lives in our
> world. To paraphrase what Luther said about the Bible, traditional religion,
> though often extrinsic and perverted, is the cradle of Christ.[28]

The degree to which many Catholic reformers have assimilated the
characteristic modes of thinking of their culture makes them unable to
appreciate the magnitude of what has occurred since the Council, or to
evaluate it with complete honesty. Liberation from tradition seems altogether too positive a gain for them to entertain seriously the possibility
that it might be destructive. The British anthropologist Lord Raglan
pointed out that, although societies are often said to decay because of the
dead hand of the past, such decay can occur even more rapidly "by
breaking away from the past."[29] The present plight of the Catholic
Church is rendered doubly perilous by the fact that so many people
whose opinions are influential cannot even seriously admit this possibility. For too many the governing mentality is that which has been accurately ascribed to the late Episcopal bishop James A. Pike, prime model
of the "relevant" churchman of modern times:

> The point is not that Pike was ignorant. We are all ignorant. But his igno-
> rance takes a certain form, the denigration and caricature of the past. He
> looks into history and finds no unfolding coherence of meaning, only a
> domain of contingency extending up to his own self-consciousness, that of
> enlightened modernity, as its culmination.[30]

CHAPTER 3

The Imperial Self

ONE of the most neglected aspects of the "renewal" which has followed the Second Vatican Council is its psychological effect on those caught up in it. The almost uncanny speed with which religious communities, especially of women, were changed after the Council owes much to what might be called the "hothouse" and "multiplier" dimensions of their lives. The former refers to the intensity with which the life of the Church was lived in these communities. Their members, unlike even the most devout lay people, literally had no life apart from their religious life; few had even brief respites from their vocations. For such people even seemingly minor changes, such as alterations in the habit or relaxations of the daily rule, could have strong personal repercussions. The closeness and intensity of community life insured the multiplier effect in that profound changes occurring in even a few members irresistibly communicated themselves to others in the community. Where the ideals of the Church were pursued most seriously, it was inevitable that the disillusionment would be most dramatic.

A New York psychiatric hospital has reported an increase in personality disorders among both priests and nuns following the Council, attributable to conflicts and anxieties arising from change.[1] Yet measurable disturbances of this kind are perhaps less important than personality changes which, though not diagnosed as pathological, were nonetheless real and dramatic. Even among those who apparently "coped" with change there occurred shifts in attitude, behavior, and style of life which often appeared irrational and compulsive, verging on the hysterical. Most striking has been the "transvaluation of values" by which beliefs once held to be precious and inviolable came to seem false and even hateful.

But then I came to realize that I spent over three-fourths of my time relieving people of guilt that the church had imposed on them! Getting people out of their Catholic bag! Telling them that much of what their pastors and grade school nuns had taught them was a bunch of crap!

I began to question whether I truly liked celebrating the Mass and preaching or whether I simply liked the stage. . . .

. . . I did go to Mass every Sunday and found it a gruesome thing. If more priests would go to Mass and see how horrible it is I think they'd change.

I live on as a charlatan for the church, a sham, an accomplice to a continuing crime against humanity.[2]

The dominant theme of Catholic confessional literature of the past fifteen years has been "liberation," the process by which the individual has been freed from "oppressive" structures and "outmoded" doctrines, and thereby enabled to live in accord with a "true" self which was previously repressed. Among the great puzzles, however, is how a disintegrating community affects the personalities of those deeply implicated in it, especially people ostensibly desirous of changing it. Perhaps the central fact of the postconciliar Catholic experience has been the way in which the personalities of many have been dramatically reorganized, a process which has been scarcely understood at all, especially by those experiencing it.

The most powerful and effective symbol of the postconciliar Church was a negative one—the many priests and religious who gave up their vocations and, implicitly or explicitly, repudiated the commitments to which they had vowed themselves for life. The messages conveyed in that symbol were varied and powerful—that the religious life was a joyless burden, that vows were not sacred, that self-fulfillment was the paramount aim of life, that this-worldly considerations alone governed human conduct. For those who abandoned their vocations without even seeking dispensation from the Church, a further message was added—that it was impossible to "lose" one's soul, that there was no sovereign authority higher than the individual will.

The inevitable failure of much postconciliar "reform" could have been predicted solely on the basis of the use of the word itself. Classically, in the Church, "reform" has meant a recalling of believers to a stricter and more demanding kind of discipleship. The men and women honored with the name of "reformers" in religious life preached revitalization through closer adherence to the original spirit and rules of the community, often in the face of entrenched worldliness and lay customs. Reformers like St. Teresa of Avila encountered resistance and opposition primarily from contemporaries who, being comfortable within a permissive ambience, felt threatened by the demand that they return to a stricter way of life. Conditions fairly common in the religious life of today—the ignoring of cloister, the abandonment of the prescribed habit, secular occupations, enjoyment of worldly amusements, sexual adventures—were precisely the conditions which the great reformers of the past found intolerable, and against which they inveighed ceaselessly.

The disastrous effects of "renewal" in certain parts of the Church, especially the near-disappearance of some religious communities, have been a direct result of the fundamental misconstruing of the nature of authentic Christian reform. It was as though the engines of reform, designed primarily for purposes of self-discipline and even self-denial, were thrown precipitously into reverse; the result was not only the failure of the vehicle to move but its near-destruction in a storm of shuddering vibrations. A Jesuit historian has pointed out the classic formulation of the Catholic idea of reform, articulated at the Fifth Lateran Council: "Men must be changed by religion, not religion by men."[3] The radical reversal of this maxim has prevented the reforms of the Second Vatican Council from being adequately realized. Virtually every ecumenical council has been followed by a crisis, usually stemming from the refusal of a major segment of the Church to accept its decrees. The Second Vatican Council is perhaps the first council to be followed by a crisis in which its teachings have been distorted into meanings contrary to their original intention.

Certain relatively minor changes of the conciliar era—the abolition of compulsory Friday abstinence, the modification of the rules of religious life—were popularly understood as signalling that the theme of *aggiornamento* would be "freedom," in the sense of a systematic loosening of whatever restraints Catholics found burdensome or irksome. The media, with scant ability to comprehend or express the deeper meanings of renewal, especially bore down on that point, to the virtual exclusion of every other. In countless news stories the drama of renewal was presented in terms of "progressives" struggling to impart greater freedom to the Church in the face of the entrenched power of evil reactionaries. This scheme of interpretation set up inevitable bitter frustrations, since this was in fact not the Council's vision of renewal at all. Thus the Church's refusal to surrender its teaching and practice on a wide range of matters—contraception, celibacy, divorce, homosexuality, women priests, democratic structure, etc.—has induced cynicism and anger in many previously happy Catholics, although nothing in the Council's program for reform in any way implied that such changes would be forthcoming, or that they were even germane to the task of renewal.

The new ethos of release from whatever binds is usually justified as a reaction against the "rigidity" of the preconciliar Church. Rigidities of various kinds did exist, but in fact the Church was probably less rigid in 1960 than at any previous time in its history. Ascetical practices, the conditions of religious life, moral casuistry, and parish life had probably never been less burdensome, more adapted to the needs of time and place, at least in the English-speaking world. (The Church in the English-speaking world was also in 1960 not a candidate for "reform" in the classical sense. Perhaps seldom in the history of the Church was the moral and devotional life of both religious and laity at such a generally high level.)

Although *religion* in its root meaning denotes a "binding," the history of modern liberal Christianity has been primarily a flight from everything in religion which is binding and powerful, everything which appears to restrict the full freedom of the individual. Within this framework no "renewal" can possibly be other than weak and ineffective, and if certain modern notions of freedom are accepted as necessary to Christianity it follows that there have been few real Christians until very recently. T. S. Eliot said of liberalism that it

> . . . tends to release energy rather than accumulate it, to relax rather than to fortify. It is a movement not so much defined by its end, as by its starting point; away from, rather than towards, something definite.

> In religion, Liberalism may be characterized as a progressive discarding of elements in historical Christianity which appear superfluous or obsolete, confounded with practices and abuses which are legitimate objects of attack. But as its movement is controlled rather by its origin than by any goal, it loses force after a series of rejections, and with nothing to destroy is left with nothing to uphold and with nowhere to go.[4]

Within a few years of the Council the battles of Catholic liberalism had become largely rear-guard struggles, warning against "rigidity," for example, when the real danger was excessive malleability, compulsively struggling to ward off any possible return to the settled conditions of preconciliar Church life. Yet the attack on preconciliar "rigidity" was possible precisely because this rigidity, compared with previous ages, had already been significantly lessened. In the postconciliar Church the burdens of authority and tradition are hateful to many people not because they are so heavy but because they now carry only a small portion of their former weight. It is vestigial authority which is the most hateful, because it is too weak to give shape and direction to the community and therefore seems arbitrary and anachronistic.

A relativistic morality and an endlessly "pluralistic" theology suit the mood of the present moment because they dictate a stance of immobility for the corporate life of the Church. Since there are few if any beliefs which the Church can with certainty proclaim to all its members, the Church functions merely as a warm matrix within which and from out of which individuals have unlimited freedom of action, without the danger that membership in the Church will make inconvenient demands on them. An official of the National Council of Churches, studying the measurable phenomenon of the declining liberal denominations, has observed that many contemporary Christians are simply comfortable in a dying Church and resist all efforts to revitalize the Church at the expense of that comfort.[5] Here is a description of the postconciliar religious climate in England:

> . . . what was before a narrow, deep, and clearly marked gully cut by a powerful and awe-inspiring torrent across the English landscape, has now become a much wider, gentler and shallower river with ill-defined banks and far less impressive scenery. This river is much more comfortable to row a boat in, but a good deal less exciting than the old stream was. . . . You will find yourselves boating with a crowd of other people who have come out for a lazy Sunday's enjoyment and from whom you are practically indistinguishable.[6]

Whatever Vatican II's renewal of the Church might be thought to mean, it can scarcely mean this.

The disappointing effects of *aggiornamento* stem in part from the fact that it has accompanied, with few people being aware of it, an almost cosmic shift in Western cultural and moral attitudes occurring at so basic a level that their full impact has been little appreciated. This shift is analyzed most brilliantly by the Freudian sociologist Philip Rieff under the rubric of "the triumph of the therapeutic."

Rieff perceives a fundamental shift from the "inhibitory" to the "remissive" mode of behavior, that is, from a culture whose dominant symbols convey moral and religious affirmations, which include interdicts or prohibitions, to a culture which systematically grants permission to the individual to transgress these interdicts in the name of personal freedom and fulfillment. The act of transgression becomes "endlessly attractive," and a reflex attitude develops in which no fixed moral or religious belief enjoys authority or commands obedience for any appreciable length of time.

The result is the emergence of a "culture of indifference" which uses the rhetoric of faith and commitment to undermine both and even to establish a counter-faith, "a secular vision of comforts that renders all salvations obsolete." Rieff asks, "In what does the self now try to find salvation, if not in the breaking of all corporate identities and in the suspicion of all normative institutions?"

Although modern Christianity has made strenuous efforts to accommodate itself to the ethic of the therapeutic, defined as "a manipulable sense of well-being," the most fundamental assumptions of the historic Judaeo-Christian religion are in fact undermined by this new cult.

> Religious man was born to be saved; psychological man was born to be pleased. The difference was established long ago when "I believe," the cry of the ascetic, lost precedence to "one feels, " the caveat of the therapeutic.[7]

The fact that the nature of this revolution has been so little understood makes its influence within the Church all the more lethal, since many Catholics have adopted the therapeutic mentality without even realizing it; little in their educations and in the traditional Catholic mode of thinking prepared them for it. Trained to be on guard against overt heresies, they had little sensitivity to ideas which were not recognizably heretical and in fact seemed to have nothing to do with the explicit doctrines of Christianity. Yet in the postconciliar Church it is the spread of the therapeutic mentality, as Rieff defines it, which is at the root of most other problems.

The modern notion of happiness—Rieff's "manipulable sense of well-being," which he calls the "age's master passion"—is itself one of the great unexamined concepts, in that what Christians have traditionally meant by that term, as well as by related terms like *joy,* goes far beyond the modern therapeutic sense and at some points contradicts it. Christian ascetical theory has always insisted that the believer's happiness is not what the world understands by happiness and therefore, as Christ promised, the happiness of the believer is something which cannot be taken from him. William James, far from an orthodox Christian, noticed that the happiness of the saints seems almost to increase as they encounter the rebuffs and persecutions of the world.[8] Suffering, for the Christian, has traditionally been treated either as irrelevant or as a sign of God's favor, while happiness and peace are given at a level beyond all possibility of worldly suffering.

The symbolism of religious vows, of the consecrated religious life, again reveals itself as central to the whole crisis of the Church. The revolution in religious life was often publicized in terms of greater "service," the desire on the part of religious to be dedicated to their ministry even more fully, beyond the limits of petty rules and structures. But in practice it was often less the desire to serve than to be "fulfilled" which motivated the changes. In a 1975 survey a majority of former nuns, asked why they had left the convent, gave "inability to be me" as a major reason.[9] It was the therapeutic attitude, also, which virtually destroyed certain religious communities, by robbing them of whatever communal and transcendent purpose they may have had and turning them into mere collections of vaguely like-minded individualists. As one member of a highly publicized "renewed" order has said,

> What's holding us together is the past. For me, I have no sense of what the future is for this group. . . . There is nothing I can do as an Immaculate Heart that I couldn't do as an individual. . . . I find the freedom of life-style we're experiencing incompatible with maintaining an institution.[10]

The failure of so many orders to attract and keep novices is surely not unrelated to their conspicuous lack of any clear and compelling communal purpose or character.

The rapid spread of the therapeutic attitude has been facilitated in the Church by a closely related phenomenon—the ability of certain persons to manipulate traditional language in such a way as to give it almost the reverse of its true meaning, as in the arguments of a seminary professor (who has since left the priesthood) that life-long commitments may often undermine "fidelity" and that, for example, it may be wrong for people to persist in a marriage which is "dead in every way."[11] There is a perverse appropriateness about such manipulations, resting as they do on the assumption that words are subject to redefinition at the sovereign will of the speaker.

It is one of the choicer ironies of the postconciliar era that, as nuns seek to become priests, priests get married, and married people get divorced in ever greater numbers. Each group regards its own "need"—for priesthood, for marriage, for sanctioned divorce—as one whose fulfillment will quiet the deep dissatisfactions which make it unhappy in its present state of life. Each thinks its salvation lies just over the horizon; none appears to reflect on whether its restlessness has roots deeper than the vocational conditions which trouble it.

Philip Rieff sees "interdictory institutions," those which embody and proclaim particular beliefs in a binding and authoritative way, as essential for the maintenance of the moral sense of society.

> Yet a culture survives principally, I think, by the power of its institutions to bind and loose men in the conduct of their affairs with reasons which sink so deep into the self that they become commonly and implicitly understood. . . . Having broken the outward forms, so as to liberate, allegedly, the inner meaning of the good, the beautiful, and the true, the spiritualizers, who set the pace of Western civilization's cultural life . . . have given way now to their logical and historical successors, the psychologizers, inheritors of that dualist tradition which pits human nature against social order.

The therapeutic mentality has developed especially in post-Protestant America because the waning of an "ascetic" culture—a culture of authority, moral demands, and self-discipline—is its most fertile soil. It is a mentality which, virtually as a matter of principle, ceases even trying to resolve contradictions or opposing demands (the stuff of tragedy) and in effect tells people, "Live within your moral means." Self-improvement, then, becomes the characteristic modern. faith. "Prophets" arise who, unlike those who classically bore the name, preach the mechanisms of release rather than control, "liberating" people rather than placing greater responsibilities on them. All deeply internalized moral demands are ultimately repudiated. The moral revolution occurs because of the weakness of the old moral system, not because of any new and positive vision.[12]

For fifteen years the "remissive mode" has been dominant in the Roman Catholic Church, in the sense that the Second Vatican Council, despite its frequent and unmistakable affirmations of ecclesiastical authority,[13] was popularly presented (even by many who should have known better) as a process by which Catholics were released from previously imposed obligations. So complete was the intellectual victory of the therapeutic mentality that many in the Church are now unable even to conceive of renewal in any terms other than further acts of release from obligations.

Priests and religious, both those who gave up their ecclesiastical roles and those who retained them but played them in "daring" new ways, were the chief "releasing" symbols of the postconciliar period, as they had been the chief interdictory figures prior to it. (One nun has related how she abandoned her habit because it seemed to unsettle a young couple kissing on a park bench.)[14] Although in the early Church bishops were "overseers," the "good" bishop now is a kindly grandfather who indulges his people, excuses their failings, and never utters a severe word. By contrast the Pope, who continues to warn, rebuke, and utter interdictions, is resented, as are religious who appear to take too seriously the traditional understanding of their vocations. The residual hold which the Church still has on some people is revealed primarily in their demand that the Church give its blessing to their transgressions and the fact that it is precisely in transgressing its interdicts that they find their religion most "meaningful."

There are, as previously noted, no more conversion stories in Catholicism, simply stories of deconversion. The typical pilgrim is John Cogley, wending his way to Canterbury because he finds, on the whole, that there he is asked to believe less, and that less less stringently.[15] As T. S. Eliot pointed out, in Protestant cultures both belief and unbelief seem to be less intense.[16] There is no longer any moral grandeur in faith crises. People merely awaken one day and realize that they no longer believe. The loss of faith seems hardly worth commenting on. They settle comfortably into a marginal relationship with the Church, never quite accepting or rejecting its teaching, merely taking from it whatever seems useful and attractive. The behavior of a John Henry Newman, ceasing to preach once he had serious doubts about the Anglican Church, and remaining away from Oxford for thirty years after his conversion, can only seem quaintly scrupulous.

The present hostility within Christianity against interdicts—binding laws—is one more example of how avant-garde Christians seek to be modern in a way which leaves them ignorant, often, of certain important directions in modern thought. A recent president of the American Psychological Association, for example, writing from a wholly secular perspective, has suggested that the psychological disciplines are more hostile to "the inhibitory messages of traditional religious moralizing" than is scientifically justified, and has asked whether such "inhibitory systems" do not serve human purposes which are as yet not well understood.[17] A distinguished legal scholar, in a work whose implications have been widely ignored, argues that law is essential to religion and that ". . . to rule law out of social relations . . . is to leave caprice, arbitrariness, and oppression—not love." Law is, in part, the means by which "transrational values" are communicated to people.[18]

The chasm which separates the Christian from the therapeutic attitude towards human nature can perhaps best be understood in terms of the idea of "character," which in classical terms was the achievement of a stable and principled personal identity, formed and given direction ascetically, and tested in the crucible of extreme experiences. Under the therapeutic rubric, however, the very idea of character becomes meaningless and even pernicious, since a continuous personal malleability is precisely what is aimed at, for the sake of "fulfillment." Thus according to Rieff, "Lacking confidence in their inherited stock of insight, the religious prefer to avoid argument in a wordy torrent of good will." The result is the production of "tame Christians" who prefer not to challenge the ascendency of the therapeutic.

> Gods choose; men are chosen. What men lose when they become as free as gods is precisely the sense of being chosen, which encourages them, in their gratitude, to take their subsequent choices seriously. Put in another way, this means: Freedom does not exist without responsibility.[19]

Within Christianity the impact of the therapeutic has naturally been felt most strongly in the area of what was traditionally called the cure of souls, the process by which the human conscience is set right in the sight of God. On one level the very notion of "character," in Rieff's sense, has disappeared—its formation was precisely the point of traditional ascetical systems, especially in religious life, and the radical unravelling of those systems (and of many of the personalities involved in them) has been dramatic testimony to their failure. Catholicism no longer has the power to form heroic souls of the kind represented, for example, by Mother Teresa of Calcutta, and to a considerable extent there seems to be lacking even the desire to form such souls. The pervasive fear of religious "fanaticism" or "rigidity," even as the opposite dangers are obviously far more serious, prevents this.

Traditional Catholicism, through its division between lay and religious life, attempted to accommodate both the heroic and the ordinary. While many lay people led heroic lives, often anonymously, it was the religious who sought to give public witness to that possibility. Certain types of "reformers," of whom the early Protestants are the best examples, have found this distinction invidious and have insisted that all Christians are called equally to lives of holiness. Yet, however appealing this might be in theory, in practice it led eventually to a general lowering of standards for everyone. The fact that so many religious in the postconciliar Church find their vocations troublesome is directly related to the mentality which is not even certain that a distinctively Christian form of heroism— sanctity—is desirable.

On the lowest level, there is not any longer any principled Catholic resistance to antinomianism, the rejection of binding laws in favor of a wholly spontaneous and "free" response to what is deemed good. Those who are not themselves antinomians often see nothing particularly wrong with that stance, or at least refrain from criticizing it publicly. The Church at present lacks any basis on which to support a moral order, a system capable of holding together communities and even whole societies, as distinct from whatever moral help it may be able to give individuals. The breakup of marriages and religious communities, the religious and sometimes moral collapse of once-fervent individuals, are viewed with a sense of helplessness, a mere acceptance of the inevitable. Much of modern life is now the systematic shucking off of burdens and responsibilities, a process towards which the Church seems to take the position either of a spectator or at best a feeble critic. (The spread of the charismatic movement is, among other things, an attempt on the part of many people to forge an interior moral and religious order for themselves, supported by small groups, to replace the patently weak order now provided by the Church as a whole.) A former Presbyterian minister, now working with drug addicts, has remarked that

> Contemporary churchmanship is awash in a kind of permissiveness which results in watered-down distortion of what true religion has been through

the centuries. Religion has to do with subduing the ego, the voluntary taking up of a self-denial and service to a Higher Power. . . .

I believe organized religion frequently doesn't get anywhere with addicts because it's not honest enough. It's caught up in niceness and gentleness and timidity and it isn't tough enough.[20]

Nowhere is the intellectual and moral revolution that has swept over the Church more tellingly revealed than in the current popularity of the word *pastoral,* which is often simply used as a synonym for *permissive.* A "pastoral" solution to a problem, a "pastoral" priest or a bishop, "pastoral" needs, are now frequently the simple equivalent of endorsing whatever happens to be current practice, a refusal to lay burdens on people's consciences.

Yet an authentic understanding of the Church's tradition of pastoral care cannot evade the recognition that, since this care aims at setting man right with God, it cannot be simply a concession to the individual's subjective sense of rightness. Authentic pastoral concern might, under some circumstances, precisely demand instructing lax consciences, even, if necessary, using sanctions and condemnations. It is doubtful, for instance, if many Catholic racists of times past felt any subjective sense of guilt. On the contrary, most probably enjoyed a feeling of righteousness. True concern for their souls virtually dictated strong and admonitory preaching and, where necessary, ecclesiastical sanctions as an effective way of dramatizing the seriousness of their sin.

A California priest, a devotee of Transactional Analysis, spends much of his time trying to rid people of their feelings of guilt, which he attributes to "negative programming" received while children. Such feelings are considered bad because, among other things, they contradict the compulsory belief that people are "born to win." Fear itself is one of the greatest "sins," and a prime purpose of this particular form of pastoral guidance is to teach people that "it's okay to express your feelings."[21] In St. Louis a nun tells audiences: "Think of your emotions, your thoughts and traits as media that an artist could work with. . . . By learning the basic techniques of effective living, you can shape these media into something of effective beauty, and become more alive to the artistry of yourself." Hearers are urged to adopt maxims such as, "I like myself unconditionally as God made me," "I never devalue myself through destructive self-criticism," "I am easily able to relax at any time," and "I am completely self-determined and allow others that same right."[22]

Apart from considerations of the truth or falsehood of these approaches from a Christian standpoint, they are trivializing and debasing from a human standpoint, offering the promise of adulthood in terms which relieve the individual of all sense of adult moral possibility. As usual, Christians eager to embrace new movements prove extremely naive about their full implications. Thomas Harris, a leading exponent of Transactional Analysis and author of *I'm Okay, You're Okay,* was in 1974 required to make a $50,000 settlement to a woman who accused him of keeping her under the influence of drugs and liquor in order to enjoy her sexual favors.[23]

The controversy over divorce within the Church has focused the question of responsibility, since in their eagerness to persuade the Church to sanction divorce some spouses fall into the habit of describing the breakdown of their marriages as though they were mechanical failures devoid of any human intervention. No one can be held responsible.

> If a couple decide they are unable to grow and mature in their marriage they should be free to divorce and remarry.[24]
>
> . . . marriages which have a built-in self-destruct mechanism that is triggered somewhere along the line by the psychic chemistry of the partners.[25]

The watchwords of the new morality are *freedom* and *maturity,* the claim that adult Christians can no longer allow themselves to be governed by laws made by others, including the Church. Yet the former president of the Canon Law Society, who advocates that annulments be more freely given and that partners in second marriages be admitted to the sacraments, also asserts that "there is a serious lessening of the possibility (i.e., the capacity) of American Catholics entering canonically valid marriages today" precisely because many people now enter into marriage with no necessary expectation that it will be permanent.[26] The American priest most outspoken in advocating that the Church permit divorce points out, however, that while annulments are now routinely granted because of the "psychological incapacity" of one of the partners, rarely is this interpreted to mean that the person in question is therefore incapacitated from marrying again. Rightly observing that this is a sham, he nonetheless is quite explicit in acknowledging that the "therapeutic" criteria—the decision by two people, based on "personal needs," as to whether they will stay together or be divorced—alone ought to govern and that it is the moral responsibility of the Church to foster this therapy. Psychiatric professionals alone have the right to speak on the subject, not the Church.[27]

The rubrics of "freedom" and "responsible adulthood" are now routinely used to justify the opposite. The freedom which people presumably possess, with the help of divine grace, to make and keep permanent commitments to one another and to God is implicitly denied, or treated as improbable. The weight of clerical authority is increasingly brought to bear to excuse and justify the breaking of such commitments. The permanency of marriage is often suggested as an "ideal" rather than a law. But it is noteworthy that in Protestant churches which officially hold this position it does not seem to be vigorously preached, even as an ideal. A therapeutic approach to marriage is alone practiced, and the dichotomy of "ideal" and "law" is simply used to justify virtually unimpeded divorce, even among the clergy themselves.

Having been for so long rationalistic in its theology and tending towards rigidity in its ascetics, Catholicism is now inundated with a subjectivist reaction, in which feelings and personal "needs" (often undistinguished from mere wants) are given primacy. While supposedly, in this new dispensation, there are no rules or obligations except those personally chosen, in fact people are denied the right to resist the therapeutic program. One is required to be "open," "loving," "creative," "caring," "compassionate," and "nonjudgmental," and a new style of ecclesiastical leadership has emerged (sometimes even including bishops) which is highly practiced in displaying such traits while at the same time wholly inept at witnessing to any fundamental credal principles. (In practice, these "loving" people often allow themselves the luxury of animosity directed at others who are nontherapeutic in outlook.) In a Wisconsin parish, for example, parishioners are asked to exchange handmade pom-poms called "warm fuzzies" during the greeting of peace, while banners ask, "Have you given anyone a warm fuzzy today?" The practice is said to "illustrate with piercing clarity fundamental messages of doctrine,"[28] although it seems precisely designed to smother all possibility of doctrine under an amorphous syrup. (The end of a rigorous ascetical tradition is uniquely suited to the production of wholly sentimental personalities.)

It cannot be emphasized too often that the greatest objection to the therapeutic approach to religion is that it does people a grave disservice by failing to communicate to them the fullness of Christian teaching. "Meeting people where they are" is a valid pastoral strategy provided they are not simply left where they are, which increasingly seems to be the case. If it is true that people do not hire expensive lawyers to tell them what they cannot do but rather to tell them how they can do what they want to do, it is also increasingly true that moral theologians are simply people who find theological reasons for justifying what is taken to be common practice. (This is true of the Catholic Theological Society of America's 1977 report on sexual ethics, for example.)[29] The refusal to "impose" things on people is hardly a service if the thing imposed happens to be true, and related to eternal life. To the desire of so many contemporary people to "be myself," the appropriate Christian response, now as always, is that no one is truly himself except in accord with the divine will, submission to which has never in the past been thought of as demeaning or oppressive. The "needs" of people are relevant to the mission of the Church but do not begin to exhaust that mission, and to the degree that Church leaders allow these expressed "needs" to limit their vision they are both derelict in their duty to God and irresponsible with respect to their own people. Compassion for sinners necessarily includes the responsibility of enlightening them about their sins.

A vastly significant shift has occurred recently with respect to the word *conscience,* which since the Second Vatican Council has been used as a shibboleth in advanced Catholic circles. The Council, even in its "progressive" decree on religious liberty, warned against a false freedom which was an excuse for license and of the necessity of having a properly formed conscience.[30] Increasingly, however, the word has been used therapeutically to mean a subjective sense of moral serenity, of self-righteousness. Classically, conscience has more often referred to uncomfortable moral demands made on the individual. St. Thomas More was a martyr to conscience in that he believed there were certain laws of God which he had no right to transgress, whatever the personal cost. Those Christians whose consciences told them to resist the Nazis also paid with their lives. Now, however, "conscience" seems to be all too often that internal faculty which assures people that they are right in doing what they wish to do. (A couple may feel justified in using contraceptives. It is difficult to see, however, in what way "conscience" requires this action.)

Philip Rieff warns that modern education, with its openness to a seemingly endless variety of moral viewpoints, tends to produce a kind of person who is morally uninvolved, "the kind that would rather switch moralities than fight about any." The greatest paradox is that the best products of modern moral education lack all conviction.[31] Christopher Lasch, a socialist historian who is scarcely an orthodox Christian, points out the disservice parents do to children by failing to impart firm moral beliefs that can serve as the basis of an adult identity.[32]

Practices associated with the sacrament of Penance are especially significant indexes of the inner state of current Catholic life. Objections to the traditional rite of Penance have been of two kinds—that it was an unpleasant and "oppressive" experience and that it was merely mechanical and thus without real significance. The two criticisms are quite different from one another and require different responses.

To the first it seems appropriate to observe that, after all, sin itself and the guilt which follows it are unpleasant experiences. While the act of confession should not be needlessly traumatic, the attempt to make it into a pleasant and wholly untraumatic experience, amidst cosmetized surroundings, is akin to similar efforts, now widely recognized as misconceived, to deny the reality of death in a plastic mortuary environment. Peace and joy are possible after sin only because of repentance and forgiveness which, until they are pronounced, leave the sinner unsettled and uneasy. Sin, if it is real, is a fearsome thing, and certain new styles of Penance tend instead to trivialize it.

The attempt to overcome the mechanical character of traditional confession seems at first promising—allowing priest and penitent more time, encouraging the penitent's heartfelt and thorough baring of his entire spiritual condition, the opportunity for real direction. In practice, however, this too seems in danger of subversion by the therapeutic mentality. Calling Penance the "sacrament of reconciliation" is obviously not wrong, provided the concept is not understood too narrowly. But in practice the word *reconciliation* is often used in modern society to gloss over the question of moral blame. Two people are "reconciled" through a tacit understanding that neither will allude to what caused their original estrangement. Such reconciliation takes place between equals. Both implications of the word are obviously false when applied to the relationship of God and the sinner, yet the style now sometimes used in administering the sacrament seems designed to beg the entire question of guilt and to short-circuit the necessity for real repentance.

As the practice of confession has declined, therapeutic practices of all kinds are on the rise—Transactional Analysis, encounter groups, psychotherapy, etc. Some of the new approaches to Penance are easily accommodated to the therapeutic mentality, so that the experience of "reconciliation" becomes subtly egocentric—the "penitent" undertakes to become a better person, more fulfilled, by resolving his past "restricting" and "destructive" experiences. Rather than seeking God's forgiveness and blessing, he attempts to excise, painlessly, all the "uncreative" parts of his personality. God becomes the power which the individual appropriates to overcome the obstacles in his life. The modern ego appears so fragile that few individuals can live with a sense of their own sinfulness; they need constantly to find ways to excise it. It is ironic that, in a culture which places high value on intimacy and the dynamism of small groups, a high-water mark of postconciliar American Catholic "renewal" is thought to be a 1977 rite in Memphis in which thousands of people were absolved anonymously, forgiven sins which had been identified in only the most general way, and with the ramifications of specific moral situations—second marriages, for example—nicely glossed over.[33] This desire to lose oneself in a moral crowd is reflected also in the liberal Christian penchant for focusing on social evils for which "everyone" or "society" is held responsible.

The literary critic John Sisk has identified the "narcissistic" moral attitude as perhaps a direct product of sustained material prosperity which systematically silences all authoritative voices from outside the self.[34] Langdon Gilkey, describing how the Catholic Church of the future ought to function, offers a concise exhortation to adopt this attitude:

> And if all human authorities are relative, it follows for any human among humans, that only *his* mind, only *his* conscience, and *his* will can have ultimate authority for him.
>
> . . . The value involved in penance, as in most of the activities of religion, is the fulfillment of the autonomous personal being of each and by each. . . .[35]

As Daniel Bell has pointed out, the problem with this kind of moral attitude is that it makes "the impact on the self not the moral consequence to society—the source of ethical and aesthetic judgments."[36]

This attitude has profound theological and religious ramifications apart from specific moral questions. At its root is the question of whether in fact God exists, as a distinct and real being who created the universe and presides over it, to whom men therefore owe homage. Modern atheism insists, with a certain logic given its understanding of freedom, that man cannot be truly free under God. Liberal Christians have sought to dispense with the problem more ambiguously, as in the manner of Gregory Baum,

> God is not the symbol of power over man but rather a symbol of power in and through man, that is, the symbol of the release of man's power and its orientation toward growth and liberation.

Otherwise, according to Baum, belief in God is "pathological."[37] The utility of his formula lies in the fact that one can thereby be a Christian without necessarily affirming the existence of any being truly distinct from the self, the possible existence of such a being left deliberately uncertain.

The new concept of revelation, incompatible with what the Church has taught and believed for nineteen centuries, works in a similar way, in that revelation is not conceived as God communicating truth to man, a divine irruption in human history, but simply as man's own reflections on his personal and corporate religious experience. Thus, for instance, Gregory Baum finds parts of the New Testament clearly false and in need of radical revision.[38] The traditional concept of revelation is a grave threat to the therapeutic personality precisely because it represents an "intrusion" from the outside, something larger than itself to which the self must accommodate. There is an arrogant and naive assumption that this generation of Christians can discover all that it needs of divine truth from its own experiences and that whatever lies outside that experience can scarcely be significant. Although lip service is paid to the experiences of past Christian ages, in practice contemporary religious experience is assumed to be normative, and everything else is judged in accordance with it. There is a willful narrowness of perspective, in which even some of the central truths of the faith are progressively discarded as no longer meaningful. Personal experience, because of its immediacy and vividness, will always exercise a disproportionate influence and hence is always in need of amplification and correction from some source outside itself. True Christians believe in the teachings of Christ, not their own experiences.

That this should be the age of the Holy Spirit is therefore appropriate, since the Spirit is thought to speak from within the self. It is He who gives divine sanction to the self's promptings. Traditionally the cult of the Holy Spirit in the Church has been problematical in the same way that mysticism is problematical—valid and profound truths must somehow be separated from what is false by reference to some outside criterion of judgment. In the present age of the Holy Spirit it was first necessary to abolish Satan (who unexpectedly returned through the back door of the popular media) in order that all the promptings of the self could with absolute confidence be attributed to the Spirit.

The Father recedes progressively from view because He is the person of the Trinity least assimilable to the self. He remains the presiding, overarching presence whose existence is a threat to the weaker egos among His children. His traditional attributes, especially as judge, are virtually banished from thought. No bright banners proclaim, "What a fearful thing it is to fall into the hands of the living God." "Finding God in other people" has become a formula to justify not seeking Him. The coziness of personal relations is, by tacit agreement, allowed to define the limits of the religious universe. God is not the God of Abraham, Isaac, and Jacob but the God of Sister Corita, Rod McKuen, and Jonathan Livingston Seagull.

But the crucial area of modern Catholicism is inevitably Christology, where the revival of Arian or quasi-Arian notions is part of a general process by which Jesus is literally being cut down to size, reduced to a plane of equality with the individual believer. The movement began in the popular media, in productions like *Jesus Christ Superstar* (accompanied by the Beatles' celebrated remark that they were more famous than Jesus) and has been abetted by certain kinds of biblical criticism which render the figure of the historical Jesus so misty and problematical that Christians are in effect free to make of Him whatever they wish. (As

Gregory Baum puts it, "While Christians define their own existence in terms of Jesus Christ, the Christian churches of our day have tried to relativize this symbol in theologically responsible ways.")[39] Many modern Christians are more comfortable with the thought of Jesus as simply a man like themselves than of Jesus Christ the incarnation of the eternal Word. Like the Father, the latter image is felt as a threat to human autonomy.

The preference for regarding Jesus primarily as "our brother" or "my friend" has some warrant in the devotional traditions of Christianity but little warrant in the New Testament. However Jesus Christ is ultimately understood, the Scriptures clearly portray Him as an authoritative and even authoritarian figure. His preaching focused heavily on sin and the need for repentance. He seemed to attach immense importance to His own person and to Himself as the only way to the Father, and never seems to have entered into relationships of equality with anyone. He warned His followers against disobedience and never engaged in "dialogue" with people except for the pedagogical purpose of eliciting from them the responses He wanted. Nowhere did He encourage anyone to disagree with, challenge, or contradict Him. There were apparently no multiple roads to truth.

The therapeutic personality in modern Christianity tellingly reveals itself in terms of its sometimes fanatical attachment to what is ordinary and even banal, at the expense of anything that reverberates grandeur, power, authority, or solemnity. Thus for some people there is a real personal need for liturgy celebrated in a very ordinary setting—a living room, a gymnasium, or a parish hall, with metal folding chairs, casual clothes, a plain table, and a conversational style of preaching and proclamation. They are at ease only with those things which seem like extensions of themselves, which do not threaten by symbolizing a world transcending their own and towards which they are called. Similarly there is a strong need, in liturgy, in theology, in religious education, to have every message recast in such a way that it speaks primarily of man and only indirectly of God. For to speak of God is to exclude those who might be described as religiously tone-deaf. Modernizing movements in the contemporary Church are sometimes inspired by the sociological phenomenon of *"ressentiment"*—dislike of what is perceived as higher than oneself and possibly unattainable.

Contemporary liturgy, following the strenuous reforms of the post-conciliar era, is consequently weak in power and symbolism, a bland conveyance which lacks the ability to grip anyone at any very deep level.[40] Classical liturgical, spiritual, and theological texts are in effect bowdlerized to make them palatable to minds unable to digest stronger food. (The translation, "Happy are the poor in spirit," is both misleading as an empirical statement and trivializing in terms of its meaning.) The urgent desire to "create" liturgies, though the products may have little merit, is a reflection once again of the need to enter into only those acts of worship which are felt to be extensions of the self. Liturgies which are given ("imposed") are somehow experienced as threatening to the self's autonomy and therefore to be resisted. There is an imaginative impoverishment which precludes the possibility of entering deeply into something which is not of one's own creation.

Insensitivity to the power of language and symbol, even a deliberate resistance to what is other than ordinary, has relevance to the vitality of Christianity at any given time. Compare, for example, Lincoln's Second Inaugural Address with the jargon-ridden, whining style of many contemporary manifestoes of social justice. In Lincoln's prose the awful threat of God's wrath directed at the evildoer is real, and there is a palpable sense of the terrible consequences of human actions, while the literary products of many modern leftist groups seem merely petulant. Compare also the awesome power of the traditional clothing ceremony of a cloistered nun, or the starkness of a Cistercian funeral, with juxtaposed descriptions of "renewed" nuns: "an elegant woman with upswept hair and an expensive dress," "the superior arrives in curlers to say grace: 'Good food, good meat, good God, let's eat.' " "She has been on television several times and is constantly flying to conferences and meetings. She has a great many men friends, says she falls in love at least once a year, and has had several marriage proposals."[41]

Perhaps the most persistent concern of therapeutic Christianity is that nothing in religion be experienced as unpleasant, constricting, or negative. Thus a former Jesuit, now religious-education director for a Midwestern parish, writes that:

> The warm reception given the musical play *Godspell* suggests a light, optimistic interpretation of the Gospels strikes a deep, resonant chord in many people.
>
> It is terrifying to read any interpretation of the Annanias/Sapphira story (Acts 5:1–11) which does not see this as a bit of Jewish humor. . . . In a tight little Christian community fund-raising can be fun now and then![42]

What is intriguing about his interpretations is the frank way in which the intended meaning of the Scriptures, as distinct from the individual's subjective reaction to them, is easily thrust aside. Since it is deemed inappropriate that God should ever communicate something unpleasant to man, obviously He did not.

Contemporary religious education has for over a decade emphasized the "positive" approach, forbearing to lay burdens on children, constantly exhorting them towards love and joy, shunning the Ten Commandments as negative, insisting that few children are capable of either understanding or committing sin. Yet one of the great child psychiatrists of modern times, Bruno Bettelheim, says,

> There is a widespread disinclination to let children know that the source of much that goes wrong in life is due to our own natures. . . . Instead, we want our children to believe that all men are inherently good. But every child knows that *he* is not always good, and that even when he is he would prefer not to be. . . .

Bettelheim regards traditional fairy tales as far more suitable fare for children than "relevant" modern stories, partly because these tales present evil as real and powerful. The polarity of good and evil enables children to grasp the difference between the two. The tales also recognize the natural human desire for eternal life (which modern catechetics has chosen to ignore almost completely) and children's natural tendency to believe in magic, and Bettelheim believes that the credulity about magic that many adolescents now manifest may be the result of having been deprived of it in childhood.[43] (The modern religious educator has an absolute horror of anything in religion which may be thought of as even remotely magical.)

The therapeutic approach to liturgy, catechetics, religious life, ascetics, and morality has the ultimate effect of making life weightless. Everything is an emanation of the self, and nothing has an objective correlative outside the self. Neither ideas nor actions have real consequences, in the sense that no decision is ever irrevocable—each can be recalled at will. Vows may be kept or broken. Liturgy may be solemn or trendy. One's life may be hedonistic or austere. All such choices refer back only to the self, and none carries any weight capable of imposing on the self. The final result is what the literary historian Quentin Anderson defines as the "imperial self," traceable in American culture to Ralph Waldo Emerson, in which "realized human greatness consists in a demand for the immediate realization of our widest visions." The result is that a sense of membership in human society and in history ultimately disappears and the horizon comes to be filled with projections of the self. According to Anderson, ". . . part of the process of becoming a self in such a culture is precisely the need to deny the efficacy of the operative familial and social constraints in fixing a sense of the self." Finally, a matter which ought to be of crucial concern to the churches but seems not to be, "human beings are now demanding the counterpart of Christian beatitude as a natural right."[44]

Preconciliar reformers argued that the Church placed too much emphasis on sexual morality, especially to the exclusion of social morality. Whatever validity that contention may have had in the abstract, in practice it has proved impossible to deemphasize sexual morality because modern Western culture is obsessed with it. Questions of sexual behavior will continue to be raised whether or not Christians wish them to be, and sexual morality will therefore continue to be of central symbolic importance. This is in fact quite appropriate, for as the historian John Lukacs points out,

> The profoundest problems of morality involve, after all, what people do (and how they think) with their own selves: in other words, what people do privately (or, rather, what they think of their acts). It is therefore that the problem of sexual, that is, carnal morality is at the center of the moral crisis of our times; it is not merely a marginal development.[45]

Philip Rieff has insisted that sexual controls were placed very near the center of the Christian symbolic and that attempts by contemporary churchmen to argue that they are not necessary are misconceived. Christian asceticism aimed at the spiritualization of the natural drives, "a liberation of the highest powers of personality from blockage by the automatism of the lower drives." Reiff also remarks witheringly that ". . . enlightened Christians . . . have a genius for accepting almost any position, so to say, that is grossly anti-Christian or simply vulgar— especially in sex and art" and that even many of the Church's leaders seem not to understand what is really at stake with regard to the question of celibacy. The "transgressive sense," that is, the sense that there are laws which one can violate and that such violations involve consequences, had first to be broken in the area of sexual behavior.[46]

Once again, therefore, the central symbolic importance of the crisis of the religious life for the postconciliar Church becomes apparent, not only in the fact that so many religious repudiated their vows (this might have been merely a quantitative change from the past) but in terms of the mystique which followed upon that repudiation as the grounds for justifying it: that the Church had no right to "impose" celebacy on people and that to live celibately is, except in unusual cases, "unnatural." Within a few years time the repudiation of vows apparently ceased being, for many people, an agonizing and momentous personal decision and became almost routine. In their public statements, and in the attitude towards these statements reflected in the mass media, it was treated as a wholly natural thing, unaccompanied by any great struggles of conscience.

Birth control was the key popular issue, since, consciously or not, the leaders of the transgressive assault recognized the importance of separating sexual experience from any necessary connection with procreation and denying the Church's right to "interfere" with sexual behavior. Although many reformers had the dream of turning the Catholic Church into a community of socially compassionate individuals, it proved inevitably easier to reach people in terms of their own self-interest than concern for others. The moral authority of the Church was battered most severely on the rock of an assertive sexual freedom, with little concern for the ultimate result of that battering. The result might simply be a rejection of the Church's moral authority on all questions. A 1972 California survey showed that more than half of Catholics disagreed with the Church's position on sexual matters, nearly half thought the Church should "stay out of" social issues, and less than half thought racial integration was a desirable social goal.[47]

To an extent which is still not fully appreciated, the drive for social justice in the past decade has been a metaphor, in the lives of many of those participating in it, for their own sexual liberation. It was in radical political circles that sometimes militant forms of transgressive sexual behavior were most fully accepted and even applauded. Many religious who began convinced that racial injustice or war was the gravest moral problem of the age ended by placing their own vows of chastity in that central place. A New York priest suspended by his archbishop because he insisted publicly on his "right" to have an intimate relationship with a woman issued a statement asserting, militantly but irrelevantly, that "Christ does not look for large cathedrals, military chaplains, or elite academic institutions in his church."[48]

Many priests and religious, after sojourns in the fields of social concern, found suitable spouses for themselves and retired to the suburbs. It is especially ironic that countless "radical" Catholics have chosen both to support the sexual revolution and to attack the consumer society, without apparently appreciating how the former grows naturally out of the latter.

The Second Vatican Council, in its "forward-looking" decree *Gaudium et Spes,* spoke of "polygamy, the plague of divorce, so-called free love, and similar blemishes; furthermore, married love is too often dishonored by selfishness, hedonism, and unlawful contraceptive practices." It recalled that "Marriage and married love are by nature ordered to the procreation of children."[49]

Like many other conciliar decrees, however, these passages were tacitly censored out of the mental world of many postconciliar renewalists. The Catholic Theological Society of America's 1977 report on sexual ethics appears to fall into the category of those sexual studies about which Lionel Trilling, in reference to the first Kinsey Report of thirty years ago, observed,

It goes with nearly conscious aversion from making intellectual distinctions. . . . We might say that those who most explicitly assert and wish to practice the democratic virtues have taken it as their assumption that all social facts—with the exception of exclusion and economic hardship—must be *accepted,* not merely in the scientific sense but also in the social sense, in the sense, that is, that no judgment must be passed on them. . . .

But then it goes on to imply that there can be only one standard for judgment of sexual behavior—that is, sexual behavior as it actually exists; which is to say that sexual behavior is not to be judged at all, except, presumably, in so far as it causes pain to others.[50]

One recent work of Catholic moral theology, published under the auspices of a Benedictine abbey, finds ample justification not only for divorce and contraception but also for unmarried persons living together, polygamy (especially for older people), "comarital" or triangular relationships, sexual therapy in nonmarital encounters, sperm banks, and euthanasia, all on the primary grounds that these are coming to be accepted in American society.[51]

The very word *chastity* has become difficult for many Catholics to pronounce without a snicker, and, despite their determination to be liberated, an unacknowledged guilt with regard to sexual matters still underlies the outlook of many "enlightened" people, compelling them to offer prim rationalizations for almost every kind of sexual behavior. Another of the endless ironies of present Catholic life is the fact that, although generations were embarrassed by the widespread clerical fornication which was one of the corruptions of the pre-Reformation Church, people are now expected to react to that same phenomenon with sophisticated equanimity. In this as in other matters, self-consciously "advanced" Catholics fail to understand what is really happening. Thus a priest-psychologist can state with assurance that "Traditional Christianity is deeply suspicious that words like 'sexual fulfillment' are euphemisms for fornication, adultery, and sheer hedonism. This, of course, can never be the case."[52]

"Liberated" Christians tend to have a naively hygienic view of sex—that it is a wholesome human power which, given proper education and the right kind of social arrangements (those liberal panaceas for every kind of moral disorder), will prove entirely healthy and benign. They have scant appreciation for its demonic qualities, for the propensities for disordered use that seem endemic to it, for its potential idolatry which has made it suspect in the eyes of many of the world's religious. In particular they fail to understand that, since sex is the chief vehicle by which traditional interdicts are being assaulted, its gentle qualities are at least temporarily submerged. In this as in other matters the liberal Christian, in seeking to bless and make holy, succeeds merely in trivializing. Modern sexual hygienists seem never to wonder why, although sexual behavior in the Western world has grown steadily less repressed for over sixty years, the goal of a totally "healthy" sexuality remains so elusive. Liberal Catholics seem not to understand that, in an age of aggressive hedonism, an equally strong and living ideal of chastity is essential for the spiritual well-being of the culture. Although preferring to emphasize the healthy aspects of sexuality, avant-garde Catholics rarely miss a step even when forced to look at its underside. Thus a prominent psychologist, a former priest, insists that "man is, after all, saying something to us in the language of pornography. . . . movies and exhibitions that make people feel a little less lonely."[53] A well-known Jesuit secondary educator pronounces the censorship of pornography as "puritanism, chauvinism, narrowness, anti-intellectualism, and all kinds of cultural fascism." He finds moral justifications for premarital intercourse "rather conservative."[54]

"Make love, not war" was a battle cry of the 1960s youth culture, but its loud and frequent repetition merely served to obscure the fundamental fallacy it enshrined. Wars have always had a loosening effect on sexual attitudes because they release hitherto repressed passions. Many enlightened Christians sincerely believe, however, that greater sexual freedom is conducive to gentleness and peace.

Philip Rieff, on the other hand, has observed that the dissolution of respect for interdicts will, for many people, also mean the dissolution of respect for themselves, as evidenced in "our cults of the criminal and drug use." People are now being educated to criticism before loyalty to what is being criticized. The transgressive imagination tends towards brutality, by which people "murder their creative sense of guilt." It is now the superego—formerly the source of moral constraint—which stimulates transgressive behavior, as virtually a duty of the truly free individual.

> Immediately behind the hippies are the thugs. They occupy the remissive space opened up by the hippies. . . . The self-absorbed therapy of the hippies clears the way for the mass-murder therapy of the thugs. . . . we will see in true light the craven aping and interminable apologies for the transgressive types at the bottom: the perverts, the underclass, all those who can do no wrong because they have been wronged. This is no Christening movement: the early Christians did not ape the publicans and sinners they tried to save.[55]

A former Paulist priest describes how ". . . I went to work as chaplain at a clinic for alcoholics. Oh, I arrived pure, powerful, sober as hell . . . I was healer, reconciler, articulator of hope for the despairing. . . . An old drunk named Bobby looked right through me one day, saying, 'Jim, boy, you need a drink.' And he was right. And that night I went to a bar and got drunk for the first time in my life. . . ."[56]

Sins of the flesh, formerly at least a useful corrective to pride, now support it, since being emancipated from the right taboos, demonstrating one's transgressive abilities, are now marks of moral prestige in advanced circles. When the "remissive mode" of behavior surfaced in the 1960s it quickly became obligatory for the avant-garde, including the avant-garde of the Church. There was, consequently, little of freedom involved in it but rather a well-rehearsed parody of freedom. In place of the traditional badge of orthodoxy, the new Christians asserted defiantly "We love more," an infinitely more arrogant claim. Every even remote hint of arrogance associated with ecclesiastical office is ruthlessly exposed, while arrogance displayed by "prophetic" or "charismatic" figures serves merely to strengthen their appeal. As Daniel Berrigan wrote, "Could it be that authority, so conducting itself, was really granting me a backhanded compliment, and every time I received an official put-down, I should wear it up and down Fordham Road like a shiny new Croix de Paix?"[57]

Unless the fact is recognized that ego-assertion—against institutions, superiors, laws, creeds—has now become more than a right, in fact a duty, much of what is happening in the contemporary Church will remain unintelligible. For the fragility of the modern ego appears to be such that everything other than itself, and especially everything which appears larger than itself, is experienced as a threat. In the Church this takes the form first of demanding constant symbolic expressions of personal recognition (the reiterated cry that the Church is "insensitive to our needs"), then an assertion of emancipated superiority over all the generations of Christians who have gone before ("we are just beginning to understand what the Gospel is all about"), finally repeated assaults on official authority in order to test its precise strength and demonstrate one's own courage. Rebellion and dissent, which may once have been thoughtful and courageous, have now become reflex actions often bringing with them greater rewards than penalties. Self-expression is the last vessel of the sacred, what the sociologist Robert Nisbet describes as the "victory of the performing self."[58] The particular theological issues over which dissent arises are less important than the need to dissent itself.

An anonymous young man, reflecting on the values of the new culture, writes,

> Emancipation has to do with power, not love; and a view of life in terms of emancipation—or liberation—will tend to be a political view. . . . Finally,

the object of emancipation is the individual, not the connection between individuals; the doctrines of this emancipation stress terms like "self-awareness," . . . terms that crowd anybody other than the "self" right out of one's imagination.[59]

With respect to religion, the time-honored strategy of the liberal churches for dealing with dissent—conceding as much as possible to the dissenter, in the hope that he will then accept everything else—virtually by definition is no longer workable, and is in fact suicidal. For since the act of self-emancipation is its own end (liberal Catholics now commonly feel embarrassed if they are found agreeing with the magisterium on some controversial question), authority, no matter how many concessions it makes, will find itself pursued still farther, until it finally admits that it has no authority. As Philip Rieff has put it, there will be "a systematic hunting down of all settled convictions."[60] Finally the only truly "flexible" morality (and hence a morality which does not impose itself on the self) is no morality at all. As *Commonweal's* Italian correspondent wrote following the 1974 referendum on divorce, "And I must confess that on that night I envied them. Who has not dreamt of the chance to say *No* to all the pseudo-fathers, the know-alls, the moralists, who know so well 'what is good for us'. . . . The Italians had that chance, and used it . . . It was certainly worth one night's roaring festivities."[61]

Aggressive behavior, hostility masquerading as love, is now common in the Church to a degree that would have seemed horrifying and totally unpredictable during the conciliar era of good feeling. The following statements were made, respectively, by a former director of family life for a Midwestern archdiocese, a Spanish-American nun, and a noted Scripture scholar:

> After a day with the good sisters, I can still retreat into a delicious dream. In this dream I put them all into one boat and start them for Rome. Here the dream varies: sometimes I put a hole in the bottom of it; sometimes I depend on a hurricane. But always, the results are the same: sheer joy because I have given these people what I have always wanted for them— eternal happiness, *now.*[62]

> "I'm frightened by what the seminaries are producing in terms of conservatism. They go overboard on intellectualism. They think they're so special. They're a cancer that we have to cut out," she said, banging her fist on the table.[63]

> Some bishops are like a drunken father. He is a constant annoyance and a financial burden, we try to hide him when company comes, and we worry about what half-wit blunder he will make next. But we will not throw the old sot into the gutter; we feed him and house him, pick him up when he falls and tuck him into bed. We love him about as much as we can, and it may not seem to be much; but it is more than any one else loves him. . . .[64]

During the interim period before all authorities lose their charism, a literary genre has emerged in which embittered Catholics blame the Church for their personal problems, for the "oppressions" which were imposed on them, another subtle testimony to the falseness of their newly proclaimed freedom, another refusal to take responsibility for one's own life. When the final discrediting of all authority has occurred, however, when human moral autonomy has finally been asserted beyond even the possibility of contradiction, the results are not likely to be the dreamed-of reign of peace and freedom. Daniel Bell points out that the great religions of the West have been religions of restraint, seeking to control the demonic and the ecstatic, while moderism—including its denial of the authority of the past as embodied in religion—embraces the demonic.[65] In the words of Philip Rieff,

> . . . evil and immortality are disappearing . . . mainly because our culture is changing its definition of human perfection. No longer the Saint, but the instinctual Everyman, twisting his neck uncomfortably in the starched collar of culture, is the communal ideal, to whom men offer tacit prayers for deliverance from their inherited renunciations.
>
> Against interdictory form, a culture organized by contempt and rancor, rather than reverence and justice, must view inhibition, the delay of gratification, all those disciplines by which self and society can be held in mutual check, as the main enemy.[66]

In the end the absence of laws and structures is apt to foster a distorted personalism, a kind of moral frivolity in which nimble minds are able to justify—to themselves and to an admiring audience—virtually any kind of behavior that can somehow be designated as "freeing." There is no possibility of reforming structures without first reforming people, which is precisely what the age refuses to do. The residue of inherited, authoritative religious morality is rapidly drying up in Western culture. It is only a hypothesis, with virtually no historical example to confirm it, that society can for any length of time sustain itself wholly on the basis of spontaneous human moral impulses. A threatening solipsism—the uncertainty whether other beings besides the self even exist, an unwillingness to permit such beings to impinge on the self—is the gravest moral problem of the age. The universe is increasingly perceived as a vast empty space waiting to be filled by an infinitely expanding self, and in this vision religious authority must be shucked off not primarily because it is false but because it is binding, because it impedes the self's continuous unfolding. In the end the promise of our culture is one the Judaeo-Christian tradition has heard before: You shall be like gods.

CHAPTER 4

The Sensation of Movement

THE loss of a sense of a living and inspiring communal past, the deliberate refashioning of traditional symbols to give them a primarily worldly emphasis, and the partly unconscious adoption of the moral attitudes here designated "therapeutic," have had the cumulative effect, among Catholics deeply affected by them, of bringing their religious life to a standstill. The streams from which members of the Church have traditionally drawn refreshment are diverted or dammed. New sources have been slow in appearing. Many people no longer understand what motive powers, over the centuries, have imparted energy and direction to the life of the Church. T. S. Eliot's point that liberal religion is much more adept at criticism and undoing than at creation and inspiration has proven abundantly accurate in the era of what was supposed to be renewal.

The primacy of the therapeutic attitude—the granting of sovereign authority to a self which is intolerant of all limitations imposed from the outside—should not be understood only in moral terms, still less only in terms of sexual morality (although it is most dramatically manifest there). The governing spirit of much of what has called itself renewal in the past fifteen years has been essentially negative and, in a quite literal sense, reactionary. The positive meaning of liturgical reform, the renewal of religious life, ecumenism, and many other things have been lost in the midst of an attitude of mind which focuses solely on the conditions of its own self-defined liberation. *Aggiornamento* has, in the minds of many people, taken on meaning exclusively in terms of a proclaimed freedom from the past—we do not need to fast any more, wear uncomfortable and conspicuous "sacred" clothing, pray at set times, follow a ritual not devised by ourselves, believe particular doctrines, submit to particular moral laws, follow the injunctions of our pastors.

Renewal has been interpreted in the liberal West largely in terms of a deeply culturally conditioned emphasis on "freedom," which is only a *leitmotiv* in the documents of the Second Vatican Council and is in any case now often understood in ways foreign to the Christian tradition. *Gaudium et Spes* says,

> Only in freedom can man direct himself toward goodness. Our contemporaries make much of this freedom and pursue it eagerly; and rightly so, to be sure. Often, however, they foster it perversely as a license for doing whatever pleases them, even if it is evil.

In their *Declaration on Religious Liberty* the Council fathers reaffirmed that

> Many pressures are brought to bear upon men of our day, to the point where the danger arises lest they lose the possibility of acting on their own judgment. On the other hand, not a few can be found who seem inclined to use the name of freedom as the pretext for refusing to submit to authority and for making light of the duty of obedience.[1]

The fact that the promised renewal has proved disappointing to many people is directly traceable to certain weaknesses inherent in modern liberalism—its far greater capacity for criticizing received beliefs than for discovering new wisdom and its tendency to make freedom the end of existence, a purely empty concept which is unable to suggest how such freedom may be meaningfully used. In the Catholic Church this has led to several quite predictable states of mind, now dominant among the most articulate people in the Church. "Renewal" is largely equated with the winning of constant victories over the "rigidities" of the past, continually opening new territories formerly deemed taboo. For some the victories come so easily that they lose interest in the contest and drift away. After a while the game seems trivial, since its aim was merely to bring Catholics to the same frame of mind that secularists or liberal Protestants have enjoyed for a long time. For others, with the low toleration of frustration bred by an affluent society, the slowing down of the parade of "breakthroughs," real or apparent signs of conservatism in the Church, induces anger and even hysterical panic. For still others the contest is merely boring. They remain in the Church but take little interest in a struggle which no longer seems dramatic or challenging.

In countless ways individuals of all shades of opinion have expressed fear that the postconciliar Church is in a condition of stagnation, that it has lost its momentum, that there are no more exciting horizons, no great ideas. To a large extent this is true, a situation predetermined precisely by the expectations which lie behind such disillusionment. It is easy to forget that twenty years ago this complaint would have been unintelligible to most Catholics. They were not accustomed to thinking of their religion as having any necessary connection with what was dramatic, public, controversial, and exciting. The Church's task was primarily to save souls, a task it could, for the most part, fulfill quietly, even routinely. Such drama as existed was often hidden in the great crises of soul that individuals experience. The contemporary expectation of tangible signs of "movement" in the life of the Church is one of the most significant evidences of the profound intellectual revolution which has followed the Council but which appears fundamentally at odds with the Council's own authentic mind.

Philip Rieff diagnosed the "panic and dis-ease" which follows the destruction of those means by which a culture maintains moral control, and the many efforts that then have to be made towards filling up the spiritual emptiness left behind after the inhibitions depart.

> In our recovered innocence, to be entertained would become the highest good, and boredom the most common evil.
>
> A social structure shakes with violence and shivers with fears of violence not merely when that structure is callously unjust but also when its members must stimulate themselves to feverish activity in order to demonstrate how alive they are.
>
> Psychological man may be going nowhere, but he aims to achieve a certain speed and certainty in going. Like his predecessor, the man of the market economy, he understands morality as that which is conducive to increased activity. The important thing is to keep going.[2]

The Second Vatican Council was, on the superficial level, a dramatic event which stimulated in many Catholics a sense of awakening from a long torpor, paralleling the political awakening from the Eisenhower years that was personified by America's first Catholic president. But since the deeper meaning of the Council could not be assimilated nearly so readily, the expectation of renewal has remained largely on the level of excitement and that almost narcotic need for outside stimulation which Rieff diagnosed for the culture at large. It cannot be overemphasized that in the present milieu an enthusiastic welcoming of constant change, or at the very least a prudent "openness" to all possibilities, is the only security. Those who have coped most successfully have been those who have exorcised from themselves the ability to be shocked or anxious. The popularity of what is called process theology derives largely from the assurance it offers modern Christians that change is, after all, the only reality that need be taken seriously, an assurance that their culture constantly drums into them in uncountable numbers of ways.

The Roman Catholic Church in the West is now decadent, in that it has lost its sense of self-generated energy and purpose, as have many of its members. The years of heady excitement have been followed either by disillusionment or a troubled boredom, a sense of treading water, of waiting for new developments which for some reason fail to appear. There is an almost insatiable need for artificial stimulus, some force which will once again get the Church "moving," although where it should be moving and why are unclear. Many Catholics have "liberated" themselves into the wild blue yonder, beyond the reach of gravity, and for them further changes in the Church—which they crave compulsively—are like astronauts doing acrobatics in outer space. There is nothing substantial at stake.

In this context a constantly sustained illusion of movement is essential, and the Church has been deeply affected by the modern mentality which repeatedly and without embarrassment announces new "break-throughs," most of them forgotten in a few years. A succession of fads in theology, spirituality, social action, education, group dynamics, and personal therapy comes and goes, each quickly used and used up, as devotees wait impatiently for the next wave. Much has been made of the Second Vatican Council's image of the "pilgrim Church," without analyzing what it means to be a pilgrim—to have a fixed and known goal, to be single-minded in quest of it, to place oneself wholly in the hands of God, to submit to a rigorous discipline which alone will make attainment of the goal possible.

In this atmosphere everything which is stable, ordinary, and traditional is a standing rebuke, to be ignored or discredited. The fact that some orders of nuns have changed relatively little, have lost relatively few members, and continue to attract novices since the Second Vatican Council is largely unknown to the American public, for example. Much publicity has been given to various "exciting" parishes, without recognizing that there are many parishes which are doing outstanding work that is simply not recognized—the Gospel is preached, the sacraments administered, people properly instructed, the poor and sick cared for, the troubled comforted, yet nothing dramatic or newsworthy ever occurs.

A priest-journalist expresses the postconciliar spirit by which movement becomes its own justification, change its own law.

I think the Church is far healthier than it has been for a long time. Those people who are disturbed by the seemingly unchecked activity in the church . . . by change, and who therefore want it all to stop, want a corpse, not a living body. No, they want not a corpse, for a corpse at least rots and therefore changes. They want a mummy. No change. . . .[3]

Catholics were formerly thought of as unusually firm, even rigid, people insofar as their beliefs and principles went. The acceptance of the new order has therefore required a substantial revolution of personality for many, especially those in religious life, which given the nature of the human psyche can probably never be achieved fully and completely without misgivings and residual guilt. Those who wish to become therapeutic personalities find themselves, therefore, in a constant struggle against backsliding, tensely vigilant against anything which threatens to pull them back to their former selves. Certain "renewalists" warn Catholics almost compulsively against possible recidivism, deliberately fueling feelings of embarrassment about past beliefs and insecurity about present ones:

> A whole book could be written about our sexual hangups on toilet habits and words for them, as well as ideas about modesty and clothes. We've made progress in these areas, thank God. Why not enjoy it?
>
> Nostalgia is great fun, and good hearty laughter is one of Catholicism's oldest characteristics. Yet a long memory helps immensely to avoid legal tyranny. The ridiculous positions we assumed officially in years past because we didn't keep up with developments in varied sciences can all too easily be assumed again. We should watch this tendency when tempted to politicize issues involving varied euthanasia methods and abortion laws.
>
> Into oblivion went much compulsive behavior tied up with our prayer life, our attendance at Mass, our use of Sacraments and also sacramentals like holy water.[4]

The sentiments are familiar, but take on special significance because they represent the postconciliar thinking of a priest who spent most of his life promoting popular Marian devotions. (One of the most interesting aspects of *aggiornamento* has been the ease with which certain of the clergy who once taught traditional beliefs in an authoritarian way set about, almost without skipping a breath, undermining those same beliefs in an equally authoritarian way. The phenomenon might be called "the emperor's *old* clothes," insisting officially that the Church was always naked, even when countless of the faithful were able to see its rich vestures.)

The largely negative thrust of so much of what has passed for renewal, its focusing on those things in the traditional Church deemed unhealthy or outmoded, has created a situation in which many Catholics are maximally susceptible to fads of all kinds. Since they no longer possess deeply held convictions of their own, they are incapable of criticizing such fads. Superficially the "liberals" in the Church appear to be affirmative in their judgments, while "conservatives" are in the position of critics and carpers. But conservatives are merely seeking to defend long-held beliefs which have come under severe attack in recent years, and are therefore profoundly "positive" in their ultimate commitments.

Self-consciously modern Catholics appear to have a compulsive need to think of themselves as "creative," "open," and "free," the authenticity of these claims constantly tested by their ability to respond affirmatively to every new development. A theologian, for example, argues that not only should the Church accept the morality of polygamy (even in the United States) because ". . . the hearts of people upon which this law of nature is engraved may well be moved to accept this practice," but should even "lead the way in agitating for civil legislation favoring polygamy."[5] Movement is regularly confused with progress, liveliness with vitality, innovation with creativity.

Like most apostles of change, avant-garde Catholics óscillate between proclamations of a radically transformed world which will scarcely resemble anything known in the past and condescending assurances that nothing essential has changed and that traditionalists are merely neurotically insecure. Increasingly, however, changes are not justified primarily in terms of the good or bad they promise, which are measurable according to some agreed-upon standard, but merely in terms of the desirability of change itself. Even if all the changes of the postconciliar era were healthy, they would cause discomfort and even agony to many Catholics, since deeply held beliefs which sustained generations of people have been cavalierly discarded. Surely change, even of a "progressive" kind, ought not to be bought too cheaply. Yet many postconciliar Catholics, sometimes even in high places, have come to resemble Evelyn Waugh's Sir Joseph Mainwaring:

> . . . a peppercorn lightness of soul, a deep unimpressionable frivolity, which left him bobbing serenely on the great waves of history which splintered more solid natures to matchwood.[6]

Venturing into uncharted waters is sometimes necessary. Doing so frivolously and with the conviction that everything that happens is for the best is neither rational nor humane.

The sense of movement, now so important to many Catholics, is illusory precisely because it is not self-generated, even while they claim that it is. The watchword is "freedom," taken to be a sign of self-generated activity, whereas the literally reactionary character of contemporary Catholicism is manifest in the fact that it relies on stimuli from the outside—movements from the secular culture—to give it purpose and direction, occasionally by providing targets for criticism or condemnation, more often by offering some other moving vehicle to which the

Church can attach itself. Much of contemporary Catholicism is bereft of any vision of its own and depends for direction on whatever "the world" churns up at any given moment. Black rights, women's rights, homosexual rights, American Indian rights, the human potential movement, the youth culture, the antiwar movement, all have served at various times to inject some vitality into the Church, but always without providing the answer to the fundamental question of what the Church should be doing as Church and not simply as an adjunct to the world. The need for a sense of movement carries with it a need for frequent victories, either over designated worldly enemies or over "backward" elements in the Church itself. Such a need once again betrays the contemporary lack of belief in eternity and the consequent sense that tangible, temporal signs of progress alone make the struggle worthwhile.

Many influential Christians are now concerned in breaking down the "rigidity" of their co-religionists without recognizing how the general culture promotes an endless malleability, an unrestrained openness against which firm convictions and the ability to resist change form a valuable personal resource. Latecomers to modernity, they do not realize to what degree the modernist impulse—in art and literature, in education, in personal values—is now spent and seems to promise little beyond endlessly repeated sterile gestures of revolt against now impotent establishments. There is always the risk in change of genuine loss, yet few "experiments" in the postconciliar Church have been acknowledged as failures and little compassion has been spent on those harmed by an often chaotic process of change. (No previous "reform" movement in the history of the Church has been followed by the sharp decline in membership and the widely expressed feelings of malaise which have followed the Second Vatican Council.)

The loss of the Church's moral center has induced in many people a frantic thrusting outwards towards contemporary causes, each of which it is hoped will inject new life into a tired body. As in any decadent society, there is a fascinated preoccupation with groups which manifest youth, energy, self-assurance, cohesive doctrines, and the strong dedication of their members, all qualities which the Church itself now lacks. An unacknowledged doctrine of progress rules, in which a deepening "adult" faith proves itself by a progressive discarding of everything from the past. That genuine growth might involve a rediscovery of things hastily discarded, or that it is often a sign of maturity to take a principled stand against change, is scarcely even considered. (The parable of the Prodigal Son, popular now because it suggests that God is not a stern judge, also seems to teach that leaving home is folly and that it is possible to go home again.)

The final end of this attitude is a voluntary slavery to history, a conservative belief not that whatever is is right but that whatever will be will be right, for as long as it maintains its cultural respectability. A theologian, for example, approvingly quotes Henrik Ibsen, "That man is right who has allied himself most closely with the future."[7] Advanced Christians are pleased to think of themselves as critics of society, constantly bringing it to judgment before the bar of the Gospel. Yet in practice they often serve merely as front runners for the next stage of social development, prudent stewards getting themselves right with history lest they be shunted aside from its swift path. Although "triumphalism" in the Church is severely condemned, the liberal Christian stance towards history is deeply and inevitably triumphalistic, reducing its movement to a series of confrontations between "progressive" and "reactionary" forces and celebrating those victories which claim to reveal a future infinitely superior to the past. The Church is made to serve these victories and, having no distinctive and ruling task of its own to perform, is urged to fulfill all manner of worldly tasks for which it may have no special competence. No embarrassment is felt more acutely than the church's having been on the "wrong" side of some past controversy.

A moral and religious premium is therefore placed on the ability to validate every new historical development, while the worst kind of sin is resistance or foot dragging. A former president of the National Coalition of American Nuns says that:

> Women are among those on the front lines of ministry. Meanwhile, the sacramental system is back at the ranch. It's time for the sacramental system to catch up with what's happening in ministry.
>
> This great bird—the Holy Spirit—is out here calling women, giving them the gifts of ministry.
>
> And the magisterium prayerfully considering its own role, making sure it seconds the actions of the Spirit. The Spirit is not famous for following the lead of the magisterium.[8]

When the *Human Sexuality* study of the Catholic Theological Society was published, the dean of an archdiocesan seminary said that it "can probably be likened to the issues of Galileo and Copernicus" and added, "It reminds me of the story of the philosophers who argued about how many teeth a horse has. Some simpleton suggested that they go outside and count them."[9] (The relevance of counting to the subject of sexual morality is unclear, except possibly on the assumption that statistical practice determines morality.) A group of English clergy rejected the 1976 papal declaration on sexual morality by affirming that "The

Church must continue to develop an authentic theology, based upon where people are, rather than where it is thought they should be."[10] When the fad of "streaking" (running nude in public) passed over American college campuses in 1974, a Newman Club chaplain dutifully and instantaneously developed a "theology of streaking" which explained how streakers were protesting against oppressive and immoral social structures and were therefore doing the Lord's work.[11]

Controversial new ideas which divide and wrack the Church with predictable regularity are never merely proposed for their own sake, however. "Revisionist" views on sexual morality, social questions, basic doctrines, and other things are essential to a certain conception of the Church because their proponents can conceive for themselves no meaningful form of membership in the Church which does not involve fighting continuing battles. The various "liberation" movements which emerge in secular society are taken literally as godsends by a certain type of Catholic. Another former president of the National Coalition of American Nuns says, for example, "We're on the threshold of renewal in Christianity and the ordination of women is going to bring it about."[12] The failure of each new movement to revitalize the Church as predicted induces temporary depression, followed by an equally ardent commitment to whatever promising development appears next on the horizon.

All of this carries with it an exhilarating sense of freedom, of being emancipated from the static categories of the past. Yet beneath the rhetoric of freedom, and the artificially induced sense of liberation which the breaking of taboos always carries with it, another kind of reality is found. The popular Anglican theologian John A. T. Robinson has said, for example, that "What the new morality is saying to us . . . is that we need not fear flux: God is in the rapids as much as in the rocks, and as Christians we are free to swim and not merely to cling."[13] But few people can swim in rapids; the invitation to "swim" is an invitation to be carried along helplessly by the current, usually to destruction.

The apparent freedom in the modernist rejection of all binding authority from the past is in reality a total submission to the movement of history. By relaxing and ceasing to struggle (almost in essence the therapeutic mentality) one is moved along swiftly and almost painlessly. It is this movement which gives the sense of freedom, but it is in fact a subtler kind of slavery, in part because the individual is not even aware of being bound. Although the modernist credo speaks bravely about the absence of ready-made answers and the necessity of thinking for oneself, in fact such a stance requires little thought, except in the instrumental terms of how previously held opinions can be adjusted to fit in with newly perceived historical imperatives. A total openness to history (one theologian has equated the Spirit, now rarely referred to as the Holy Spirit, with the spirit of the age)[14] also relieves one of the anxiety of trying to defend values which seem doomed to defeat.

The young nun in dungarees and a patchwork poncho who believes that "any sort of habit is dressing up. . . . You're no longer yourself"[15] is deliciously unaware of how she has merely exchanged one badge for another and how her new costume symbolizes a sensible submission to the now reigning American culture. A priest who sees the increasing divorce rate as a sign of "the positive evolution of a new kind of marriage" preaches submission to the inevitable: "The water is already coming over the dike. I think we Roman Catholics should take our fingers out and learn to swim in the new human era."[16] As the noted French Protestant theologian Jacques Ellul has pointed out, Christians are merely obeying a historical necessity to become part of secular culture, and as Christianity is demythologized the culture itself is divinized, its imperatives made absolute.[17]

One of the great untold stories of *aggiornamento* has been the virtual persecution of those who have proven insufficiently flexible in their attitudes to change—nuns in "updated" communities subjected to harassment, theologians pressured into early retirement, parents made to appear benighted fools in the eyes of their children by aggressively avant-garde teachers. The postconciliar Church has been awash in talk about "compassion," yet it is a highly selective kind of compassion, directed mainly to the deserving, that is, those who can be defined as on the "correct" side of ongoing historical battles. There has been much publicly expressed agony over the sufferings of racial minorities, women, homosexuals, and married priests but nothing beyond the most formal regrets about those who feel themselves tossed upon the scrap heap of history. Avant-garde Christians cannot afford to waste compassion on those who do not appear to be going anywhere, whose presence in the Church merely retards forward movement. A university professor and lay minister of communion writes,

> One unlearns ancient idiocy quickly—I recall my real shock and slight trauma last year when, while distributing communion, I encountered an elderly lady who with tight-shut eyes and protruded tongue insisted on a gesture I had almost forgotten. The atavistic insistences are merely foolish, however, and are doomed.[18]

A well-known priest and spiritual writer explains how parish councils should not be established in parishes where the people are likely to resist the pastor's desire for change.[19] A bishop tells parents that he hopes that his diocesan schools will not produce Catholics like themselves, people whom the diocese is "frantically" trying to "update."[20] The qualities of "maturity" and "compassion" generated by a commitment to the new are well captured in the remarks of a Chicago nun:

> We have a number of parishes in Chicago dragging their tails. This year the personnel board placed deacons in these parishes, with the hopes of moving some of these cuddly Cody pastors. . . . The whole mess has held-up the visions of the liturgy and CCD offices. . . .
>
> Come to Chicago for a pre-Vatican [sic] vacation with Cody.[21]

Although proclaiming freedom, the rhetoric of the avant-garde is replete with words like *must, cannot, imperative,* and *untenable* as applied to change and those who resist it. The historical fact of change is routinely transmuted into a moral imperative. (The total investment of self formerly required by the Church from its members is now shifted to movements like Women's Liberation. It is no exaggeration to say that certain communities of nuns now seem to be held together by nothing more than their shared feminist ideology.)

It is important to recognize that much more is involved here than mere faddishness or vulnerability to fashion. The passion, even fanaticism, which characterizes many "progressive" movements in the Church bespeaks sincere conviction. The problem is, in fact, far worse than faddishness. The sincerity and fanatic energy which these fashionable movements generate stem from an absolute faith as deep as that which the same avant-garde (especially the avant-garde religious) once had in the Church. It is an absolute faith in the essential rightness of history's movement, which it is almost blasphemous to challenge. The traditional category of heresy has been discarded. Yet those who deviate from what is perceived to be history's correct path are often dealt with by condemnation. Apostasy on the part of those who once held the truth is even worse—when Michael Novak, once a leading spokesman for liberal Catholicism, questioned the validity of women priests, he was met with a deluge of abusive replies, including several suggestions that his essay should have been censored.[22] Those who resist change are deemed merely insecure, blind, or self-interested. The possibility of a principled attachment to tradition is scarcely even conceivable.

Christopher Lasch tellingly dissects the prevailing American attitude towards change, which is closely linked with the prevailing faith in technology:

> The real value of the accumulated wisdom of a lifetime is that it can be handed on to future generations. Our society, however, has lost this concep-

tion. . . . The older generation has nothing to teach the younger, according to this kind of reasoning, except to equip it with emotional and intellectual resources to make its own choices and to deal with "unstructured" situations for which there are no reliable precedents or precepts. It is taken for granted that children will quickly learn to find their parents' ideas old-fashioned and out of date, and parents themselves tend to accept the social definition of their own superficiality.

. . . the growth experts compound the problem by urging the middle-aged to cut their ties to the past. . . .

This is a recipe not for growth but for planned obsolescence. . . . The new therapy provides for personnel what the annual model-change provides for its products: rapid retirement from active use.[23]

The 1960s was so extreme a youth-oriented decade that older people almost had to apologize for their existence. The spirit of the age affected the Church deeply, and there was no lack of religious "leaders" who thought the institution could be salvaged by tying it to the youth culture. (There were Christians who were terribly flattered, for example, by the fact that the pop-music industry condescended to bestow some attention on the Savior in *Godspell* and *Jesus Christ Superstar.* Alas! like some other superstars His contract was now renewed beyond a season.) In the 1970s the "problem" of the aged was discovered and some of the same neophiliacs sternly lectured society on its neglect of the elderly. Religious who earlier had found it impossible to live with elderly members of their own orders and had moved into small, selectively chosen communities suddenly emerged as prophets concerning the needs of the elderly. They were willing to grant them every consideration except that of taking their values seriously.

Avant-garde Christians have invested heavily in an image of themselves as independent, iconoclastic critics of prevailing social values, particularly those associated with industrial capitalism. It is odd, therefore, that most of these same people fail to recognize the degree to which the religious values they now support—impatience with dogma, rejection of tradition, pragmatic preoccupation with social problems, intense concentration on the conditions of self-liberation—are primarily generated by "late capitalism" and the "consumer society." Langdon Gilkey has expressed quite candidly his belief that these mores are authoritative, with modern Christians obligated by history to submit to them:

. . . the church [is] in that world of modernity and, for good or ill, believes in that world. . . . The principal reason the Curia may not see the point is that the world of modernity in which we live here and in northern Europe has not yet penetrated spiritually very far south of Milan, though with *Autostrada* and Fiat, it will be soon enough![24]

Liberal Christians earn the contempt of the modern world by their public admission that any failure to participate in modernity in all its fullness can only be the result of timidity or ignorance, never of principled conviction. They offer themselves as hostages to various "progressive" movements, which not uncommonly use them as long as they remain useful, then casually discard them. Having clergy willing to lend their names to the various movements of political, moral, or personal liberation is often only a necessary tactic for gaining respectability. A triumphant modernism has no need of Christians, no matter how flexible. The world has no incentive to take Christianity seriously, since Christians themselves indicate that, at those points where they are in conflict with the world, they will sooner or later make their accommodations.

The history of liberal Protestantism offers Catholics a preview of what happens to religious bodies that pursue such accommodations relentlessly, but it is a preview from which many Catholics do not wish to learn. For at least 300 years there have been elements in Protestantism that have, in each age, created a synthesis of sacred and secular that, to its creators, appears final and definitive. Certain "peripheral" elements in the faith, certain very obviously "culturally conditioned" forms, have been sacrificed in the interests of preserving the inner core of belief which is alone deemed important. Often it has been a process which has gone forward under the rubric of "purifying" the faith rather than compromising it. But compromise it has been, and those walls which one generation thought to be impregnable and essential to the security of the whole fortress the next generation found expendable. By the last quarter of the twentieth century there is little left to defend, and those who are cast in the role of defenders have no taste for the job. The death of God theology was the logical outcome of modern liberal Christianity. The fact that it was widely rejected even in liberal circles indicates merely that it was premature; it raised questions which liberals were not yet ready to face.

Liberal Christianity is, offensive though this be to pious ears, religiously bankrupt. This is not to say that liberal Christians themselves are bankrupt, since many of them are highly moral, idealistic, and sincere people. But liberal Christianity simply has no resources of its own. It has bartered its patrimony to the point where there is not enough left to support the family. What has been lost has neither been wisely invested nor generously given to the poor. Rather it has been lavishly squandered in the hope of attracting the respect of outsiders. That strategy is obviously unsuccessful, and the liberal churches are now largely forced to subsist on crumbs from the secular table, whatever spillovers from secular movements are suitable for churchly use.

Given the liberal Christian frame of mind, the Church will always by definition be "behind" the secular world, castigating itself for its backwardness, frantically running to catch up, eagerly devising new strategies for coping with new phenomena. For certain types of Christians this condition alone provides a built-in meaning for their faith, the process of constantly measuring the gap that exists between Church and world and struggling to close it. Expectation of change becomes simply a habit of mind and after a time ceases to require any particular thought or conscious decision. Nothing is easier than predicting a glorious and daring future, a secular millenium which, if it remains elusive, can nonetheless always be perceived beyond the horizon.

The following analysis of the "younger generation" could be duplicated endlessly from ecclesiastical writing of the past fifteen years:

> There can, I think, be little question as to the truth of the general impression that something has happened to the religion of our young people. They do not believe what their predecessors did. . . . Most important of all, they are not interested in the religious things that interested the older generation. Their grandfathers believed the Creed; their fathers a little doubted the Creed; they have never read it. . . .
>
> . . . The vast majority of college students are not interested in the church. They have no sense of the importance of the church. . . .
>
> . . . If you ask them whether they are orthodox or heterodox, they may hardly know what you mean, and certainly will wonder that you should care.
>
> . . . there is much more of gain than of loss in the change. . . . they spend evenings teaching English or arithmetic to newly arrived immigrants . . . or they study social conditions with a view to the betterment of society and the prevention of evil. They talk less about saving their souls, but they far outstrip their predecessors in actual social service. . . . They are mentally a far more wholesome lot than our narrow-minded, prejudiced fathers were.[25]

These comforting words, familiar as they are, were written in 1929, about the fathers and grandfathers of today's youth, precisely those generations so severely censured in the past decade for their hypocrisy, moral callousness, and refusal to change. Liberal Christians regularly bet on the future and, when it fails to win for them, simply transfer their bets to the next race. They are often unaware that their current enthusiasms have a history, or that there are any precedents by which to evaluate them. Everything must be treated as a fresh discovery and, to the degree that attention is given to past thinkers, no higher compliment can be paid a man than to say that he was "ahead of his time."

Within a few years, dissent within the Catholic Church has moved from a cautiously proffered possibility to almost a duty. The presumption of orthodoxy has shifted in the public arena, and to a great extent even among scholars, from defense to attack of traditional doctrines. (The question of women's ordination is a particularly apt example.) Dissent begins to supply its own promise of certitude and, even more important, the promise of a bright future. "Thoughtful" people demonstrate their thoughtfulness by their willingness to dissent and soon form themselves into what George Orwell described as a "herd of independent minds."

Almost unnoticed, a reverse kind of missionary activity is taking place, as various influential persons in the Church come to see their role not primarily as preachers of the Gospel to nonbelievers but as agents, within the Church itself, for outside influences—various political orthodoxies, schools of therapy, "liberation" movements, etc. The socially defined role of "change agent" has been highly congenial to many religious professionals, many of them unable to conceive of any other role which would give their work meaning. In their stance towards their fellow Catholics these missionaries of secularity have permitted themselves all those characteristics which they condemn severely in missionaries to the heathens—arrogance, authoritarianism, lack of respect for the native culture. Many Catholics today are being victimized by ideologies they do not even know exist, proffered in pseudoreligious language by persons whom they have been conditioned to respect.

There is a remarkable paucity of discussion as to precisely why Christianity is obligated to adapt itself to the culture of each new age, why the *Zeitgeist* should be conceded such authority. The great theologians of the past rarely spoke of this need. St. Thomas Aquinas had little to say about the social system of feudalism which dominated his own society. Historians, with the benefit of hindsight and professional ingenuity, can postulate various ways in which the great minds of past ages reflected their times. But the reflection is far from complete, often debatable, and almost never a conscious or deliberate accommodation to the spirit of the age. The greatest minds are in fact usually those which in some meaningful way transcend the limitations of their own culture.

St. Thomas's synthesis of Christian doctrine with Aristotelian philosophy is often pointed to as the model that later theologians ought to follow, given the great Dominican's courage, serenity, and open-mindedness in the face of the unfamiliar. But the Thomistic synthesis was not the first attempt by medieval Christians to deal with these new ideas, and in their uncritical openness many contemporary Christians more closely resemble those medieval thinkers like Siger of Brabant and David of Dinant whose attempts at accommodation proved premature and destructive of faith.

There is also a very ancient Christian tradition of writing treatises *contra,* a tradition of which St. Thomas was also a part but which the postconciliar age has chosen to regard as somehow un-Christian. And who, surveying the history of Catholic theology over the past eight centuries, can think that St. Bernard was altogether wrong when, defying the palpably growing spirit of his age, he dared to oppose the Scholastic spirit and warn of what was being lost?

CHAPTER 5

The Illusion of Pluralism

THE full acceptance of this "world of modernity" implies in a profound and intimate way the mastery of one of the most important features of that world, namely, the organs of publicity and the techniques of public relations. This requirement has been understood both by liberals and conservatives in the Church. But it has been the former group which, by an often instinctual understanding of the realities of power in the contemporary world, has unerringly learned to use them. In almost every encounter they have shown themselves far more skillful than their rivals, and traditionalists in the Church have suffered defeat in almost every public-relations battle of the past twenty years.

The reasons for this are partly remediable, in that many traditionalists, especially in the hierarchy, failed to acquaint themselves with the elementary rules of successful publicity and do not understand how their beliefs can be presented to the larger society in terms which will command attention. But the problem also goes deeper. By virtue of the very fact that they are traditionalists, many of them are psychologically debarred from fully appreciating the immense importance of publicity and even more from effectively making use of it for their own purposes. What they fail to comprehend is that, in a world where attitudes are largely shaped by the kinds of technological change which Langdon Gilkey extols, truth in the traditional philosophical meaning of the term is rendered irrelevant. Since there is finally no way by which any individual can be thought successfully to transcend the perceptions of his own historically determined culture, the "official" opinions of that culture become immensely important. The familiar philosophical debates by which, in the past, it was assumed that objective truth was progressively discovered increasingly lose significance. In the churches, the 1960s brought this process to full maturity, as theologians and others seeking to affect the future course of Christianity discovered that what they published in cautious, technical form in learned journals had far less impact than what they were able to convey to the general public through properly orchestrated publicity campaigns.

In the Roman Catholic Church this process began even before the Second Vatican Council, during the papacy of Pope John XXIII, when legions of journalists—some out of sincere ignorance, others with fully conscious manipulative purpose—succeeded in establishing a public image of that pope greatly at variance with the reality of his personality. Every papal word or gesture that could possibly be given a "revolutionary" significance was interpreted to death in the media, more often than not on the basis either of Vatican gossip or the free imaginations of journalists. Inconveniently "reactionary" deeds, such as intervening in the Council to insert St. Joseph's name in the Canon of the Mass, commanding the use of Latin in all seminaries, or suppressing the worker-priest movement in France, were glossed over. The world today, including many Catholics, knows little of the real John XXIII, as found for example in the pages of his *Journal of a Soul.* They know mainly a media-constructed image.

However, the Council itself was the most effective example of this process at work. Attracting a degree of interest from the secular media unprecedented in the history of the Church, it soon ceased to be an event primarily defined by its convenors and participants and became a media event whose meaning was determined largely by the propaganda image which it projected, an image over which the Council fathers had little control. The Church was not victimized, however, primarily by secular media personnel who did not understand its inner meaning (although there were such people in abundance). Rather what occurred was an alliance of convenience between secular technicians of communication who simply wanted an exciting and, if possible, sensational story and Catholics, including some Council *periti,* who realized that the actual thrust of the Council would not achieve the revolutionary ecclesiastical changes they deemed essential and that what was finally contained in the Council documents was far less important than what the world could be led to think had been the "real" meaning of the Council. (The highly influential writings of the pseudonymous Xavier Rynne in *The New Yorker* and of *Time* magazine's Robert Kaiser especially used this technique very effectively. Despite impressions to the contrary, the Council was probably one of the worst-reported major events of modern times.)

Few Catholics, even perhaps few priests and religious, have ever carefully studied the conciliar documents. Their understanding of the most important event within the Church in the past 400 years is largely dependent on impressions, gained at one time or another, from either secular or religious media. When the Council ended, some bishops and *periti* who had helped shape its decrees found themselves accused of betraying its spirit or of seeking to sabotage its effects. In vain did they appeal to what the Council had said about liturgy, religious life, ecumenism, and many other things. They soon discovered that what was supposed to govern the postconciliar Church was a certain "spirit of Vatican II" which could not be found in the Council's documents but had emerged from the endless commentaries on them.

Such was the euphoria of the conciliar years that it was scarcely possible at the time to understand the immense importance of the public-relations triumphs which accompanied it. It is probable, for example, that in 1960 most Catholics had scarcely heard of the Roman Curia; still less did they regard it as chief obstacle to progress in the Church, even in the unlikelihood that they considered such progress desirable. The media deliberately made famous such men as Cardinal Alfredo Ottaviani solely in order to establish him as the principal villain in a drama. They "educated" people on abstruse issues like collegiality solely in order to enlist their sympathies on one side of the struggle. Every discussion was cast relentlessly in terms of a conflict between "progressives" and "reactionaries." Every vote was assessed as either a victory or a defeat for the respective forces of light and darkness. The immense subtleties of the questions at stake, and above all the call to spiritual renewal which was the Council's chief exhortation to Catholics, did not lend themselves to effective media presentation and were passed over as irrelevant.

One of the choicest of all the ironies of the conciliar era presented itself here, since in its decree on communications, *Inter Mirifica,*[1] the Council warned severely against precisely those misuses of the media which the conciliar excitement was in the process of inspiring. There developed an almost universal conspiracy of silence about that document. The journalists who fed the public's seemingly insatiable hunger for information about the Church's new era deliberately kept that same public in the dark about the one document which bore directly on their own work. Although certain conciliar documents were employed as clubs with which to belabor the intransigent, a document which was too blatantly "reactionary" to be of strategic use was in effect repealed by the media themselves.

The conciliar experience impressed on many strategically placed Catholics the fact that the successful manipulation of publicity was perhaps the single most valuable weapon for effecting changes in the Church. Many bishops and religious superiors learned to dread an unfavorable notice by the media above almost every other evil. Few had the stamina to show themselves able to accept a consistently hostile press as

the price of doing what they conceived as their duty. Almost impercepti-
bly, public-relations considerations began more and more to govern
decision-making at certain levels in the Church, and proponents of
change were able to make maximum use of the fear of bad publicity.

A leading American theologian has described how, as rumors of the
imminent release of a papal encyclical on marital love and contraception
circulated in 1968, "We tried in vain to raise enough publicity to prevent
the issuence [*sic*] of any encyclical." Learning that the encyclical, *Humanae
Vitae,* would be issued on a Sunday, he organized by telephone a national
network of persons prepared, without having as yet seen the document,
to subscribe to a public dissent from its contents. After a reading that
must necessarily have been hasty, a dissenting statement was forged on
Monday, 600 names subscribed, and on Tuesday morning a press conference was held. The theologian concludes with satisfaction:

> The day after the encyclical was promulgated American Catholics could read
> in their morning papers about their right to dissent and the fact that
> Catholics could in theory and practice disagree with papal teaching and still
> be loyal Roman Catholics.
>
> There was absolutely no virtue in delay.[2]

A milestone in the history of the modern Church was reached on that
day. The "right of dissent," which, to the degree that it had been recognized in earlier eras, had been exercised cautiously and only after long
deliberation, was now consciously tied to the demands of the moment,
the pressure of deadlines, the need to make "news" before the "story"
had gone "stale." For the first time in the history of the Church, Catholics
were told that they should seek authoritative guidance about what it
meant to be a Catholic not from their Supreme Pontiff but from their
morning papers. To have actually seen a copy of *Humanae Vitae,* much
less to have studied it, had become irrelevant in a world where prepack-
aged theological opinions were available with breakfast. A notion gained
credence that somehow the authentic meaning of Catholic teaching was
understood better by particular religious journalists than by the pope
himself.[3] The dissenting theologians, in this case as in others, failed to
inquire into some of the possible motives of their eager allies in the
secular world. (The theologian who orchestrated the dissent from
Humanae Vitae acknowledges "the inestimable generosity of the law firm
of Cravath, Swain, and Moore of New York City."[4] A few years later that
same firm became the defendant in a lawsuit charging that it systematically discriminated against Catholics in hiring over a period of nearly
seventy years. The case is still pending.[5])

That a concern to make known the truth was less important than the manipulation of publicity for strategic purposes was frankly acknowledged by one prominent lay theologian who, three years after *Humanae Vitae,* argued that, although press coverage had been "useful in breaking open closed institutions," the more "progressive" movements in the Church should be shielded from "premature" publicity that might harm them. Religious journalists were openly enlisted as allies in this campaign.[6] When the Catholic Theological Society of America issued its report *On Human Sexuality* in 1977, it arranged for no advance copies of the volume to be available. Thus those who "dissented" from its contents were forced to wait several weeks before saying anything authoritative, which cost them the necessary publicity edge. The bishops of St. Louis stated appropriately,

> The book was kept quite secret—from the Bishops and even from some of the most interested members of the CTSA until it could be publicly announced to the press. . . . We find this a strange manner indeed for the CTSA to "dialogue" with theologians and bishops.[7]

A short time later the Canon Law Society of America reached yet another level of achievement in the effective use of publicity by announcing the possible results of its study of marriage before the study had even begun. "Maybe we're going to be able to say this marriage failed and should be dissolved." "Maybe Christ didn't mean a marriage is forever when love dies."[8]

Amidst this sometimes frantic maneuvering to extract the maximum strategic benefits from publicity, certain Catholic "leaders" became in effect celebrities—largely created by the media in the sense that their public images, and their ability to attract and keep media attention, became crucial to their effectiveness within the Church. A whole series of such celebrities—William Dubay, James Kavanaugh, Sister Corita, Ivan Illich, Sister Jacqueline Grennan—enjoyed brief periods of popularity during which their pontifications about Church and world were treated with the utmost seriousness. Just as quickly they sank back into obscurity, unless they were nimble enough to leap from one publicity vehicle to another at the right moment. By 1977, the former priest James Kavanaugh was "a poet who makes as much as the vice-president of General Motors." His volumes of "poetry" were said by his publisher to be "moving closely in on Rod McKuen's," and Kavanaugh said of himself, "The black man's way to get what he wants is to lie; my way is to be charming."[9]

The most effective practitioners of this art of public relations were those who, consciously or otherwise, seemed to be modelling themselves on show business. An interview with Hans Küng, for example, conveys his opinions on contraception and celibacy but concentrates even more on his clothes, his exercise habits (he has the use of a private swimming pool), the decor of his house, the food prepared by his cook, and the worshipful attitudes of his secretary. At one point his assistant makes the obligatory point that the famous theologian is "fed up with publicity," "hates travelling around," and "likes to live simply"—yet another star martyred by his duties to his fans.[10] The following is a description of Ivan Illich by an adoring journalist:

> Doctor Illich . . . finding a few minutes a day—like a surgeon making his rounds—to administer some devastating aphorism to each of his patients; or to give them short discourses on Saint John of the Cross, Wittgenstein's philosophy of language, the relationship between tenth century monastic groups and twentieth century hippie communes.

The same journalist neatly juxtaposes the beautiful people to the not-so-beautiful.

> The [Catonsville] Nine's good humor increased further at the appearance of the Government's two material witnesses, Mrs. Murphy and Mrs. Mos-burger. . . . Confused and drawling models of outraged respectability, the two matrons provided the first comic relief of the courtroom drama.[11]

Those unable to discourse about Wittgenstein can nonetheless serve a useful purpose in the world by keeping their betters entertained. Media attention is crucial to the therapeutic personality, who seeks constantly to demonstrate his flexibility and unpredictability. One of the obligations laid on him by history is to be a performing self.

The dependence of avant-garde Catholics on the favor of the media is not the result merely of a hunger for personal fame, however. Whatever elements of vanity may have been present in the activities of the Berrigan brothers, for example, their acts did have high serious intent. However, all those (the present author among them) who extolled the new kind of witness which the Berrigans provided failed to notice how completely dependent that witness was on media interest. Had the Berrigans done what they did in an unfashionable cause (anti-abortion, for example) they would have been treated by the media as mere fanatics. After a brief flurry of largely unfavorable publicity they would have disappeared into prison remembered only by a few faithful disciples. Curiously, suspicious though the Berrigans are of established institutions, they seem never to have asked themselves why the media chose to lionize them.

Dependence on publicity for the achievement of one's goals soon passes into something subtly different—the tailoring of those same goals to whatever is likely to generate publicity. Those who emerged as celebrities in the frenetic religious world of the 1960s quickly discovered that they had a required role to play just as rigid as the traditional ecclesiastical roles they were rejecting. To maintain their positions in the public eye required a constant supply of fresh tricks. A priest publicly challenging the papal teaching on contraception soon ceased to be news. The pressure to dissent on more and more doctrines, and in more and more daring ways, grew always stronger. Few people adopted opinions merely for the sake of the media. However, among the many subtle factors which enter into the adoption of an opinion, the fulfillment of public expectations is not unimportant. For those who had decided that they would take their case to the public, dissent became not a right but a duty.

In the process, reality—in the Church as well as in the world—tended to become to a large extent media defined. In 1972, for example, the semiannual meeting of the American bishops was criticized as insignificant because the religion editor of the *New York Times* (a Presbyterian minister) did not deem it lively enough for him to file a story.[12] A little later the cardinal archbishop of Utrecht was quoted as saying that it would be a very bad sign if the Church in Holland ceased to be news.[13] The importance of constant publicity lies not merely in its tactical usefulness or in the desire to maintain a public identity but in the fact that media attention is a confirmation that something is "happening" in the Church, movement is indeed taking place. Where the guideposts of authentic development have ceased to be internal to the Church itself, drawn from its own traditions and structures, and where Church people are always on watch for signals from the larger culture, the degree of publicity received is roughly a measure of one's relevance. Movements which fail to get or sustain media attention almost literally cease to exist. Motivated by an insatiable craving for "news," the media can respond to reality only in preformed categories. That which does not readily fit those categories is either ignored or forcibly reshaped to make it fit (reshaped, sometimes, not by the media themselves but by people in the Church desirous of publicity). The question of women's ordination, for example, can scarcely be explained to a mass audience in properly theological terms, and the media do not even attempt to do so. The "issue" is discussed solely in terms of the secular ideology of women's liberation and democratic process. The very terms of the discussion are falsified in the interests of attracting outside attention.

Ultimately the Church is effectively prevented from maintaining its own teachings, since the media, which monopolize so much of the attention of even most Catholics, inculcate a mode of thinking that is thoroughly alien to properly religious ways of thinking. In effect the media have the power to jam the Church's broadcasts, which are restricted to the pitifully weak outlets of the Sunday sermon and the weekly diocesan paper. Typically a media "story" on, for example, women's ordination will state the papal teaching in one paragraph, then move immediately to a lengthy discussion of the various dissents already registered against it. Endemic to the journalistic approach is a presentation in which the "opinion" of the pope on a fundamental theological issue is accorded equal status with that of an instructor of theology in an obscure college, or the president of a self-constituted lobbying group. The full teachings of *Humanae Vitae,* to cite merely the most blatant example, remain largely unknown even to the Catholic public, while the various dissents against it have been publicized exhaustively. The inability of institutions like churches to maintain doctrines contrary to what the media present as truth should be a grave concern to all thoughtful people, even those who disagree with the substance of Catholic doctrine. Yet, because they have mainly benefited from this state of affairs, avant-garde Christians seem complacently willing to allow the media to become the unchallenged molders of public opinion in modern society. Numerous individuals who claim prophetic status for themselves are now lionized by the media, which is a self-contradictory absurdity and ought to lead to a complete reconsideration of the phenomenon of prophecy.

In areas other than "hard news," that is, daily events like murders, fires, court decisions, or legislation, most journalism (now and in the past) is primarily propaganda. It is propaganda because, in trying to assess "trends" or to probe the "quality of contemporary life," journalists are responding to things in the culture which lend themselves easily to dramatic presentation. Any attack on, or dissent from, an "establishment" automatically becomes news because it has built-in motion. The situation of conflict, the familiar stereotype of the courageous dissenter versus the insensitive guardian of orthodoxy, the shock value of the ideas set forth ("theologian announces death of God"), all provide a "story" automatically. Any affirmation of traditional beliefs is, correspondingly, either not news or is relegated to an inconspicuous position. Personal animosity towards traditional religion is not rare among journalists. In 1971, for example, the religion editor of the *Times* ridiculed the Synod of Bishops and compared the church to an "underdeveloped country" because it failed to support fashionable social causes.[14] A more typical form of manipulation is the publishing of opinions in the guise of news. Thus in 1977, United Press International told its readers that Pope Paul VI would like Cardinal Giovanni Benelli of Florence to succeed him and that his efforts to achieve this "have not been popular,"[15] although the first statement was mere speculation and the second failed to answer the obvious question, "not popular with whom?" The wire service also quoted a British Jesuit critical of Cardinal Benelli, without revealing that the man was no longer a Jesuit or a priest.

Journalists, because of the nature of their work, must inevitably seek out whatever is dramatic or sensational and soon develop an instinctive insensitivity to whatever does not lend itself to such treatment. (Thus the real meaning of the Second Vatican Council was not conveyed to the public.) The profession of journalism seems also to attract people who are by temperament iconoclastic and cynical, or who become so under the conditions of their work. A successful journalist is often someone who thrives in chaotic situations, able to live rootlessly and without firm personal convictions, thus able to exploit each new issue for as long as it retains its news value. Of necessity few such people are able even to understand, much less to sympathize with, the kind of principled adherence to tradition which characterizes authentic Catholicism, and they almost invariably depict such fidelity as mere stubbornness or personal insecurity. (*Newsweek* once got a psychiatrist to pronounce, at a distance, that Paul VI was emotionally unfit to continue in office.)[16] In recent years religious journalism seems also to have attracted a disproportionate number of people who have personal quarrels with their own religious traditions which they endlessly pursue in public.

Although changes in the Church have often been urged on the grounds that "the people" desire them, many reformers have come to realize that what the people may or may not want is ultimately irrelevant and that the acceptability of a particular new idea depends primarily on winning the battle of public images. A stereotyped journalistic form has developed in which innovators are represented as warm, loving, humorous, pragmatic, sensible individuals, the defenders of orthodoxy as rigid, remote, unfeeling, and out of touch with reality. In their personal lives bishops whose characters have been publicly assassinated may in fact be wholly admirable. But they have consistently lost the public-relations wars to opponents who understand how to project themselves for benefit of publicity.

Catholic liberals who pride themselves on their sophisticated understanding of modern society either do not understand, or do not wish to understand, how publicity actually functions. Its point is not, as is often piously stated, simply to make information available to the public. The media constantly censor available information, withholding what they judge unimportant. The aim of publicity, whether conscious or not, is to tell people what they ought to believe, what the "sensible" opinion now is on any particular subject. Since these opinions change with some rapidity, close attention has to be paid in order to avoid being left behind. In a mass society whose traditional institutions and communities are rapidly decaying, the media serve the indispensible function of determining what is or is not thinkable. They send out the signals whereby confused people can align their own opinions with what the "best" minds (i.e., the most articulate and up-to-date people) are thinking. The concept of "trends," so tirelessly employed in all forms of journalism, is crucial, since by projecting a trend the journalist signals to readers what the future will be like and how they can adjust to it. Without always using such terms, the media are in fact constantly signalling that certain ideas, persons, or movements are in the process of losing authority, credibility, and influence, while others are gaining at their expense.

It is essential to the successful functioning of the media that they minimize their own influence, insisting that they merely report what is happening and do not shape events. Thus critics of the media are often told that they are irrationally attacking the messengers who bring them bad news. The media foster the myth of what might be called atomistic public opinion, in which each person individually is supposed to observe what is happening in the world, commune with his or her own conscience, then form an opinion based on personal experience. Gradually, through this process, a "consensus" emerges, which must be accorded respect because it supposedly represents the thoughtful conclusions of a large number of independent-minded people.

In practice, the formation of public opinion is indeed atomized, in the sense that the weakening of traditional communities like churches and families leaves people with few spiritual and moral resources on which they can rely. However, this atomization process does not serve to produce the celebrated autonomous individual. Rather it renders people almost totally vulnerable to the pressure of public opinion and extraordinarily dependent on the way in which questions are formulated by the media. The "independent-minded" person is more and more the person who manages to embrace new ideas just slightly in advance of their becoming common currency, relying on media signals that are easily readable by anyone anxious to know what the world of tomorrow will be like and how to adjust to it.

There is nowadays a highly developed process by which the necessity of accepting new ideas is enforced in American society, a process in which the media play the crucial role.[17] The key to the process is the establishment of the belief that the new, whatever it may be, is in fact inevitable and irresistible. Thus, even though many people find a particular proposed change personally distasteful, they are pressured to accept it as the price of themselves becoming obsolete or being forced into a long, unpleasant, and ultimately futile stance of resistance. "Do not resist change. Resistance will only make life unpleasant for you," is a working principle that the media emphasis on "trends" relentlessly enforces.

Central to this process of conversion to the new is the implication that the "best" people—those who are considered sensitive, compassionate, open-minded, and courageous—are themselves being converted, while those who resist are insecure, hysterical, bigoted, and callous. Within a remarkably brief period of time, accepted wisdom (for example, about the morality of homosexuality) is put on the defensive, while the formerly avant-garde position is made into a new orthodoxy, increasingly immune from attack.

The media in effect provide a score card, constantly being updated, in which various movements in society are charted either as rising or declining. Once so characterized, movements are expected to follow the appropriate direction. A beleaguered establishment is expected to be apologetic, self-accusatory, diffident in its rhetoric, tolerant of and even hospitable to its enemies. It will be accused of repressing its members and failing to allow them to be fully themselves, and in the face of such accusations it will be expected to loosen its discipline and relativize its doctrines. It will develop a sceptical, even cynical attitude towards its own past, and in time its very right to exist will be called into question.

By contrast a new and ostensibly rising movement (for example, in favor of women's ordination) is not only permitted but expected to employ an aggressive, hostile, even strident rhetoric for the purpose of discrediting and psychologically undermining the establishment. The rising group does not indulge in self-criticism, except at the level of strategy, and it demands loyalty and discipline from its members. (Rising political movements in particular are sometimes rigid in their discipline and puritanical in their attitudes towards personal morality.) Whereas any demand that an establishment makes on its members is automatically resisted as an infringement of personal liberty, to sacrifice for the sake of a new movement is deemed a privilege and willingness to do so a test of sincerity.

The ability to articulate one's ideas, and especially to articulate them in terms acceptable to the media, is indispensable to this process and the grounds on which so many traditional Catholics have lost their battles over the past twenty years. The skill at presenting one's ideas in such a way as to fit them harmoniously into the current cultural mood is both a condition and a result of being personally flexible, not tied too closely by settled convictions. Genuine conservatives, struggling against cultural changes which they consider deleterious, usually find themselves unable to enter the avant-garde world even on the level of imagination. Hence they cannot formulate their beliefs in such a way as to gain a fair hearing in the media or, if a hearing is granted them, they are easily disposed of in ways which make them appear stupid or morally obtuse.[18]

Many Catholics were flattered at the immense interest which the media showed toward the Second Vatican Council and the Church in the period following. But they failed to comprehend the root of the media's interest, which was the journalists' perception that a seemingly close-knit institution was unravelling, that the Second Vatican Council was essentially a process by which Church leaders were systematically admitting that their doctrines had been in error for many years. (Thus the anger over the issuance of *Humanae Vitae,* which frustrated this expectation.) During and after the Council bishops who failed to play a diffident role, like Cardinal Ottaviani or Cardinal Patrick O'Boyle of Washington, were savagely attacked in the media, and the lesson was not lost on bishops who came after them.

Although liberal Catholics profess "pluralism" as one of their most cherished values, they fail to understand the real nature of pluralism, which in a mass society can only mean the existence of a number of strong, cohesive, well-defined groups which work out a social relationship with one another through compromise but also through tension and a tenacious defense of their own interests and values.

Instead of real pluralism, many liberals have, willy-nilly, chosen to support a homogenized society in which a series of unstable consensuses develop on various public questions, succeeding each other in rapid succession. Put another way, if a group like the Catholic Church is not interiorly cohesive, with strong leadership and firm beliefs, it will be ineffective within the overall pluralistic framework of society. Its members, having "liberated" themselves from the authoritative teachings of pope and bishops, are rendered "free" to acquiesce in those values which the media promote at any given moment. The anti-abortion campaign is particularly important here, because it represents an authentic "grass roots" movement (often with only lukewarm clerical support) which has been remarkably successful despite the overwhelmingly unfriendly attitude of the media towards it and the "neutrality" or active opposition of prominent Catholics like Senator Edward Kennedy and the Jesuit Congressman Robert Drinan. The hostility of the media towards the anti-abortionists is intensified by annoyance at how the movement has successfully defied that hostility and managed to establish a large zone of public acceptance independent of media control.

Even at the peak of its preconciliar strength, religious life in the United States (including the secular clergy) never encompassed more than a tiny fraction of the population, far less than one per cent. The average graduating class of a parochial grammar school was considered unusual if it produced more than a single religious vocation; many produced none. In terms of pluralism, therefore, the survival of traditional religious life, as an "alternative life-style" radically at variance with many of the prevailing American cultural assumptions, should have been considered highly desirable even by those who had no particular sympathy with Catholic doctrine. So also the effectiveness of Catholic education in inculcating "counter-cultural" beliefs in students—about the reality of the supernatural, about ritual, about moral authority, about sex—should also have been valued as a distinctive contribution to a pluralistic society. (Catholics comprise somewhat over twenty percent of the population of the United States, believing Catholics presumably less.)

Although "enlightened" American opinion reacts with profound regret to the extinction of the most obscure species of flora or fauna, or to the destruction of even the most pedestrian example of Victorian architecture, the apparent unravelling of the moral fabric of American Catholicism has not been accorded a like consideration. Religious who have repudiated their vows, former believers turned agnostic, practicing Catholics rejecting official teaching about sexual morality are endlessly celebrated in the media as heroes, people who have learned to think for themselves, rebels and nonconformists. It is an odd sort of nonconformity, however, which involves the abandonment of a beleaguered minority position in favor of the dominant assumptions of one's culture.

The media's alleged commitment to "pluralism" is at base a kind of hoax. The banner of pluralism is raised in order to win toleration for new ideas as yet unacceptable to the majority. Once toleration has been achieved, public opinion is systematically manipulated first to enforce a status of equality between the old and the new, then to assert the superiority of the new over the old. A final stage is often the total discrediting, even sometimes the banning, of what had previously been orthodox.

The real purpose of pluralism is therefore to forge and enforce new uniformities. Enlightened American opinion, especially as it is expressed through the media, is highly intolerant of whatever diverges from the orthodoxies which it has itself constructed. Religion and sexual morality are among the most sensitive tenets of this orthodoxy. Hence the media have bestowed massive attention on traditional Christianity, primarily in order to discredit it. Almost limitless hospitality has been extended, for instance, to any former Catholic (especially a former religious) willing to testify to the "inhumanity" of the system in which he or she was raised. Those inclined to tell an affirmative story about these same realities have been largely ignored. Meanwhile, the media's portrayal of "trends" in the Church serves to reinforce the idea that the old Church is dying and that no prudent person should want to continue being associated with it. The fact, for example, that certain traditional communities of nuns are still healthy and continue to attract novices, or that radical changes in religious orders or parishes tend to cause loss of membership rather than the reverse, is rarely noticed in the media.

"Enlightened" opinion is in fact hostile to genuine pluralism and has, for over two hundred years, fostered the destruction of those traditional communities which alone would make real pluralism possible, since such communities are by definition "backwards" and resist enlightened opinion. Genuine pluralism, in the America of the 1970s, for example, would require (*pace* Father Curran) that Catholics pay more attention to their pope and bishops than to their morning newspapers. Yet the modern churches have few resources for coping with the influence of the media, and when that influence is hostile to a particular religious teaching only the most committed church-members, those in whom the traditions of their faith are deeply inbred, can adequately resist. The effect of the media, allied with other segments of the "enlightened" consensus, is to undermine genuine pluralism by insuring, for instance, that as few people as possible are impelled by "narrow" religious motives in their public behavior.[19] When a church, or an individual church leader, proves particularly recalcitrant, the media are fully capable of mounting a systematic campaign of vilification.[20]

By helping to undermine traditional communities like churches, the media also help create a deep hunger for group identity among people, a hunger which in turn the media alone are able to fill. Since the idea of the atomized, wholly self-sufficient citizen is a chimera, individuals are eager to associate themselves with some identifiable group which grants credibility and security to a particular set of opinions. One of the most destructive effects of the media has been the degree to which reality is no longer even recognized as such until it has been accorded media attention. People cut off from their roots no longer know who they are until the media inform them. It is from the media that one now learns what it means to be a woman, a "modern Catholic," a college student, a black, etc. The media alone are capable of fulfilling the function that at one time churches, families, and other communities fulfilled—holding up models of behavior deemed worthy of emulation. The final aim of the media is the total homogenization of culture, the creation of predictable, stereotyped opinions on all sensitive questions. What the media then celebrate as "liberation" is the process by which individuals give up the distinctive values of their own inherited communities, churches in particular, and make themselves part of the great emergent enlightened consensus. Those Catholics willing to go through that process publicly are given abundant media rewards—recognition, sometimes money, fame, influence. (A new kind of stage Irishman has been created by the media, exemplified by Jimmy Breslin—an individual whose claim to attention derives almost entirely from his group identity but who makes his living undermining his group's values at the behest of the dominant elite.)

Pluralism is largely defined as the willingness to dissent from the values of traditional communities, never as dissent from the enlightened consensus itself. Much attention is given, for example, to Catholics who favor the ordination of women to the priesthood or who reject the Church's teaching on contraception or abortion. Such dissent is taken to be the sign of healthy honesty. Yet there is a conspicuous lack of dissent on the opposite side. Rarely are there reports of members of the National Organization for Women who oppose having women priests, for example, or members of Planned Parenthood who have doubts about abortion. The enlightened consensus, finally, recognizes only one position as being a truly valid one. It discourages the holding of private moral views at odds with those towards which the society as a whole is evolving.

American Catholicism has suffered grievously in the postconciliar era because so few of its leaders seem to understand the true nature of a pluralistic society and how to act within it. As latecomers to the notion of pluralism, many of them have made the fatal mistake of assuming that the proper stance of the Church is one of diffidence and accommodation, when in reality any group choosing such a stance ends up crushed in the machinery of group conflict, the mechanism which in practice propels a pluralistic society. A number of these leaders, intellectual leaders especially but also some bishops, have unwittingly accepted the role of presiding over a declining, even a dying, Church. Their attempts to earn the goodwill of those who have traditionally been the Church's cultured despisers, their concern lest any hint of conflict with the enlightened consensus develop, predictably have the opposite effect. Having hastened the weakening of the internal authority of the Church, and having colluded in discrediting many of its traditions, they now find themselves at the mercy of a merciless publicity, wielded with flawless skill by persons determined either to mold the Church to the specifications of the enlightened consensus or to kill it.

The popular media are the most direct organs by which this consensus is formed and enforced, but they are not alone. During the past fifteen years the whole educational system, at all levels, has experienced a remarkable process of "liberation." Platoons of new young teachers armed with messianic convictions about changing the world by changing the young have entered the system. Numbers of older teachers have been "radicalized," both politically and morally. The scope of thoughts and actions permissible in schools has broadened significantly. From the standpoint of the enlightened consensus, therefore, the educational system has been rendered truly "pluralistic" for the first time.

Yet there are certain peculiar lacunae in that pluralism. A teacher who expresses controversial political opinions in the classroom, or who espouses moral causes like homosexuals' rights, will attract strong legal support and favorable publicity if any attempt should be made to discipline him. Yet a teacher suspect of engaging in religious proselytization in the classroom would not only be dismissed, civil libertarians would regard his dismissal as a triumph of justice. Planned Parenthood sponsors sex-education programs in many public schools; requests by anti-abortion or anti-contraception groups to be allowed equal time are routinely denied as violating the separation of church and state. Teachers regularly assign required readings which violate the moral sensibilities of some parents; assignment of explicitly religious material would, however, automatically arouse grave questions which a prudent teacher or educational administrator would rather avoid.

For very tangled historical reasons, the doctrine of separation of church and state (a phrase which does not appear in the Constitution) has been interpreted in an absurdly rigid way by American jurists, to the point where it now often amounts to placing legal obstructions in the way of religion's free exercise. This is perhaps the only area in all of constitutional law where liberal opinion favors a strict as opposed to a flexible approach to legal questions, where upholding an abstract doctrine is given precedence over meeting obvious social needs.

Although many people sincerely hold to the doctrine of strict separationism, it is also true that a plain antireligious bias (traceable to some of the Founding Fathers themselves) finally lies behind it. Two reasons are commonly offered to support the wisdom of the doctrine—that there is potential for grave and destructive religious conflict if each "sect" is not kept at arm's length by the government, and that taxpayers who are nonbelievers should not be required to support, even indirectly, religious institutions whose tenets they do not accept.

The absurdity of the second position is immediately obvious—taxpayers have to support many programs of which they do not approve, and if each citizen were allowed to reject those government projects to which he had moral objections almost no one would pay a full assessment.

The first objection is merely anachronistic, left over from the era of bloody religious wars of which the Founding Fathers had strong memories. Partially religious conflicts, such as those in Ireland or the Near East, still occur. However, in the twentieth century purely political struggles, and purely political ideologies, have been far more bitter and wasteful of human life. The attempt to prevent the outbreak of religious conflict by putting legal obstacles in the way of religious activities should, if followed logically, lead to the suppression of democracy itself, since any controversy which erupts in the public arena—race relations, for example, or war—has the potential of becoming "divisive" and even violent. Strict separationists are people who have a peculiar horror of what they deem religious fanaticism, which may well turn out to be any kind of deep religious conviction. They share an inherited Enlightenment prejudice against organized religion, which they have succeeded in building into law.

This too marks a massive failure in pluralism. In the postconciliar era the parochial schools have been subjected to a ferocious battering in the media by "Catholics" chosen for their eagerness to denounce the schools' allegedly oppressive character. For a variety of reasons, many Catholic schools have had to close, while the future of the entire great system is problematical. A statesmanlike concern for a genuine pluralism of social values would seek to devise ways to save them. Not only are such efforts not being made, but some influential persons look forward with unconcealed eagerness to the eventual demise of what they regard as "backward" institutions which foster an undesirable "rigidity" in their graduates. Meanwhile, the Catholic schools themselves have experienced an internal crisis, especially at the college and university level, in which they have come to doubt their own worth. Throughout the 1960s many Catholic colleges could conceive no higher ambition than to emulate the most prestigious secular institutions, a process which by the late 1970s had become, in many cases, virtually irreversible.[21]

The enlightened consensus favors policies which, if not reversed, will destroy pluralism by eventually destroying all genuinely private, independent social institutions. Yet there has been no corresponding move to make public institutions genuinely pluralistic in spirit. Public education remains the most obvious test case. Virtually any sociologist, anthropologist, or historian, who need not be a believer, would admit that religion is one of the strongest and most enduring dimensions of human existence. On a purely academic level no education could possibly be complete which did not take this dimension into account. Yet many universities which would be embarrassed not to offer instruction in, for instance, Slavic linguistics, have no department of religion and no intention of establishing one. Students learn about religion, if at all, in a very fragmentary and haphazard way through history, sociology, and literature classes. They may spend four years in college without ever encountering a single professor sympathetic to Christianity. The American educational system not only does not form believers (which, of course, is not its purpose), it produces religious illiterates, people who cannot even understand the terms of Christian belief and for whom such belief remains a bizarre phenomenon with which they cannot even empathize. While the Catholic schools have vigorously, and often uncritically, striven to make themselves more open in the past two decades, there has been no corresponding effort to make the secular schools genuinely open to religious values.

Where secular colleges have chosen to recognize religion as a respectable academic discipline, this has almost invariably been done in the primmest of academic ways. Professors are chosen for the "objectivity" of their method, and there is an unspoken agreement that the worst of evils would be to unleash "fanatics" or proselytizers on the students. The method of instruction used in religion courses is almost guaranteed to relativize, and hence render less credible, any particular religious belief. All beliefs tend to emerge as roughly equivalent, none having any particular claim to truth. Religion ends by being studied essentially as a series of historically developed metaphors for the "mysteries of human existence," without any real divine referrant.

Many religious persons have enthusiastically acquiesced in this approach to education, and not uncommonly the most severe critics of religious orthodoxy on campus are professors of religion, many of them clergymen. Yet, ironically, these same "enlightened" individuals have failed to notice how American higher education actually operates, as distinct from the official versions of how it is supposed to operate. With relatively few exceptions, for example, departments of philosophy are dominated by practitioners of Anglo-American disciplines of logical and linguistic analysis. For years this has been the ruling orthodoxy, and devotees of these philosophical schools are quite frank in asserting that their own beliefs reflect truth, other schools of philosophy varying degrees of error. Behaviorism enjoys a similarly entrenched position of dominance in most psychology departments. In general the spirit of positivism permeates higher education, and other philosophies are scarcely even discussed. In newer programs like Women's Studies, or among faculty who consider themselves Marxists, the classroom is often used explicitly for proselytization. Under such conditions, some of which have prevailed for many years, it is almost miraculous if any student emerges with a conception of reality significantly at variance with what the supposedly pluralistic colleges and universities have set out to impart. Catholic institutions of higher learning at one time sought to be alternatives to, and even adversaries of, the prevailing secular academic orthodoxies. But that ambition has been abandoned with embarrassment by all but a few unreconstructed individuals. The suggestion that the Catholic schools might contribute to American pluralism by creating an educational environment consciously hospitable to religious belief now makes many Catholic educators profoundly uncomfortable. When a young Jesuit founded a program based on traditional Catholic studies at the University of San Francisco, some of his fellow Jesuits demanded that his "mental health be evaluated" by university authorities.[22]

T. S. Eliot observed, even before the Second World War, that "Paganism holds all the most valuable advertising space"[23] and, despite an apparent reversal of that condition during part of the postwar era, the situation is more serious now than when Eliot wrote, and it is getting worse. There is much basic hostility to Christianity, and especially Catholicism. For many years it was somewhat muted and subterranean, except on college campuses, but it is gaining in boldness. For a large part of the population, even many people who harbor no particular hostility towards it, Christianity is like a foreign language which they cannot decipher and do not really care to. As the most important agencies of opinion, especially the media and the schools, either fail or refuse to make genuine Christianity intelligible to their clientele, the interior disarray of the churches renders them also increasingly impotent for the task. Most fatally, the churches have allowed their declining influence to persuade them to adopt the policies which declining groups are likely to fall into, and which only accelerate their decline.

With some exceptions, mainly those Protestant groups which are broadly designated as fundamentalist, the churches do not try to counter the prevailing secularism in anything like aggressive terms. Certain aspects of the secular spirit, for instance, the consumer mentality, are still denounced with passion, but only those aspects which enlightened secular opinion also regards as open to criticism. The new pagansim, which is full of self-confidence because it senses that it is winning its battle with Christianity, has chosen to make sexual morality its principal battleground, and here it has consistently encountered only very half-hearted opponents, some of whom surrendered at the earliest opportunity. Only a few decades ago, self-confessed unbelievers were rare in American society and were often put on the defensive. Now the tables have been turned, and believers—except in a very attenuated, essentially humanistic sense—are increasingly forced to defend their own "backward" and "incredible" beliefs. Liberal Christians are in the now habitual position of approaching secular society hat in hand, endlessly apologizing for past and present failings;· grateful for any sign of recognition or approval; eager to separate themselves, in the world's eyes, from their still unenlightened brethren within the churches. This stance has in fact become so habitual that many modern Christians would not know how to live any other way.

The sociologist Peter Berger has identified very acutely what is perhaps the central social and cultural problem of modern Christianity. All socially constructed worlds, he points out, are precarious, in that they depend for their plausibility, and therefore for their continued existence, less on the coherence or inherent credibility of their underlying ideas as on various social factors. In religion the authority of tradition has always been one of the most important sources of legitimation. In a pluralistic society, religion lives in a viable subsociety which gives it social credibility, as a substitute for the scepticism and indifference shown towards its teachings by the larger society.[24]

Those who believe in the supernatural are now a "cognitive minority" in Western society, holding to beliefs which the total society does not share and which therefore always threaten to become implausible even to those who profess them. Berger points out that ". . . Protestant theologians have been increasingly engaged in playing a game whose rules have been dictated by their cognitive antagonists." There is an underlying question which is usually not asked overtly, "Who is the stronger party?"

> In this country the maharajas of this world of true sophistication are mainly individuals whose baptism in secularity has been by total immersion. The theologian who wants to take his cues from this source is unlikely even to be recognized short of abject capitulation to the realities taken for granted in these particular circles—realities hardly conducive to the theological enterprise in any form.[25]

To face the implications of this situation would require the kind of courage and imagination which all too many Church leaders now appear to lack.

The university has in many ways replaced the churches as the would-be moral center of American society, and consciously or not it is directly in competition with the churches for the formation of young minds, a competition which for the most part it is winning with ridiculous ease. From this dominant position, the university, and all that it symbolizes in terms of the full acceptance of the prevailing suppositions of modern culture, exercises an almost hypnotic attraction for certain influential Christians. It is the model of intellectual respectability against which they believe the Church must constantly measure itself, usually with discouraging results.

A measure of this hypnotic influence is the fact that universities are so often extolled by progressive Catholics as models of freedom, especially in contrast to the supposedly narrow and authoritarian character of seminaries. Oddly, however, at precisely that time, around 1970, when many religious orders were moving their philosophates and theologates to university campuses, sometimes secular university campuses, the universities were themselves embarrassing examples of the suppression of freedom, as classes were forcibly disrupted, speakers prevented from delivering their messages and sometimes physically threatened, buildings burned, bombs planted. That so many liberal Christians either sided with the disrupters or appeared not to notice what was happening suggests that they were less concerned with finding a haven of freedom and more with being fully a part of the prestigious university world.

The inadequacies of preconciliar Catholic education are nowhere more manifest than in the conditions of its supposed coming to maturity. In retrospect it is now obvious that the Catholic schools did fail to prepare their students for life in the modern world, but not in the way their critics have charged. Instead they (seminaries included) seem to have imparted to many of their students only a very superficial kind of Catholicism, which crumbled in the face of its first major cultural challenge. Many self-consciously intellectual Catholics can conceive of no better sign of their own liberation than the full acceptance of the wisdom currently received in higher academic or journalistic circles. The Jewish journal *Commentary* represents a level of genuine intellectual maturity which the American Catholic community has yet to attain, in that—from an unimpeachably high intellectual level—it has been free to criticize the shoddy thinking of intellectuals themselves, while most Catholic journals with intellectual pretensions still serve chiefly as messengers from the avant-garde to the Catholic community, endlessly flogging the dead horses of clerical authoritarianism and immobility. It is symptomatic, for example, that while certain nuns feel compelled to offer a sweeping defense of contemporary art—"never before in history have the arts pursued the undisguised truth and sincerity as they have in this century"—the most perceptive secular critics, like the late Harold Rosenberg, are free to point out how much of what passes for art is faddish and even fraudulent, proclaiming breakthroughs where none have occurred.[26]

If the consciousness of "modern man," mainly as defined in the universities and the media, is taken as normative, Christianity will by definition remain in a defensive and apologetic stance. The loss to the Church of massive numbers of young people in the postconciliar era has less to do with the Church's alleged backwardness (the fundamentalist churches do not appear to have experienced a similar problem) than with the fact that, at a crucially sensitive period in their lives, young people encountered a church that seemed confused, timid, and irresolute even with regard to its own basic teachings. This internal weakness, the exact opposite of the rigidity from which it was alleged to suffer, deprived many young Catholics of what should have been an important element in their personal growth. Instead they were left wholly prey to the pressures of the youth culture, with no traditions of their own to fall back upon. Thus young Catholics whose priests claimed they had no interest in the supernatural ended by joining a variety of exotic cults. Bishops and other Church leaders who connived in the destruction of folk Catholicism, on the dubious grounds that they were replacing it with something religiously purer, similarly helped create a situation in which many of their people are wholly formed by the culture around them and have no living traditions through which they can withstand that culture.

The present emphasis on "religious experience" as the basis of faith is inadequate in the same way that the talk about modern man is inadequate—it assumes as normative a model which is the limited product of a particular culture (despite the horror so many progressive Christians háve of being "culture-bound"). If the categories of thought and expression acceptable to modern secular society are taken as the necessary starting point, or are accorded more than a limited validity, the problem of belief will continue to turn back upon itself. Authentic Christian doctrine will seem less and less credible, and Christians will find themselves increasingly giving way in the hope of winning approval for what little they have left, continually forced to assure secularists that they are not fanatics.

The modern relativist mentality can be tolerant and relativistic about everything except the basic terms of its own thinking. An absolutist claim, especially in religion or morals, is the one thing it cannot tolerate and against which it is fully prepared to employ censorship both of a gross and a subtle kind, using all its power to make absolute beliefs appear sinister and deformed. To break out of this cul-de-sac requires believing Christians once again to assume an aggressive stance and requires the secular mind to take belief seriously on belief's own terms.

CHAPTER 6

The Triumph of Bureaucracy

COMMON sense would suggest that, were modern Christianity suffering a crisis of belief, there would develop a tension between those who can be broadly designated "religious professionals"—priests, educators, church bureaucrats—and lay people, with the former group struggling valiantly to maintain the Church's official doctrines, from within their institutional ghetto, against a spirit of scepticism growing among lay people forced to live their lives amidst the secularity of the world. Some commentators have in fact described such a division despite little empirical evidence to support it.

Here common sense is in error, and the above division, to the degree that it exists, is almost the reverse of what might be expected—on virtually every question it has been the religious professionals who have espoused avant-garde and iconoclastic positions, the laity in the pews who have resisted or remained passive and bewildered towards change. Thus a 1977 survey of sexual beliefs by a Jesuit sociologist reported that "The groups the least in agreement with the pope's authority are the parish staffs" and "The parish councils, generally composed of the most active, are the most orthodox in agreeing with the official Catholic stance on sexual mores."[1] Even on issues like contraception, where there has been an obviously massive defection of the laity from official doctrine, it is questionable how strong that defection would have been if many religious professionals had not prepared the way for it either by attacking the official teaching or by predicting its modification, and if these same professionals had made any serious effort to uphold *Humanae Vitae* once it was issued.

The expectation that religious professionals represent the "establishment" and thus are forced to uphold an official "line" misunderstands both the historical character of the Church and the nature of modern bureaucracy. Innumerable studies have revealed that bureaucracies are at best only tenuously responsive to commands issued by their nominal superiors. They operate, usually, under their own momentum, in accordance with their own priorities, sometimes in direct contravention of official policy decreed from on high.

Until the Second Vatican Council the Catholic Church retained some of the characteristics of an absolute monarchy, although even in absolute monarchies the ruler finds it impossible to control the bureaucracy as firmly as he would like. Liberal Catholics never tired of charging that a reactionary Roman Curia was thwarting the will of a progressive pope. The Council brought an end to this absolutism. However, the effect was not to "liberate" the laity from arbitrary control, which was the media's favored version of this process, but rather to liberate the ecclesiastical bureaucrats, especially at the national and diocesan levels, from accountability to an international authority. The Roman Curia had to be discredited in order to allow national and diocesan bureaucracies to flourish unimpeded. Prior to the Council, the chart of authority in the Church was clear and simple—from the pope at the top, down through the various bishops, to the ordinary parish priest. After the Council the flow was jumbled and uncertain. Church bureaucrats then began to behave much like bureaucrats in any other large modern organization. Skilled in the use of the media, they were able to present their own newly found autonomy as evidence of a new freedom in the Church.

The preconciliar Church was very imperfectly bureaucratized, and thus doctrine was not conveyed to the laity primarily through conduits from on high but was in reality communal, something which the postconciliar bureaucrats hold out as the promise of the "new Church" but which they have actually destroyed. The most exalted exercise of papal authority in modern times—the proclamation of the dogma of the Assumption in 1950—did not impose anything which was not already fervently believed by the mass of the laity. Although the preconciliar Church was often accused of being a totalitarian institution holding its members in mental bondage, it was in reality something quite different—a community with genuinely shared values and beliefs which could be maintained even without an authoritarian structure. But this "folk Catholicism" was as hateful to reformers as was hierarchical authority, and they waged a massive and successful campaign against it.

Liberal Catholics, behind the times as usual, still tend to think of bureaucracy in outmoded terms, as rigid, inflexible, legalistic, backward, and immobile. Under certain conditions bureaucracy may be all these things. However, modern bureaucracy, more often than not, tends to be quite different. John Lukacs has defined this new reality:

> . . . it is quite possible that the age of aristocracy has been succeeded not by the age of democracy but by the age of bureaucracy. . . .

> What we are faced with is the bureaucratization of intellectual life, and of the *entire* intellectual profession—a new phenomenon, this. We are faced with a new kind of man who thinks that the principal purpose of his mind is to represent or exemplify applications of ideas that have become public and current—current among intellectuals and possibly becoming current in the mass media.[2]

The bureaucratization of the American Church since the early 1960s is a phenomenon of major importance, scarcely even alluded to in most of the vast literature dealing with renewal. Bureaus already existing in 1960, such as the diocesan school offices, have been expanded geometrically, with the addition of more and more specialists dealing with matters which were not even recognized twenty years ago. New offices have been created to deal with matters—liturgy, for example—which were formerly thought of as self-regulating and not requiring any special bureaucratic oversight except in rare instances of abuse. Parishes were formerly quasi-paternalistic, quasi-communal organisms which had quite simple structures. Now the "ideal" parish not only has a pastor and several associate pastors but a permanent deacon, possibly a temporary deacon from the seminary, a religious-education coordinator, a liturgical coordinator, and other assorted members of the pastoral "team," plus various committees. Most striking, however, has been the growth of the national bureaucracies centered in the National Council of Catholic Bishops and the United States Catholic Conference, two bodies which house innumerable committees, special offices, and designated experts in every conceivable area of both ecclesiastical and social life. There has been no serious effort to assess the impact of this burgeoning bureaucracy on the life of the American Church; its monetary cost alone must be enormous.

The major revolution which has occurred in the American Church is one which, characteristically, the media have failed to notice, except vaguely and without understanding its implications—the revolt of middle management, the growing tendency of ecclesiastical bureaucrats to behave like bureaucrats everywhere and consequently to function as independently as possible. It has been priests and nuns, as well as lay people who operate within the Church in some professional capacity, who have been the principal locus of discontent, resistance, and outright opposition to papal decrees. Similar manifestations of rebellion appear elsewhere in the Church, mainly emanating from these professional sources.

Modern bureaucratized professionals are, as John Lukacs points out, people who are maximally susceptible to received opinions of a certain kind. Educated to a degree, but not intellectuals, they are unlikely to be original thinkers or even particularly daring in the thoughts which they entertain, but highly conscious of their positions "in advance" of what ordinary people are thinking.

The modern professional's status depends intimately on the notion of expertise, on having certain competences which the "client" of his services does not possess. There is hereby built into the very notion of professionalism the assumption that people are incapable of managing their own affairs without help and that what the average person "knows" is in fact subject to correction by the expert. Professionalization, especially when it is bureaucratized, is thus almost of necessity opposed to "folk" culture and seeks always to weaken that culture in the name of "purifying" it. In a certain sense the ordinary lay person exists, in the mind of the professional, primarily for the sake of being enlightened or instructed.

Almost equally of necessity, professionals do not consider themselves finally accountable to their clients, since if the clients' need is based on ignorance the clients themselves can have no basis for evaluating the services they receive. Indeed, many professionals provide services which clients are not even aware of needing until the professional has pointed out the need. Modern bureaucracy has adopted the rhetoric of service and accountability, and an able professional understands how to create an aura of "openness." However, in a democratic society such a style is finally a better guarantee of retaining control than outright authoritarianism could ever be.

The two most sensitive areas of bureaucratized professionalism in the American Church are liturgy and religious education, and it is probably fair to say that most American Catholics, at the time of the Second Vatican Council, were unaware of any particular needs in either area. They were deeply committed to their traditional forms of piety and found the instruction in faith which they had received adequate to their needs. (Later some lay people would confess how oppressive and inadequate their upbringings had been, but only after they had been enlightened by the professionals.) The first task of professional liturgists and professional catechists was to destroy the credibility of the traditional ways so as to make room for their own programs.

The role of the professional in such a situation is exactly parallel to that of the professional reporter—he or she is the bringer of "news" to the community from the outside, news which the members of the community may find disturbing, confusing, or threatening but which the messenger assures them will be, if properly prepared for and accepted, liberating. The worst sins become resistance, closed-mindedness, clinging to the past. If the professional no longer has any news to impart, if there is nothing substantial to criticize in the religious life of the community, his task becomes superfluous.

The professional's role is therefore also directly tied to sources of information from outside the community, and he functions primarily as agent from those outside sources to the community. Although supposedly at one with the people he "serves," the professional is in fact virtually by definition an alien or semialien presence, a missionary, someone who seeks to change the community to bring it more into conformity with the larger culture. The parish director of religious education, for example, periodically attends diocesan workshops at which the newest and "best" ideas and materials are explained and mandated. The diocesan bureaucrats in turn are familiar figures at regional and national conventions where they receive this information from recognized national experts, who in turn represent a larger, possibly international, community rooted in the universities. This latter group looks for its principal signals from outside the Church altogether, and seeks to develop a modern form of Catholicism based on what is taken to be the best secular thought in a given discipline, for example, educational psychology. At this level experts are also likely to be self-consciously very ecumenical, impatient with what they regard as the meaningless and petty barriers which separate one denomination from another.

The immense growth of bureaucracies in the postconciliar Church has been rendered possible by the confusion of the conciliar changes. The bureaucrats are charged with establishing the policies, the guidelines, the procedures which will help people to survive the confusion. They explain the meaning of change to those who thought the Church could never change. But an even more important point is overlooked—much of the confusion of the postconciliar period has been created, or at least greatly exacerbated, by these same bureaucracies, who in the crucially sensitive areas of liturgy and religious education chose to emphasize discontinuity over tradition, ridiculed and denigrated past beliefs and practices, sometimes interpreted the conciliar decrees in ways which directly contradicted the texts of those documents. The role of the expert became inflated after the manner of nineteenth-century private-enterprise fire departments—fanning the blaze in order to demonstrate skill at controlling it.

The immense increase in the number of functioning experts has paralleled a marked decrease in the number of professional Catholic missionaries, a symbolic kind of symmetry, in that many priests and religious after the Council began to conceive their roles not in the traditional sense of converting unbelievers but in the sense of acting as missionaries to their own people, agents of the larger culture devoted to transforming and broadening the "narrowness" of Catholic life. The democratic emphasis which emanated from the Council has nowhere been more effectively thwarted than here, by professionals who are disposed to "listen to people" only in order to enlighten them as to the inadequacies of their thinking. Those lay people opposed to the new catechetics, for example, have in general encountered a solid wall of unyielding bureaucratic determination. As one Jesuit educator has written,

> Diocesan and parish school board members are not likely to exercise great power in the development of new instructional programs, and this may not be a bad thing, since most of them don't know very much about Vatican II anyway.[3]

The professional likewise does not consider himself ultimately accountable to his nominal superior in the bureaucracy, the bishop. (The same Jesuit writes, "Given the present state of the hierarchy in the U.S., centralization [of education] might be very risky indeed.") In the immediate conciliar period, professionals assumed authority on the grounds that they alone had made a thorough study of the conciliar documents and were thus transmitting to the parishes the official messages emanating from Rome. The pretext that Rome sets policy, which the local churches merely follow, has long since been abandoned, however, and experts in areas like catechetics and liturgy tend more and more to emphasize the needs of the local church, which they deem themselves uniquely suited to interpret.

Despite the emphasis on episcopal collegiality, the authority of the bishop within his own diocese has in reality diminished since the Council, due mainly to the growth of bureaucracy. As a general rule, the more complex the structure the more difficult it is to control from the top, and in large modern dioceses the various bureaus often seem to operate with something approaching total autonomy. It is not unusual to hear of dioceses where the bishop is known to be personally out of sympathy with the prevailing philosophy of catechetics, for instance, but believes he is powerless to change it. Here again the power of expertise, which becomes almost mystical in a technological society, reigns supreme. Many bishops have had impressed upon them, over and over again, that they are not theologians, not liturgists, not educators, not canon lawyers, and that they are consequently not competent to lay down policy in these various areas of Church life. The bishop's role is merely one of ratifying whatever his bureaucracies do and defending them from the criticisms of irate lay people. When the American bishops collectively dared to amend the proposed draft of the National Catechetical Directory in 1977, a nun complained that they had "almost ravaged" a document "that we spent hours, and sometimes years, developing,"[4] as though bishops have no authority to oversee the teaching of the faith.

Religious professionals have been the primary beneficiaries of the changes which have occurred in the Church. Not surprisingly, therefore, they are generally the loudest in extolling the unalloyed benefits of those changes and in calling for further changes still. Bishops, who now find themselves more effectively insulated from the laity than ever before, precisely because of the elaborate structure of bureaucracy (protocol demands, for example, that a bishop not listen to complaints about liturgical practice but instead refer them to the liturgical office), are under constant temptation to act as though, for all practical purposes, the religious professionals *are* the Church. On a day-to-day basis the bishop finds himself dealing mainly with professionals, whose point of view and whose ability to interpret for him what the laity really want and need tend to crowd out information he may be receiving from other sources. Unless he is an extraordinarily self-reliant man, his own viewpoint will be inevitably reshaped to fit theirs. He also finds the professionals in his diocese, priests and nuns, organized effectively to function as pressure groups, while the laity have no such organization. At the national level the situation is even more extreme. A host of professional organizations—the National Federation of Priests' Councils, the Leadership Conference of Women Religious, the Canon Law Society, the National Catholic Education Association, etc.—regularly bring pressure of various kinds to bear on the bishops, and there is no lay group even remotely comparable in terms of influence and organization. The measurable "liberalization" of the American hierarchy in the 1970s has much to do with the skewed perspective which this state of affairs tends to create.

If the professionals are not accountable either to their "clients" below them in the hierarchy nor to the bishops above them, to whom are they accountable? The answer, as with all bureaucratized professions, is: to each other. A vertical accountability has been replaced by a horizontal accountability.

It should not be overlooked that there are important elements of power involved here. Bureaucracies create vested interests which are self-perpetuating. Apart from every other consideration, no bureaucracy will seriously entertain criticisms of its policies if they jeopardize its continued authority. Countless professionals in the American Church are now committed to the new liturgy or the new catechetics because their own continued ascendancy depends on them. This does not imply conscious bad faith. However, to them all criticism is merely based on ignorance and is not to be seriously entertained.

In the bureaucratic world recognition and rewards come primarily from one's peers, and it is to the peer group that one looks both for signals as to what constitutes correct behavior and for confirmation of professional success. The national convention, various national publications, the national organizations are the organs which lay down guidelines for correct belief and behavior and grant recognition to those who follow them. Not infrequently, opportunities for professional advancement, and higher salaries, accompany this. Again, conscious bad faith is not implied. One of the products of professionalization is an environment in which it becomes almost literally impossible to think in ways different from the way the profession as a whole thinks. Deviations, especially by nonmembers of the profession, are regarded merely as evidence of benightedness or willful wrong-headedness. In such a situation it becomes far more important to be identified with a program which enjoys prestige than one which pleases the people it is supposed to serve.

The stereotyped image of bureaucrats as timid people who deliberately try to retard change has given way, in almost all areas of modern life, to the reality of the bureaucrat as "change agent." Bureaucrats are still blamed for being obstructionists because there are always people who would like to move faster than the bureaucrats consider practical and who favor direct action independent of institutional control. But modern bureaucrats recognize that lasting and significant change usually takes place under their own auspices and that they possess the necessary skills for implementing changes in such a way as to upset the fewest people.

Modern bureaucracies strive to identify themselves closely with "creative" programs. On the basis of this image of creativity professional bureaucrats tend to gain advancement. Sometimes the image is merely cosmetic. More often, however, bureaucrats are willing to experiment with as much innovation as they estimate their clients will tolerate. In the postconciliar Church few incantations have been repeated so frequently as the term *creative,* applied to countless new programs, ideas, books, courses of study, etc. By definition modern bureaucrats must always be "ahead" of their clients in their thinking. There must be a constant flow of new "guidelines" and "position papers," often enough contradicting those which have gone before. The laity are condescendingly lectured for holding attitudes inculcated into them by an earlier generation of professionals.

The absence of professional accountability is fundamental to the modern bureaucratic reality. Although in principle they are accountable to their professional peers, in practice no profession polices its members rigorously. Professions dealing with "hard" data, like medicine, are notoriously lax. Professions concerned with "soft" subjects, like catechetics, have no standards of professional responsibility at all. The aim of the modern professional is in fact to escape any kind of control except the opinion of his peers. Harsh criticism of the pope or the bishops still passes as a sign of honesty in advanced circles. Those who object strenuously to innovative catechetical programs are not uncommonly denounced as divisive and uncharitable. Although numerous professionals have told the laity that the Council gave them the right to dissent, it is soon discovered that this right ends at the point where it challenges programs with which the professionals themselves are closely identified.[5]

In certain ways the laity now have less of a voice in the administration of the Church than in the past. Traditionally, for example, there was an implied contract between the people of a parish and the nuns staffing the parish school—if the people built the school and maintained it, there would always be a supply of religious teachers. Now, however, religious communities often unilaterally decide to abandon a particular school, which may force its closing, not merely because of the shortage of nuns but often also because the community in question has decided that it has more "important" work to do than instructing children. The needs of the parish are rarely given primary weight in this decision, despite the rhetoric of service which modern religious so strongly espouse. There is a similar lack of accountability about money. Religious communities have, in numerous instances, freely given up for secular use institutions paid for by the laity through many years of sacrifice, based mainly on the religious' own desire not to be burdened with the institution any longer. In recent years many religious communities and church agencies have used money for purposes which donors would probably find objectionable, and no one has begun to account for the vast sums spent on clerics and religious who obtained expensive educations but afterwards gave little or no service to the Church.

The maintenance and expansion of bureaucracies is now one of the major priorities of the American Church, although it is a priority nowhere publicly stated and one which it is doubtful that most lay people would think important. Part of the modern professional style is to express concern for the needs of the poor, and lay people are often sternly reminded that the building of expensive churches, for instance, or owning two late-model cars, involves a selfish expenditure of money which could be better spent on those in need. Rarely, however, do these same professionals seriously suggest that money spent on travel to national conferences, speakers' fees, pursuit of advanced degrees, office staffs, official publications, or photocopying equipment could better be given to the poor. No figures are available, but it seems likely that the amount of church money spent on such bureaucratic necessities has risen enormously in the past twenty years. The bureaucratic sensitivity to new "problems" which are constantly being discovered also enters here—according to an iron-clad modern law, each new problem discovered inevitably generates new bureaucracies. As the number of priests and religious in the Church continues to decline, the number whose work is primarily bureaucratic continues to increase.

The triumph of bureaucracy has given rise to a new style of episcopal leadership in the Church (happily not universal)—the bishop who is known to be personally orthodox, pious, conservative in many ways, but who is also concerned to be maximally "open," "flexible," and "conciliatory" in his exercise of authority, who in effect makes a sharp distinction between his personal beliefs and his official policies. Such bishops appear to conceive their role as that of reconcilers, but it is a role which is predefined for the bishop by his bureaucrats. "Reconciliation," for example, will rarely mean candidly admitting the damage done by certain experimental catechetical programs and apologizing to those whose children were not instructed in their faith. As self-conceived "moderates," such bishops are always at the mercy of those "extremists" who are most aggressive in pushing their own ideas—the "middle" is defined by those most successful in shifting the whole axis either right or left, a process in which the moderate bishop is a purely passive participant, a merely symbolic figure whom each side seeks to capture for its own use (and whom the bureaucrats almost always end by capturing). Each age tends to produce the wrong administrative type—too rigid in times of stability, too flexible in times of change.

The struggle to enlist episcopal prestige—a usually quite unequal struggle between sophisticated and well-organized bureaucrats and naive and poorly organized lay people—involves a process which is also endemic to modern bureaucracies but has not been noticed in the Church: the use of authority to undermine authority, the last stage of authority's decline. Newer programs in religious education, liturgy, and other sensitive areas have not triumphed, as their proponents would like to think, because of their self-evident superiority. They have triumphed because they have been officially mandated, and numerous sceptical lay people have been cowed into submission by the implication that resistance is a form of disloyalty. Although proclaiming an end to blind obedience in the Church, the professionals have invoked obedience to enforce the necessity of change. However, through a yet even more dazzling irony, the new ideas whose acceptance has been enforced through obedience are themselves then used to further undermine the concept of obedience. The bishop who lends his prestige to new programs in religious education, for example, is perhaps unaware that these

same programs tend to inculcate attitudes which cannot tolerate episcopal authority in any form, nor any of the religious beliefs close to the
bishop's own heart. Modern bureaucracies are generally impatient of
their nominal superiors, whom they regard as not as qualified to wield
authority as they themselves are and whose existence is tolerated as necessary mainly to lend legitimacy to the bureaucrats' own actions. As
Philip Rieff has brilliantly said,

> In their numbers and spread, beyond our schools into the more and more
> heavily capitalized bureaucracies of the welfare state, of business enterprise,
> and of the mass media, the social scientists . . . paratherapists . . . repre-
> sent everything a priestly theorist cannot be and everything a prophet can-
> not announce. A true prophet is called to conserve what is being destroyed.
> Problem-solvers parody prophecy; they call themselves to destroy what may
> be possible still to conserve.[6]

In common with other self-consciously advanced modern professionals,
church bureaucrats now often consider themselves critics of the capitalist
system, and a good deal of bureaucratic activity (especially at the national
level) aims at instructing the faithful in the inadequacies of that system.
But these same bureaucrats fail to notice how their very existence, and
the style in which they operate, is itself a product of late capitalism and
depends upon the underlying cultural assumptions of that system.

The bureaucratic system of governance which now dominates the
American Church exactly parallels what advanced capitalist thought con-
siders sound management practice, and in some cases consciously models
itself on it. Particularly significant is the tendency to treat every form of
dissension which arises not in credal terms—that there is a true and a
false position and the Church must uphold the one and condemn the
other—but in purely administrative or personnel terms. All kinds of
"problem" people in the Church—parents upset over what their children
are being taught in the parochial schools, priests experiencing a crisis of
vocation, divorced people demanding that their second marriages be
blessed—are responded to therapeutically, in terms of sympathy, cajolery, and symbolic gestures of "concern," but rarely will the issues they
raise be discussed substantively. Good management practice seeks to
avoid situations where it is necessary to make fundamental judgments
about the rightness or wrongness of a particular course of action and
prefers, if possible, to rely on sophisticated manipulation of people's
psyches as a way of overcoming dissension. In an ecclesiastical situation
this means, among other things, that important doctrinal questions are
often shunted aside in the interests of good management (as Rieff has
put it, "problem-solving is anti-credal.")[7]

A leading clerical defender of the postconciliar experiments embarked upon by the Church in the Netherlands has explicitly invoked what he terms the "excellent principles" contained in a book entitled *Strategic Maneuverability and Strategic Management*. Among its principles are the following:

> Continuous adaptation to "surroundings" is called strategic behavior.
>
> the appointment or schooling of managers who are open to change;
>
> "brains" carry a very great responsibility in professional decision-making—in spite of this "brains" do not have an equal status with the managers who take their decisions and regulate their implementation;—this difference in status is an important source of many conflicts between designer and executioner;
>
> —developing and programming is a continuous process; it can be compared with a ship changing course at sea;
>
> [there are] internal resistances to change which must be broken down;
>
> —the acceptance of business risks;
> —systematic and expert-controlled decision preparation;
> —strategic thinking and acting as a continuous element in top management,[8]

The bureaucratic model of Church government closely parallels those institutions in secular society which are identified with the illusory pluralism of modern life discussed in the previous chapter. The key to the bureaucrats' triumph has been their claim to have liberated Catholics from the narrowness, rigidity, and authoritarianism of the preconciliar Church and to have introduced a new pluralistic regime in which all points of view can be accommodated. The revolution is now being ratified by the claim that there are "two magisteria"—that of the hierarchy and that of the theologians, with the latter in most cases to be preferred to the former.

The close link between this bureaucratic style and the culture of an advanced capitalism is manifest in the very terms in which the new professionals seek to advance the cause of Christianity, which are similar to the terms in which advertisers seek to promote the purchase of goods. The doctrine of progress is assumed, in which each new model is another step toward an anticipated apex of development. Outdated models are ridiculed as quaint and those who still use them made to feel abnormal, and when new models are introduced older models soon cease to be available even to those who want them. The right kind of packaging and promotion—an image of brightness, contemporaneity, youthfulness, and vitality—is rated essential. Finally, the new model is offered to the consumer on the basis of its promising a happier, more fulfilled life—modern evangelists would no more dream of trying to sell Christianity in terms of the doctrine of sin and redemption, or obedience to the commands of Christ, than soap manufacturers would advertise their product as gritty but effective. In short, many of those who are most eloquent in criticizing the consumerist mentality have most deeply assimilated it to their own thinking about religion.

American capitalism may be politically and economically right-wing, but culturally it is left-wing, since in principle it recognizes no restraint on its activities except law and profitability. Business success to a great extent depends on the ability to break down consumer resistance to new ideas, and the greatest rewards often go to those who are most daring in their innovations and least respectful of established patterns of thinking and acting. Advertising is perfectly suited to the therapeutic mentality, with its emphasis on immediate self-gratification and the acceptance of planned obsolescence. The therapeutic mentality, now so influential in the Church, in fact grows directly out of the consumerist mentality, as another mutant of late capitalism.

The perfect bureaucrat is "anti-credal" in that there are no fixed principles or dogmas to which he is committed which might impede the development of the institution to which he is committed (the great cautionary example from the capitalist world being Henry Ford's commitment to the Model T rather than to the profitability of the Ford Motor Company). The liberal Catholic charge that traditionalists in the Church idolize the institution here completely misses the mark and is a charge much more relevant to themselves. For what traditionalists—the orthodox—value in the Church is the truth which they believe it embodies and teaches. In extreme cases they may break with the institution if they believe this truth is not being honored. It is in fact the liberals who are committed to the institution itself, in that they are prepared to accept with equanimity, and even to promote, all manner of changes in its doctrines and practice while continuing to be a part of it and even to earn their livings from it.

It is interesting, in this context, to notice that one form of the Modernist heresy of the early twentieth century was really a kind of ultra-Catholicism which was precisely an idolizing of the Church. The priest-theologian Alfred Loisy, condemned by Rome along with other Modernists in 1907, proposed, in reaction to the Protestant emphasis on the authority of Scripture, a theory of the Church in which it could in effect do anything. The evolving religious consciousness within the Church was bound by no higher authority, and the Church in each age could therefore become something quite different from the Church in the previous age.[9] The same belief is present among many contemporary Catholics who argue for the morality of homosexuality, for instance, the legitimacy of divorce, or the reopening of the question of the divinity of Jesus Christ.

Modern bureaucracies require people who are maximally flexible, which means that they commit themselves totally to present official policies but are prepared to abandon them on short notice and commit themselves with equal fervor to new policies which may run contrary to past policies. Clients of the bureau in question then earn the contempt of the professionals if they fail to show a similar flexibility and remain stubbornly attached to the old policies. Thus professional liturgists of twenty years ago extolled the beauties of the Roman and Latin liturgy but have now in effect banned the Latin and argue the necessity of an authentically American liturgy. In matters of doctrine, morals, and spirituality many priests and religious are now telling their people almost the opposite of what they were telling them before the Council.

The current Catholic preoccupation with process, which reaches its peak in the so-called process theology, also reflects the prevailing attitudes and practices of the business world, in which a mastery of the techniques of management are far more important than expertise concerning a particular product and executives regularly and successfully move from company to company, almost without regard for the particular product which the company sells. Here too great a belief in the product, as distinct from the process by which it is produced and marketed, reduces the executive's mobility and usefulness. This attitude is reflected in, among other things, the ease with which modern Christians move back and forth among denominations, in contrast to the lengthy agonizing which afflicted converts of past ages like John Henry Newman.

The bureaucratic mind is preoccupied with movement or signs of movement, since it is through such activity or pseudo-activity that the bureau's own legitimacy is reaffirmed. Competent bureaucrats are highly adept at creating the illusion of movement, and the postconciliar Church has been dominated to an almost suffocating degree by reports, commissions, white papers, guidelines, meetings, conventions, programs, etc. Those who thrive on such ephemera have thereby gained a disproportionate influence in the Church, while those who find such things debilitating and demoralizing (who often enough are deeply devoted to the Church in its fundamental religious meaning) are relegated to inconspicuous corners. The life of the Church is coming more and more to be viewed wholly in functional and managerial terms (the concept of the personnel board now so important in many dioceses, for example), with little sense of the transcendental and mystical sources of the Church's structure. The goals of "dialogue," "process," "openness," "input," "flex-ibility," etc., seem often merely self-validating, not leading to any deeper or more vital manifestations of faith.

The bureaucratic mind therefore confronts, as an enemy, the mental-ity of the client or lay person who does show evidence of being too overly credal in his commitments, and in the postconciliar era religious profes-sionals have probably spent much less time in opposing unbelief in the larger society than in attempting to dampen down the "fanaticism" of their own people. For perhaps the first time in the history of the Catholic Church members of the clergy have been convinced that one of their most serious problems is that their people are too religious. (Liberal Protestant clergy have been convinced of this for a long time.) The con-certed campaign against folk piety and the new catechetics were both battles in this war. Another front is the "emotionalism" of the anti-abortionists. The ranks of religious professionals in America are hon-eycombed with persons who would like to desensitize their fellow Catholics on the subject of abortion, looking to a future time when the Church will belatedly join the emerging enlightened consensus on that subject.

By its nature modern bureaucracy cannot tolerate genuine pluralism, both because it seeks to maintain control over its society (more suavely but in many ways more effectively than old-style rulers) and because the bureaucratic style of operation is ultimately incompatible with certain traditional ways of thought. The secular world's fostering of an illusory pluralism which ultimately proves to be an enforced uniformity is paral-leled by a similar phenomenon within the Church. In both cases the claim of pluralism is first used to gain tolerance for new ideas, then to permit the new to displace the old, finally in effect to outlaw the old. Actual censorship is sometimes employed, as when universities or the media simply exclude certain ideas from serious consideration, or when ecclesiastical bureaucracies outlaw traditional catechisms, for example. More commonly, however, uniformity is enforced by creating conditions in which certain ideas become literally unthinkable while others are made to seem the only natural ones.

The purpose of much of postconciliar religious education, whether recognized as such or not, has been to create a situation in which no one is deeply attached to any particular set of beliefs, maximum credal flexi-bility is achieved, and possible outbreaks of religious fanaticism are fore-stalled. Religious educators have rarely been fully candid about the impli-cations of their programs, preferring instead to insist that they are merely altering methods of teaching, not content, or that they favor the instillation of "faith commitments" rather than mere ingestion of information. The doctrines for which so many martyrs have joyfully accepted death—the divinity of Christ, the Real Presence, the authority of the papacy—are now treated as speculations of a merely secondary importance, readily adjustable to fit the presumed needs of the time.

Genuine pluralism would dictate that, in every diocese, perhaps in every school, a variety of catechetical approaches be used, including some equivalent of the *Baltimore Catechism* for those who want it. However, except for a few unusual places where a bishop has kept close personal control of the machinery of religious education, this is not the case. In almost every instance where catechetics professionals have been allowed full control of the diocesan program, traditional approaches have been banned. Choices have been available, but only within the limited range of the newer methodologies themselves. Pastors who have attempted to resist the guidelines of the diocesan school offices have in case after case been defeated. Within the relatively brief period of about fifteen years almost the entire vast Catholic school system in the United States has been remolded, a remarkable example of bureaucratic power and unanimity of purpose.

The national professional organizations are the principal instruments by which bureaucratic orthodoxy is established and enforced, and in practice they probably wield more authority over their members than do the bishops. Despite so much talk of pluralism, there does not appear to be significant disagreement or real debate within these groups. There are no published reports, for example, of catechetical groups seriously discussing the merits of a more traditional approach to instruction, or liturgists debating the use of Latin. News accounts of meetings of the Canon Law Society suggest a near unanimity among its members as to the desirability of the "experimental norms" for annulling marriages. There is little evidence of bodies like the Leadership Conference of Women Religious or the Conference of Major Superiors of Men candidly discussing the effects of the many experiments in religious life made over the past fifteen years.

Every professional organization quickly develops its own consensus on major issues, and afterwards certain questions become effectively closed. Those who disagree with the consensus learn to live with it. Often those who seriously dissent from the consensus are made to feel uncomfortable or unwelcome in the organization. They are relegated to the margins of their profession, unofficially placed on a list of people who are considered eccentric, unreliable, or fanatical.

Professional bodies possess real powers of censorship, and thousands of working professionals throughout the nation obtain their own impressions of what is or is not sound practice from censored sources. For example, a new journal designed to review the religious media effectively scuttles every publication of an even slightly traditional kind, freely employing epithets like "sexist and racist," "unbelievably inadequate," "not too creative or exciting," "rather minor," "lacking an open mind," and "extremely juvenile."[10] The committee appointed by the Catholic Theological Society of America to write its 1977 report on sexual ethics included not even a token individual prepared to uphold traditional teachings. Members of the association who were concerned with this lack found it impossible to gain a hearing—their inquiries to the chairman of the committee went unanswered, their suggestions unacknowledged. The contents of the document were kept even from members of the association until it had been released to the press.[11] As early as 1972 a prominent ex-priest boasted that

> the liberal movement is giving clear evidence of having gained control of the Roman Catholic Church in America.
>
> Liberal Catholics have a lock-tight grip on the publication of catechisms and religious formation texts, and a similarly tight grip on the university religious education departments which train religion teachers for all levels.[12]

Although the movement for the renewal of the Church often went forward under the banners of love, peace, and gentleness, in reality a power struggle of sometimes vicious dimensions was taking place. The losers in that struggle—certain hitherto highly respected theologians, canon lawyers, liturgists, and educators—in effect became nonpersons, their very names almost forgotten. More importantly, certain ideas for which they stood were also frozen out of the permissible universe of discourse.

It would be untrue to imply that religious professionals operate solely in their own interests or that they disregard totally the wishes of the laity. Rather, the professionals are part of a broader cultural phenomenon, and they feel close spiritual kinship with certain segments of the laity who are like themselves—educated, geographically and occupationally mobile, employed in bureaucratic structures, self-confident, ambitious, and articulate. When the professionals in the Church solemnly warn the hierarchy that they must "listen to the people," it is people like themselves whom they have in mind. A liturgist, for example, will commonly hear the voices of those who want newer and more experimental liturgies but not those who want Gregorian chant. A catechist hears those who fear "rigidity" and "narrowness" in religious instruction but not those who want more explicit doctrine. A moral theologian is attuned to those who wish the Church to be more "realistic" in its teaching about sex but not to those who think such realism is destructive of family life.

Until about the time of the Second Vatican Council, the Catholic Church was remarkably successful in imparting to its professionals a kind of education which, however rarified and remote it might be in some ways (Scholastic theology and philosophy), did not alienate them from their roots within the Catholic community. Once, however, the conciliar changes came to be understood primarily in terms of discontinuity with the past, and once the professionals began to conceive of their role as that of "change agent," the process of alienation began. The alienation was in fact deliberately exacerbated, in that the newly understood role of the professional required that he or she be always in advance of the majority of the laity on most questions, and unfamiliar or even shocking ideas became many professionals' stock in trade. By a strange twist of history, the seminary and the convent became places not where, as had long been the case, pious young people underwent a deepening and refining of their faith, but often enough now a loss of faith, or at least the mutation of that faith to make it seriously alien to the faith of their own families.

The growth of religious professionalism in the postconciliar era has been in many cases a process by which individuals of simple and pious backgrounds have been initiated into the mysteries of membership in the great modern bureaucratic class. They have systematically imbibed the ideas, attitudes, and styles proper to that class. Membership in that class has come to seem to many like salvation, the distance between their origins and their present "liberated" state a measure of progress. At its 1977 convention, for example, the National Assembly of Women Religious rejected a proposal that it enter into official cooperation with the National Council of Catholic Women. The N.C.C.W., it said, had "different goals." (It had also committed the unpardonable sin of not supporting the Equal Rights Amendment.) The N.A.W.R. also rejected a proposal to ask President Carter to intervene on behalf of American servicemen held prisoner by the Soviets. "If we support this we are supporting the right of the U.S. to send its men anywhere and then expect to get them back," one nun explained.[13]

In the immediate postconciliar period criticism of the "suburban captivity of the churches" was a favorite reformist theme, and reformers only slowly came to realize that in reality the suburbs were potentially the most fertile fields for the sowing of new ideas. The following describes a parish which became famous for feuding with its bishop:

Good Shepherd is teetering on the edge of the future of the American parish. The effort, while precarious, is exhilarating, unsettling to some, and a viable model that, while tinkered with each year, seems to hold together and work at the nitty-gritty people level.

> The liturgical style, like the pastor, is often flamboyant. Celebration in church is just that—mime and merry-go-rounds, dance and dixieland bands, floats and flowered forklifts, even an orange Volkswagon—enough to drive some folks away (several hundred by [Father] Quinlan's count) and attract others.

> Good Shepherd is a sophisticated parish in the northern Virginia suburbs. . . . The average annual income is around $20–25,000 per year—mostly highly paid government civil servants, professionals, and military brass (the Pentagon and Fort Belvoir are nearby).[14]

Superficially, there are some sociological surprises in this account—well-to-do suburbanites are supposed to be conservative in their attitudes, "military brass" even more so. But, as Philip Rieff has pointed out, the old alliance in America between technological radicalism and cultural conservatism has now been broken. And he adds, ". . . the propertied classes are not conservative. . . . Modern culture is constituted by its endless transitionality; the people at the top have learned to want it that way."[15]

Modern bureaucrats and quasi-intellectuals serve the cultural function of release rather than interdiction—they grant permission to transgress the old taboos to those alert enough to understand their message. Suburbia has heard the message of release, of self-gratification and self-fulfillment, ever since the end of World War II. Until recently it was limited primarily to material consumption. Now, however, as the inevitable outcome of capitalism and a consumer economy of sustained prosperity, it has raised expectations of spiritual gratification as well, and the religious professionals are on hand with the good news that what was formerly forbidden is now permitted, even indeed required.

Capitalist America is not religiously conservative, or at least not necessarily so. Large corporations which admit nuns to their boards of directors know that such a step will do far more to change the nature of convent life than to change the life of the corporation itself, and they have no reason to regret this. The staunchly capitalist *U.S. News and World Report* treats the Catholic crisis not much differently than liberal *Newsweek*—in an article entitled "A New Vitality Emerging Out of Ferment" its readers are informed that the Church is "moving towards democracy," that Rome is out of touch with the people, women should be made priests, priests should be allowed to marry, and married people to divorce, and Good Shepherd parish is held up as the example of what a parish should be.[16] Such are now merely the conventional opinions of a broad segment of the prosperous American middle class. Belonging to a parish which boasts an avant-garde liturgy can bring the same prestige and personal satisfaction that comes from wearing a Paris fashion six months before it appears in U.S. stores. Conversely, it is embarrassing to belong to a parish that has a stodgy image.

The entire mentality of the paradigmatic "modern Catholic" is a product of the capitalist and technological perspectives which are so often fashionably criticized. The following are descriptions of two "liberated nuns," the first of whom still belongs to her order, the second of whom has returned to the lay state:

> Although it is a Sunday, Liz has half a dozen rollers in her hair. She is wearing a flowered top and knee-length green Bermudas. Her toenails are painted, she wears pretty rings, and she drives much too fast.
>
> Liz is just thirty—which she hates—and lives with a girl friend in a modern apartment a block off Hollywood Boulevard. . . . she has started her own advertising agency. . . . She has been on television several times and is constantly flying to conferences and meetings.
>
> . . . Today she [Midge] is college editor of Glamour magazine in New York, and looks every inch the part—streaky blonde hair, expensive scarlet suit, modern jewelry. . . .
>
> . . . She sips her martini reflectively amid the palms of the Waldorf-Astoria Hotel and says that not only did she enjoy that time in the convent but "I wouldn't be here now if I hadn't done that. I'd have been married at eighteen, have five kids, and be living in the suburbs running car pools." She does not want to marry, although she has been living with the same man for several years.
>
> . . . She says with some satisfaction, "I went to Charlotte Ford's wedding party. I know a lot of the big names; I consider them my friends."[17]

Langdon Gilkey's linking of advanced theological attitudes with the spread of capitalist technology is accurate, in that the modernization of the Church has been pushed forward for some of the same reasons that people embrace a modernizing technology—convenience (the Saturday evening Mass), ease (the end of private confessions), an up-to-date image (liturgy), and a maximum allowance for individuals to "fulfill" themselves (any number of innovations in moral theology). Sometimes motives of profit and motives of theology neatly coalesce, as in the proposal by two management consultants that "underused" church property be converted to "alternative uses." ("Once a management system is in place and functioning, a church manager . . . can receive the feedback necessary to evaluate the church's programs and resources.")[18] To the incurably technocratic mind, the "empty" spaces which churches are for most of each week can only be wasteful and irrational. What is odd is that so many professional liturgists have come to agree.

The Anglican priest-sociologist Robert Harvey has perceptively analyzed the emergence of a new "random-directed" type of personality in America. For true individualists, the encounter group—beloved, in its many variations, by so many religious professionals—is a traumatic experience. However, the ideal modern personality soon learns to find all groups roughly interchangeable, differentiation of one from another largely an accident. The random-directed person is in fact embarrassed by differences in tradition, class, race, or religion.

The old rugged individualism was inner-directed only with regard to man, not with regard to God—obedience to God was one of its cardinal tenets. The new random-directedness reverses this priority, claiming emancipation from divine laws in the name of conscience but accepting the values of the prevailing human society. Situation ethics is its inevitable expression. Having a weak sense of community, random-directed persons cannot believe in the existence of absolutes, which are therefore offensive. Myth, symbol, and tradition are constantly assaulted, in order to eliminate them, and group dynamics is finally an experiment in living without governing symbols. Transcendental symbols are particularly threatening to random-directed man because they link him to something beyond the fleeting community with which he has chosen to identify himself.[19]

A graphic illustration of Father Harvey's thesis was the 1976 "Call to Action" conference in Detroit, summoned by the National Council of Catholic Bishops after months of preparation and at a cost of over $400,000. The conference, with few exceptions, followed a predictable path, calling for the ordination of women to the priesthood, married priests, passage of the Equal Rights Amendment to the Constitution, the sanctioning of the practices of contraception and remarriage after divorce, acceptance of homosexuals into full rights of Church membership (including employment as teachers), and orthodox liberal positions on assorted economic and political questions. Among the resolutions voted down were those affirming the moral right of Catholics to serve in the military and the right of nations to arm themselves against invasion.

What was significant about the conference was less the contents of its resolutions than its style, structure, and purpose. (The author would personally find somewhat over half the resolutions to be acceptable.) From all over the country 1300 delegates were gathered for a three-day meeting in which they were asked to consider hundreds of proposed resolutions. Beside the delegates, numerous observers or lobbyists were also admitted to the proceedings, and in the discussion groups appointed to cull through these resolutions participants were ceaselessly pressured to adopt those favored by the various well-organized interest groups. In plenary session there was so little time to consider the various proposals that debate on any one resolution had to be drastically limited, and on the last day of the conference a large number of resolutions were approved without any debate at all.[20]

A former president of the Catholic Theological Society of America said the conference heralded a new vision of the Church.[21] Perhaps, but hardly a very attractive one. The style and substance of the meeting could appropriately be called totalitarian democracy. It is difficult to perceive much of value in a process which herds people together and then pressures them to vote on questions they have been given almost no time to study. The maximum interest of the conference seems to be precisely as an exercise in group dynamics, a means by which diverse people were manipulated into supporting the "correct" position on all manner of questions, and in which giving support to group aims and entering into the predominant group spirit became a self-validating experience.

There was more to the process than was immediately apparent, however, for in reality it also represented a brilliant propaganda victory for the Church bureaucrats, effectively designed to weaken the authority of the American bishops by confronting them with expressions of "popular will," many of which they could not possibly accede to and coincidentally striking a further blow at papal authority in the United States.

The process began with the national distribution of a booklet which was to serve as the basis for discussions in each parish. The subjects which the booklet's authors deemed worth discussion, and the manner in which questions were posed, already largely determined the likely response. No one knows how many parishes attempted the discussions or what percentage of parishioners participated. Scattered reports suggest that no more than a small minority of American Catholics even knew the process was going on. Quite predictably, such lay people as were attracted to participate were the well educated, the articulate, the affluent, those most at home in the midst of the endless committee meetings which characterize a certain kind of modern bourgeois life. (The author was once invited to lead a discussion group in a working-class parish and found the people alternately bewildered and angry at the contents of the booklet sent out from the N.C.C.B.)

Meanwhile only persons who had participated in parish discussions were supposed to serve as delegates to the national meeting, which meant that the great silent majority was in effect ruled out in advance. Those who religiously attended the parish meetings (sometimes there were diocesan meetings as well) tended in particular to be people with a grievance of some kind—women's ordination, homosexual rights, the rights of the divorced. Several clerical commentators judged that the "rank and file" Catholics had little to contribute and need not be listened to anyway.[22] But there were further catches still—over half of the delegates (appointed by the bishops) were priests and religious. Nearly two-thirds listed "church" as their principal work, suggesting a high proportion of bureaucrats. The lay delegates reported above-average incomes.[23]

Meanwhile the bishops had also been holding a series of regional hearings, taking testimony from interested parties. A number of "experts" were invited to attend, the overwhelming preponderance of whom were evidently chosen (by the bureaucrats who organized the hearings) for their unflinchingly "progressive" stands on most questions. The hearings also attracted in great numbers lobbyists on behalf of all the currently fashionable causes—the themes of women's ordination or homosexual rights, for instance, were raised over and over again, often in highly abrasive ways. People basically satisfied with the Church and happy in their faith had no particular reason to attend the hearings and thus were not heard. No effort was made, evidently, to seek them out.[24] Finally, in the summer prior to the Detroit conference, various committees met to sift through the recommendations which had emerged from the regional hearings and the parish and diocesan meetings and to formulate recommendations for the national meeting. These bureaucratically chosen committees were again composed mainly of those known to hold properly progressive views (although the author himself served on one of them).

Even apart from the group dynamics at Detroit itself, the results of the meeting were almost foreordained, given the process by which both the delegates and the proposals were chosen. For their skill in orchestrating the conference for maximum public-relations value, their success in persuading the media to equate the Detroit meeting with the will of the Catholic people, the organizers of the conference deserved high praise. They demonstrated manipulative abilities of which the Roman Curia might well be envious. In incidentally providing a glimpse of what the "Church of the future" might be like, once the musty authority of pope and bishops has been cleared away, they also gave reason for all thoughtful Catholics to take alarm.

Meetings of this kind are not intended to be taken seriously, in the sense that the American bishops are expected to implement all the recommendations. They are rather battles in a continuing propaganda war, designed to encourage one's own troops, demoralize the enemy, and create a climate in which "right-thinking" people are all perceived as sharing the same beliefs. The Call to Action Conference marked the triumph of fraudulent pluralism. One headline in a Catholic newspaper proclaimed "Speaker Compares 'Call to Action' Proposals to Declaration of Independence."

Many commentators (the author included) have tended to delineate the present division in the Church as between "intellectuals" and "ordinary people," an analysis which is just correct enough to obscure an even more important aspect of that same division.

For it is important to recognize that what is involved here is not, for the most part, genuine intellectuality, in the sense of original, profound, and creative thought, although originality and creativity are routinely claimed for what is merely novel or shocking. Ultimately the roots of the changes which have swept over the Church can perhaps be traced back to the arcane writings of certain theologians or other modern theorists. However, the way in which their ideas have been translated into practice is often far removed from their own intentions (the process of liturgical renewal is a particularly glaring case in point) and represents instead certain fashions largely derived from popular culture, to which the names of important thinkers are attached mainly because the child needs a name.

What passes for intellectuality in much of American society—what is taken to be such by the media and throughout much of the academic world—is in fact middlebrow. It involves the essentially uncritical acceptance of ideas which are mediated in quasi-popularized form, and it especially involves the inability or unwillingness seriously to confront or consider possibilities radically different from received assumptions. This failing is especially notable in discussions of sex and is strongly present in the Catholic Theological Society of America's 1977 report on sexual morality.

Twenty years ago the average educated American may have been an essentially unthinking traditionalist on most questions, but that situation has now practically reversed itself. At present many people consider themselves thoughtful and open-minded who simply cannot imagine the possibility of an intelligent traditionalism and are unaware of the existence of formidable minds committed to it—the very names Voegelin, Nisbet, Oakeshott, or Strauss are unknown to them. The profound conservatism of a Dostoevsky or an Eliot is not understood. So thorough has been the censorship (often unconscious) which prevails in educated circles that certain modes of thinking have been rendered literally unthinkable and the human mind thereby narrowed and cut off from some of its deepest roots. It is symptomatic in this regard that so many liberals, especially in the Church, fail to grasp the profundity of the cultural revolution that has occurred in recent years and continue to fight the battles of the 1960s, their minds permanently locked into those particular struggles.

Liberals consider a commitment to liberal ideas to be automatically broadening and liberating and fail to realize how, past a certain point, those same ideas become an orthodoxy as rigid as any they may have displaced. On a wide range of questions—political, moral, cultural, and religious—liberal "thought" in the 1970s is merely sloganeering, the throwing up of catch phrases designed to halt real thought, to protect liberal dogmas. There is a systematic refusal to probe deeply into the implications of various kinds of change, which are espoused for the short-range gains they seem to promise or simply out of a need to sustain the momentum of change itself. Many American Catholics now have no working vocabulary and no working set of ideas except those of liberalism and must automatically translate every religious question into those terms (women's ordination being a primary example).

Half-educated people are those who most brightly reflect the spirit of their age, in that the truly educated are capable of transcending it and the uneducated remain in certain important ways insulated from it. It is no accident that the "new Church" is most conspicuously popular with younger Catholics who are college graduates and often suburbanites. It is also the case that the most "well-adjusted" people—those who are bright, extroverted, friendly, and competent—tend also to be drawn towards a mode of religion which is self-consciously up-to-date. The convent-educated girls who in the 1950s wore white gloves, walked in May processions, and considered their virginity the proudest sign of their faith have, without great trauma, learned to be comfortable with the liberated and irreverent life-styles of the 1970s, the nuns who once taught them the old ways now showing them how to make the transition to the new. Conversely, conservative Catholics have a generally bad image precisely because they are alienated people and suffer the personality dislocations which such alienation inevitably produces. Put another way, only people who are not well adjusted, socially, have the ability to withstand the emergence of a new cultural consensus.

The anticredal aspects of contemporary Christianity are themselves an important reflection of antiintellectualism, in that a certain kind of personalism now regards any doctrinal formulation of faith as a distortion and deems beliefs to be insignificant in comparison with actions. There is a close connection here to the bureaucratic preoccupation with process and the spirit of group dynamics which accompanies it. Langdon Gilkey says that "we should recall that love *does* involve respect for the neighbor and thus a relativizing of one's own opinion when it differs from his."[25] The moral implications of this principle are staggering. The "togetherness" theory of liturgy, and the refusal to recognize any sins but socially measurable ones, those that disrupt group life, are examples of this mentality.

The quintessential "modern Catholic" in America was John Cogley, and his odyssey is instructive in several important respects. Sprung from a rather impoverished Chicago Irish background, Cogley was nonetheless alienated from ordinary Catholic life. After once delivering a speech in a parish where he felt insufficiently appreciated, he never repeated the experience and after a while preferred attending Episcopal services, in part because the churches were "half-empty." As early as 1957 he sought to become an Episcopalian but was dissuaded by friends for strategic reasons (he was advised to stay with Rome and try to bring the two churches closer together). His near-conversion did not prevent his continuing to function as the "enlightened Catholic spokesman" on a whole range of questions, and in 1960 he drafted the famous statement in which candidate Kennedy promised not to allow his religion to get in the way of his politics. Towards the end of his life Cogley did become an Episcopalian, and was ordained a deacon. He noticed how the Episcopal Church was always "ahead" of the Roman Church on questions like contraception and women priests (he did not mention abortion or homosexuality), and also loved the Book of Common Prayer (which the Episcopal Church was tossing out the back door as he was coming in the front).[26]

Cogley was not an unintelligent man, but what is most remarkable about his autobiography is his almost total failure to reflect on his own cultural and social role. He had critical things to say about the Church of his nurture and about various people connected with it, like Cardinal Newman (an inferior mind, in Cogley's opinion), but almost nothing negative to relate about those formidable modern institutions which employed him—the *New York Times,* the Fund for the Republic, the Center for the Study of Democratic Institutions. It seemingly never occurred to him to ask why he, as a particular kind of Catholic, was employable by these organizations while certain other types of Catholics would not be, or for what role he was hired. In his bland, innocent prose he delivered such judgments as:

> . . . of course the thousands of priests and nuns who were brutally butchered by the Loyalists [in Spain] only strengthened the Catholic conviction that Christianity was facing one of its historic tests. They could not understand how kindly, church-going Protestants and Orthodox could not grasp the point, it seemed so obvious to them.

> Sometimes, it seemed that Roman Catholicism did represent a kind of anti-American infiltration in this country. But to believe this would be to ignore the millions of Catholics who lived peacefully under the stars and stripes.

> It had already dawned on many Catholics that the pontificate of Pius XII was far from a model of contemporaneity.[27]

John Cogley's story, told with such disingenuous simplicity, is revelatory of a major dimension of the American Catholic crisis, the process by which persons of often humble and "narrow" origins made their way into the mainstream of professional America and how this affected their faith. For it is finally necessary, in modern bureaucracies, that people be essentially interchangeable in their various roles, so that in time the articulate professional representatives of a wide variety of ideas, movements, and institutions come to resemble one another. The bureaucrats staffing the national offices of the many denominations seem mainly to share the same viewpoint on most questions of social import, and doubtless in private they commiserate with one another over the way in which their respective churches fail to value their work sufficiently. In recent years clergymen of practically all denominations have discovered how easy it is, once one is no longer a credal person, to flourish in the bureaucracies of the government, the university, or the social-welfare agencies.

This professionalization tends severely to skew the ways in which realities—ecclesiastical and social—are perceived. In order for a particular segment of the community to be recognized and heard it must produce the kind of leaders who are at home in the great world of the media and the bureaucracies, who can present their constituents' case in terms which bureaucratically minded individuals are able to respond to. But in the very process of doing so the reality of life as it is actually lived by the group is in danger of being distorted. More important, their recognized spokesmen tend themselves to become close in outlook and attitude to the bureaucratic class they are trying to influence. The various individuals claiming to speak for blacks, women, Chicanos, the elderly, etc., gradually take on a sameness of rhetoric, personal style, and categories of thought which are essentially interchangeable. They behave in the way the media expect members of each particular group to behave, and those who do not behave in the appropriate way are ignored as unrepresentative.

The following sentiments, from a rural New Mexican priest, can scarcely be thought uncommon among people whose devotional life has perdured remarkably unchanged through four centuries:

> And I know a truly agnostic or atheistic person. I don't want to win such a person over. I respect them. . . . I simply want to stand up for my own beliefs, and I do not want to fool myself or fool the families who come here by giving the name Catholic to a porridge of secular notions, any of which may be valuable and important, but none of which are meant to be worshipped in Christ's name, in the name of our Lord and Savior.

Everyone listens to the men of outrage and alarm. Few pay much attention to the millions of Catholics all over the world who are not unlike my own parishioners—or to priests like me, who are so quickly dismissed as out-of-date.[28]

Yet almost nowhere in the large sea of rhetoric generated by the newly militant spokesmen for Spanish-American Catholicism will such sentiments be found expressed, just as officially recognized spokesmen for black Catholics in America nowhere speak for those many blacks who became Catholics precisely because they did not want to be Baptists. For better or for worse, the needs of blacks, Chicanos, and other culturally distinct Catholic groups are being defined by those "leaders" who are themselves closest to being assimilated into the dominant culture, who are most at home in the world of universities, national bureaucracies, press conferences, and workshops. The author once heard a prominent Chicano priest publicly ridicule the devotional practices of his people, stopping just short of saying that they would be better off as Protestants.

The bureaucratic mind also tends to skew perceptions in the Church in terms of the very problems which it is able to identify and which, once identified, then dominate public discussion and sap disproportionate amounts of energy. It is doubtful, for example, that many parishes, left to themselves, would spontaneously identify the rights of homosexuals as among the most pressing questions facing the contemporary Church. It has become such chiefly because religious professionals, constantly scanning the enlightened secular culture for signals as to what is important, have made it one. Great bitterness and division have resulted from what is in certain ways a false problem, or a problem which has been falsified in the process of being politicized. The question of women's ordination, although of wider interest, has emerged in a similar way, due largely to Roman Catholic women, mainly nuns, who look to the Episcopal Church for their signals. (One characteristic of bureaucratic culture is the view that, just as personnel are largely interchangeable, so are problems—what is happening in one denomination should be happening in all denominations.)

The bureaucratic approach to problems necessarily results in Church leaders expending a disproportionate amount of time and energy on either the elites of the Church or its marginal people, with whom the elites feel a good deal of kinship. An unspoken assumption of many bishops is that the mass of ordinary believers can in effect take care of themselves—given minimal pastoral services their religious life will go forward under its own momentum. This is largely true, and has been one of the great strengths of the Catholic system. However, in the process the fabric of parish life is also being weakened, many Catholics have begun to experience a strong sense of alienation from the bureaucratic centers of the Church, and problems which do concern many ordinary believers are being ignored. For over a decade, surveys of all kinds have shown a majority of Americans to be concerned over a perceived erosion of moral authority, especially as it affects young people. Religious professionals, partly because they think this perception reflects on their own work, have tended to regard this as a false problem and have prevented the Church from coming to grips with it in any very serious way.

Finally, however, the principal evil effect of the overbureaucratization of the Church is to rob it of vitality and character, to make it fit the great cultural consensus of which organized professionals are the arbiters. The rhetorical style of papal documents has often been criticized as cold, Olympian, stilted, and obscure. It has, however, at least possessed character. It is a style used today by few other institutions in the world, and there is a certain grandeur and timelessness about it which are appropriate both to the papal office itself and to the subjects about which the pope speaks. T. S. Eliot remarked that "good prose cannot be written by people without convictions,"[29] and the anticredal bias of modern bureaucrats has a direct relationship to the kind of bureaucratic prose which has become a joke all over the Western world. A former president of the National Coalition of American Nuns writes literal non-sense: "Yet, with their usual magnificent refusal to be circumscribed by any time, place, culture, or community, the persons are moving not only in the church but in the total culture of the U.S. implementing forces that caused the paradigm-transition of 1968 pre-and-post."[30] The impoverished quality of the American English version of the Mass and the execrable condition of music in the American Church are not due primarily to the fact that liturgical reform was carried out by committees, nor to the literary and musical deficiencies of the individuals who served on those committees, but to the whole state of Catholic faith and culture in the postconciliar era. Never in the history of the Church has so much veneration been offered to what is deemed creative, original, or dynamic. Yet this rhetoric often serves to puff up what is merely novel. Analyzing the rhetoric of the Catholic left, the distinguished historian Jacques Barzun notes,

> There is a habitual overuse of the word "creative" to dignify small things. These busy revolutionists seem sure that what they write is *poetry*. They accept capitalist-industrialist notions with the tainted vocabulary and speak of "updating" a religious order. Pouring blood on Selective Service records is an "educational act." They use the words "humanize" and "informal" with

the same vagueness as Madison Avenue does in an ad for whiskey or perfume. . . .[31]

There is no creativity in the Church, and all is bland, because despite appearances there is no real tension. What is called creative is merely fashionable.

The state of language in the Church is not of merely esoteric concern, nor is it a merely arbitrary index of religious vitality. The general imposition of bureaucratic prose on the Church is representative of the wider impositions of the bureaucratic mind, a significant case in point being the outlawing of the venerable Christian word *charity* and the substitution of the weak and misleading term *concern*. The cultural implications of this shift are profound, involving as it does the abandonment of a properly theological word for one borrowed from the therapeutic vocabulary. The reasons offered to justify it are even more significant, however. The word *charity,* we are told, has certain implications which the modern mind misunderstands, and Christians ought not to place unnecessary barriers between themselves and nonbelievers by making use of an unfamiliar vocabulary. But in all social intercourse, one side is always imposing its vocabulary on the other, and that side which is able to force its own terms on the general public has already won half its battle. The abandonment by many Catholic spokesmen of a properly theological and ecclesiastical vocabulary is as clear a sign as possible that they now act not as emissaries from Church to world but the reverse, agents of the great modern cultural process by which all differences are covered over, all distinctions denied, in the interests of bureaucratically controlled homogeneity.

CHAPTER 7

The Road to Utopia

ONE of the great oddities of intellectual life in the contemporary Western world is the degree to which individuals who are acutely sensitive to the faintest signs of injustice and repression in their own societies—often classic representatives of the therapeutic mentality which can tolerate no restraints on the self—are nonetheless imaginatively and emotionally drawn to totalitarian regimes where the very idea of personal freedom has no meaning and naked coercion is systematically used to enforce conformity to official policies.

The phenomenon is so widespread and of such long standing (dating back at least as far as the time of the Russian Revolution of 1917), that it cannot be explained as merely the quirks of certain individuals but must instead be seen as a permanent part of the emotional and intellectual equipment of liberal Western intellectuals. Prior to the 1960s it was a phenomenon largely unknown in the Roman Catholic Church, however prevalent it may have been in other Christian denominations. The postconciliar period brought an enormous increase in the political awareness of many Catholics, however, and in this process some of those Catholics who were "behind" their Protestant brethren not only overtook them but soon surpassed them in a zeal often approaching fanaticism. From being notoriously and militantly anti-Communist, some Catholics—clergy in particular—became forthright apologists for Marxist regimes. A few examples:

> When President Carter announced his policy of using American influence to favor human rights throughout the world, a prominent Catholic newspaper published a full-page article in which the policy was denounced as "simplistic." Fidel Castro was quoted as saying that capitalism alone is responsible for denials of human rights. Idi Amin, the murderous dictator of Uganda, was described merely as "rambunctious," and his demand that the United Nations investigate human-rights violations in the United States was pronounced meritorious. The suppression of political rights in "developing"

countries like Algeria and Tanzania was defended as necessary to prevent "demagoguery" and to maintain essential polical unity. Castro was lauded for having chosen to suppress political rights in favor of economic rights.[1]

A major Catholic newspaper published an article about the Church in Cuba in which it was reported that, although Catholics at one time had a "persecution complex," they had come to support the Castro regime unreservedly and found that for the first time they had the opportunity to live as genuine Christians. Official Government restrictions on religion were treated as minor flaws in an otherwise perfect system.[2]

A leading Catholic journal also reported on the Church in Cuba. The closing of the parochial schools, and the consequent government monopoly on education, was characterized as "positive and nationalistic, not negatively anti-religious. . . ." Parochial schools had, in any case, been rendered unnecessary by the high quality of public education under the new regime. The revolution was pronounced as doing "the work of Christ" and the solidarity existing between Church and Party was said to be unequalled anywhere outside "the Democratic Republic of Vietnam."[3]

When Cuban exiles in the United States asked the United States Catholic Conference to denounce human-rights violations in Cuba as well as in Chile and Brazil, an official of the Conference blandly replied that he had no information about such violations.[4]

Another U.S.C.C. official openly ridiculed the idea that it was possible to establish criteria by which the relative degree of freedom enjoyed in a particular country could be evaluated. Political freedom, he asserted, was relatively trivial in comparison with various economic freedoms. In America such freedom made little difference because there were, he thought, no "genuine alternatives to the ruling groups." The decline of individual freedom in progressive countries was offset, he insisted, by an increase in "social or communal freedom."[5]

When ninety Americans who had opposed the American war effort in Vietnam issued a statement calling on the new Communist government of Vietnam to end its repressions, Daniel and Philip Berrigan (who were among the signers) protested that the statement should never have been made public, because the former government of South Vietnam was more repressive than the current government. ("There's a great difference between reeducation camps and tiger cages.") The Berrigans later characterized the protest statement as "irresponsible" and said, "We have received new materials from the Vietnamese that give us confidence that the new government is deeply concerned about human rights. . . ."[6]

Don Luce, an officer of Clergy and Laity Concerned, the chief religious antiwar group in America, toured Vietnam in 1977 defending the "reeducation camps" as benign institutions. He also relayed to the press the claim by the archbishop of Saigon that Catholic Relief Services, an official American agency, was "narrow" and "elitist" in its program and should channel its aid through the official Communist government of Vietnam. Luce apparently saw no particular significance in the fact that the coadjutor archbishop of Saigon was being kept in prison.[7]

A former president of the National Federation of Priests' Councils engendered "wild enthusiasm" at the group's annual convention when he extolled Ho Chi Minh, the late dictator of North Vietnam, as an example of "freedom" for Catholics to emulate.[8]

A Minnesota priest, visiting North Vietnam, concluded ". . . people are free to worship, free to teach religion, free to care for the poor and those in need. They are not *completely* free [emphasis added] to criticize the North Vietnamese government. But neither are we in the United States."[9]

A Ceylonese priest wrote in an American Catholic journal that the North Vietnamese were rightly suspicious of South Vietnamese Catholics because they had failed to support the revolution wholeheartedly. There was no need for refugees to leave the country, he insisted, because "the new regime has not created the image of being intolerant." The principal task of Catholics was to cooperate with the new regime, and he hoped that "Rome will not push the local churches to a point of uncompromise. . . ."[10]

An American Quaker, writing in the same American Catholic journal, reported that Buddhists and others who had worked for peace in South Vietnam were now eagerly and freely joining the Communist Party and that to be "invited" to join a "reeducation session" was " a great honor."[11]

A former president of the Association of Chicago Priests enthusiastically predicted a glorious future for Vietnam under the spirit of Ho Chi Minh. Later he rejoiced that "*Marxism* is being studied everywhere—*Leninism—Maoism-newism.* Great!" On another occasion, writing with unconscious deadly accuracy, he complained that there seemed to be many Catholics who "like dictators."[12]

Despite reports of atrocities perpetrated by the Communist government of Cambodia, a prominent Catholic magazine published an article urging that Americans either be "cautiously optimistic" about the regime "or else shut up."[13]

The official organ of the Christian Democratic movement in Spain published an article insisting: "As long as there are people like [Alexander] Solzhenitsyn, concentration camps will have to continue. Perhaps they should even be patrolled so people like Solzhenitsyn cannot get out of them."[14]

The absurdity of so many Western liberals willfully suspending disbelief in the face of "progressive" regimes lies in the fact that none of these regimes even claim respect for political freedom or individual rights. The traditions and philosophies on which they base themselves, especially Marxism, have no room for such concepts, and in their systems individual people count for nothing, society for everything. There is not a single historical example anywhere of a dictatorship, no matter how lofty its ideals or allegedly humanitarian its purposes, which naturally evolved into a free society, nor do the leaders of such societies envision this as a desirable goal. A Vietnamese group calling itself "Movement of Catholics for Peace" has stated that "every citizen has the right to make his own choice and reject that of others, but he cannot in the name of his faith act against the choices of his compatriots."[15] Information about repression in Cuba, China, Vietnam, and other "progressive" countries has been consistently available,[16] but certain types of Western liberals have just as consistently chosen to ignore it.

However intrigued Westerners have been with the social "experiments" being conducted in Vietnam and Cuba, these countries have meant less to them than China, the country which will, for an indefinite time to come, dominate the imaginations of those who believe that there must exist, somewhere, the perfect society. Here again American Catholics have not been exceptions:

> A priest who is "director of human development and rural life" for a Midwestern archdiocese returned from China to proclaim that America's social system "is geared to destroy people and resources," while China's is organized "to serve the people." Christianity failed in China, in his opinion, not because of persecution but because "it's a Western ideology."[17] (Apparently Marxism is not.)

> A leading American Catholic newspaper published an interview with an elderly former Y.W.C.A. worker in China who asserted that only under Communism could Chinese Christians be real Christians. She also lamented that, while Americans had the opportunity to pattern their system after that of the Chinese, they blindly refused to do so.[18]

> The publisher of the same newspaper visited China and reported an interview with an Anglican bishop who told him that religion flourished freely and that problems only occurred with Christians who were not "patriotic" enough.[19]

> The same newspaper published a special section on China. In one article readers were informed that the Chinese people were characterized by a uniform and unflawed spirit of hard work, self-sacrifice, morality, cleanliness, good temper, cooperation, friendship, and unselfishness and that this spirit was maintained with only occasional gentle reminders from government officials. The violent cultural revolution was deemed necessary to check "degeneration." A high-ranking Roman Jesuit, although admitting the persecution of religion, also found the situation very hopeful.[20]

> A writer in an English Catholic magazine, while condemning Northern Ireland as a country suffering from an excess of religion, extolled China as a place "where you are truly a member of a group; where in all your actions you are aware of your responsibility to the group."[21]

The oddity of such willful credulity concerning totalitarian regimes lies in the fact that it is wholly at odds with the usual ways in which these same progressive Christians respond to developments in the Western democracies and in the Church itself. Descriptions of Communist China—the physical simplicity and cleanliness, the demure politeness of the citizens, their cheerful hard work, total indifference to personal desires and meek acceptance of whatever assignments they are given, their predictable repetition of official slogans on all possible subjects, their apparent valuing of chastity, the overall spirit of orderliness—resemble in extreme form the spirit which used to characterize Catholic convents, monasteries, and seminaries before the era of "reform." Yet it was precisely these characteristics which were denounced as inhumane, oppressive, and un-Christian and which were systematically eradicated, often at great cost to the community thus "purified." Whereas a spirit of individualism sometimes bordering on anarchy is routinely extolled as essential to contemporary religious life, the spirit of collectivization and discipline decreed from on high is admired, as it incarnates itself in distant regimes, as the social model towards which the Christians of the world should look for inspiration.

Part of the explanation for this seeming contradiction, which, like so much else in the contemporary Church, would require the satirical talents of an Evelyn Waugh to be savored properly, lies in the general moral decadence that characterizes Western bourgeois society. A culture in which people progressively lose the spirit of self-restraint and self-discipline, in which virtually all possibilities seem open to them merely for the asking, soon also loses any sense of purpose or direction in life. Boredom, a feeling of futility, and pent-up energies with no meaningful outlet through which to express themselves eventually begin to cry out for some transcendent purpose, some overarching meaning for life, to which the individual can give himself unreservedly. Love affairs with totalitarian regimes become expressions of nostalgia—so long as the anarchic Westerner does not actually have to abandon his therapeutic lifestyle, he can fantasize imaginatively about a purer, simpler, and better kind of society which embodies all the virtues which his own lacks. Instead of projecting this society into the past, as conservatives have always done, he projects it into the present or the future. This phenomenon has produced a new type of Catholic who virtually divinizes the forms of parliamentary democracy within the Church, while remaining contemptuous of them in advanced secular politics.

The moral emptiness which the therapeutic inevitably engenders—the compulsive reflex by which the individual seeks to reject whatever threatens to impose restraint or responsibility in an authoritative way—is also directly related to totalitarianism's appeal. Lacking both a viable and authoritative tradition and a highly developed sense of conscience (the former characteristic of classic Catholicism, the latter of classic Protestantism), the therapeutic individual gradually becomes morally stupid and is able to respond only to gross evils which have become "causes," that is, which have been designated by the enlightened consensus as moral issues deserving of support.

Liberal Christianity lacks the capacity to inspire genuine repentance in its followers, although the rhetoric of repentance is freely employed. The moral awakening of therapeutic Christians depends on their being regularly chastized from the outside—by designated social groups accusing them of immoral behavior and attitudes. Although consciously committed to a morality which is totally "free," liberal Christians in fact experience the need to be coerced in order to do their moral duties. The self-indulgent spirit of therapeutic society engenders residual problems of conscience for those who may embrace it at the rational level but whose Christianity leaves them uncomfortable and acutely aware that they are bereft of the resources—personal, institutional, and cultural—which would make real moral conversion possible. The capitalism against which avant-garde Christians now react with such antagonism should perhaps be understood as a metaphor for the unsatisfying epicureanism which therapeutic culture has created. Consequently, it also serves as an expression of self-hatred on the part of people who have consciously embraced an ethic which at some deeper level they know to be wrong. The moral disorders endemic to the permissive society—drug abuse, divorce, rape, teenage pregnancies—cannot be blamed on the spirit of permissiveness itself and are instead laid on the doorstep of a particular economic system.

For centuries political philosophers have made the point that people who refuse to rule their own passions cannot expect to be truly free. This point is dimly perceived even by those who consciously reject it, and the fascination of totalitarian regimes in part lies in the attraction of a society which will force the weak and undisciplined individual to be good. For Christians the orderly obedience of Mao's China is a surrogate for their own lost religious rigor.

The most important fact about the social gospel—the belief that the Christian vocation is action in the world on behalf of social betterment—is that it is the last frontier of the absolute, the last point at which advanced Christians can articulate positions and embark upon actions with total conviction and passion. It is the last point at which heresy is still not permitted, at which it is still required to condemn those who hold false doctrines.

As E. R. Norman has pointed out, what is called situation ethics has scarcely been applied outside the realm of sexuality.[22] (To this might be added the increasingly sensitive area of right-to-life, as it applies to unborn children, the elderly, or the ill.) Situation ethics has been promoted, and has won a measure of popular support through media, because it has sought to justify the actual sexual practices of contemporary society. Its strictures against the "rigidity" of Christian morality have been understood, rightly, primarily as coded attacks on traditional notions of chastity.

The insincerity of this moral viewpoint (not necessarily conscious insincerity) is immediately apparent if its principles are applied to the dominant issues of contemporary social morality. Logic would seem to dictate that liberal moral theologians continually insist that, under certain circumstances, Christians might indeed support racial segregation, war, capital punishment, the consumer ethic, the profit motive, the subordination of women, or any number of other social positions which avant-garde Christianity has condemned. Occasional theologians may quietly suggest that not all these questions are as closed as the most passionate moralists believe. However, there has been no serious effort to extend the principles of situation ethics into these realms, where for all practical purposes the mental framework of an absolutist ethics still reigns. This illustrates another of Norman's observations—that the positions of contemporary theologians often merely reflect the prevailing prejudices of the intelligentsia, whether in matters of sex or of politics. [23]

Perhaps the most striking indication of such absolutism is the general absence of anything like an ecumenical consciousness as it applies to social issues. Progressive Christians are convinced that, on doctrinal matters like the divinity of Christ, the sacraments, or the authority of the papacy, as well as on disputed personal moral questions like abortion or homosexuality, there are no differences which justify permanent divisions, and animosities or conflicts engendered by such questions are scandalous betrayals of the Gospel. The governing belief is that all theological positions are relative, no one denomination possesses the whole truth, and sincere believers should be able to put aside their differences to work together in love and harmony.

Yet the same spirit ceases to govern where questions of social morality arise. There is little ecumenism between segregationists and civil-rights workers, for example, antiwar activists and Green Berets, women's liberationists and "male chauvinists," proponents and critics of capital punishment. Here it is assumed that the divisions are deep and real. There can be no accommodation short of one side's capitulating to the other. Compromise is considered morally tainted and "openness" towards the other side tends to mean merely strenuous efforts to convert one's opponents rather than condemn them. Disapproval, condemnation, even hatred of the opponents are considered understandable and admirable signs of true conviction and moral passion. In an age of religious ecumenism, the passions and animosities which once expressed themselves in religious terms now find an outlet in political orthodoxies, often with theological sanction. A common social phenomenon of the times is the cocktail party where the participants warily circle one another looking for clues about each other's political orientation, and where the espousal of the wrong opinion can result in angry words or the abrupt termination of conversations.

Many Christians are now comfortable only with political absolutes, because these are the only kind their culture allows. A Catholic professor in a secular university, for example, is likely to be acutely sensitive to his obligation not to proselytize his students, and a professor who lectured from an openly Catholic point of view would create a scandal. Marxist professors, or advocates of women's liberation, commonly feel no such inhibitions. They believe they possess the truth and that students' failure to share this truth is merely the effect of a "false consciousness" which it is the professor's duty to elevate. Where issues of social justice are perceived to exist—racial or sexual discrimination, for instance (but not, normally, religious discrimination)—the full use of the coercive powers of the state is deemed just and necessary. The usual rhetoric about trusting people, allowing them to make their own mistakes, showing respect for human freedom, etc., suddenly dissipates. The preferred approach is often punitive—example should be made of those who have dared to transgress the demands of social justice. The idea of listening to the people who may favor segregation or capital punishment (or, in times past, slavery) is not even entertained, although it is ritualistically invoked on many other kinds of issues.

Social activism is the rear-guard struggle of traditional moralism, which is one of the reasons why so much religious passion has been invested in it. Leaving all questions permanently open, remaining constantly on guard against the recrudescence of "rigidity," ultimately paralyzes action, a fact which progressive Christians have recognized and which has led them in practice (if not in theory) to assume absolutist positions on social questions, from which no dissent is permitted. Contemporary politics on a wide range of issues—race, war, economics, sexual minorities, women's rights, environment—has been turned into a morality play, a continuing struggle between good and evil. Christians who would be horrified at the suggestion that they ask their neighbors whether they attend church or believe in Jesus Christ have no compunction about asking them if they have voted or whether they support the latest cause. As questions of personal morality are increasingly seen to be too complex to admit of easy answers, the great issues of politics seem precisely to yield up easy answers, often virtually on demand. Parochial schools whose graduates remain in doubt (or in ignorance) about the Trinity, the divinity of Christ, or the nature of the Church are praised for their openness. Those whose graduates emerge insufficiently attuned to contemporary social questions are quickly condemned as ineffective and un-Christian. Advanced Christians are convinced that no one, because of religion, should ever be made to feel uncomfortable or guilty; but feelings of this kind are continually generated on behalf of political causes.

The dominance of the social gospel requires that influential people in the Church protect the absolute character of social morality by correspondingly damping down possible manifestations of absolutism elsewhere. Gregory Baum, for instance, who did so much to promulgate the idea that Catholics must make their own religious and moral judgments independent of hierarchical "dictation," on the Vietnam War regretted that "the local congregations and churches do not follow their ecclesiastical authorities in this matter," and was shocked that the expressed opinions of Pope Paul VI were being disregarded.[24] In England a few years later a prominent Catholic journalist angrily demanded a "thorough shakeup" of a major archdiocese because its archbishop had not physically intervened in a public demonstration where racial strife erupted. ("There is only one Christian response to fascism and racism, and that is to oppose it with every nerve in the ecclesiastical body. Anything less is a dereliction of duty. . . .")[25] Although the use of ecclesiastical authority to condemn or discipline people has been widely denounced ،since the Council, an antiwar organization in Washington demanded that the Holy See excommunicate William Colby for the sin of having formerly directed the Central Intelligence Agency. "Colby deserves the most severe kind of ecclesiastical punishment," the group declared.[26]

The newly awakened Catholic social conscience suffers from, among other things, a failure to make clear the bases of its own commitments. In an age of rampant moral scepticism, when people are systematically encouraged to doubt every surviving scrap of traditional wisdom, the demands of Christian social concern are treated as though self-evident and are rarely even discussed in dispassionate ways, much less rigorously analyzed. A nun who advocates ordaining women to the priesthood states that, while it may be tactically useful to offer arguments on behalf of this innovation, there is no obligation to do so, since those in authority are morally wrong and their prejudices do not deserve to be thus dignified.[27]

Asked why the Christian is obliged to become involved with social change, the "committed" are likely to respond, with some exasperation, by quoting Christ's command to love one's neighbor or to offer a cup of cold water to the thirsty. Yet many of these same avant-garde Church members have already sought to inculcate in the faithful certain reflexive responses which can be invoked in uncomfortable moral situations: Did Jesus really pronounce the words attributed to Him, or are these later creations of the Church? Are His words to be taken literally, or merely as general guides to conduct? Is it appropriate for mature believers slavishly to follow the text of a book written many centuries ago? Do not changed times demand changed responses? Are not certain moral demands made in Christ's name overly rigid and thus inhumane? Are they realistic? Is not the concept of loving one's neighbor culturally relative? (Many societies in the world's history seem to have lacked it.) Is it not finally necessary for each individual to decide what is his own proper response to the Gospel? In the end, whether the social gospel is believed to be right or wrong from a Christian perspective (and there is much in it which is right), it turns out to be the mere result of a cultural prejudice, an excrescence of the prevailing preoccupations of Western intellectuals in the last part of the twentieth century.

As such it is an act of faith, not only in the sense of a commitment based on a foundation which has not been rationally established, but also in the sense of a commitment which makes total demands brooking no doubt or opposition. It is a classic manifestation of Eric Voegelin's thesis that modern "gnosticism" offers "counterfeits of faith," of which the creation of a terrestrial paradise is the most seductive.[28]

The appearance of an almost fanatical Marxism in the Church is classic illustration of Christ's warning about the hidden dangers of casting out devils. As the Church, and particularly the religious orders, "purified" itself after the Council—from "superstition," "repressiveness," "outdated" practices and beliefs—it created a spiritual and psychological vacuum crying out to be filled. Few things on the contemporary scene have been strong enough to fill the aching void left by the rapid disappearance of an all-pervasive traditional piety. Certain types of therapeutic activities have served that function for some people. Marxism, which appeared to be waning from roughly 1945 to 1965, has experienced a sudden rejuvenation in part because of its strong appeal to avant-garde Christians.

It is important to recognize that, for some, Marxism is not simply a useful tool of historical analysis, nor even merely a social philosophy. It is a religion. In 1972, for example, a group of American Jesuits drew up a document which spoke of the need for "the construction of a revolutionary social strategy for the Society of Jesus which is explicitly neo-Marxist and Maoist. . . . To effect this role authentically," the document went on to say,

> the Society of Jesus must purge itself of its bourgeois consciousness and identify itself with the proletariat, acknowledging that only the proletariat, as the living negation of advanced monopoly capitalism and as the subject of history, can achieve correct and objective social knowledge—the proletariat simultaneously knows and constitutes society. It is at this point that we are very close to understanding the mystery of Jesus' own proletarian background.

The document was extensively publicized in the official American Jesuit newspaper, and responses were solicited. One Jesuit high-school teacher replied, "I am excited about this statement, and I think the key to its success lies . . . in our official demand (even pressure) to come to a metanoia, a conversion, back to the original Ignatian vision."[29] Marxism, whether well or badly understood, is now the only creed capable of eliciting discipline and commitment from certain people of deeply religious temperaments. At the same time it also, in Philip Rieff's terms, acts "remissively," in that it justifies still further acts of iconoclasm against traditional Christianity.

The fierce anti-Communism of preconciliar Catholicism sometimes had as a corollary, especially in America, the defense of capitalism as the single best economic system and the most effective bulwark against Communism. Since capitalism was Communism's chosen enemy, the argument often ran, it must be Catholicism's friend. Not surprisingly, therefore, the new Catholic philo-Communism identifies capitalism as *the* enemy, not only because Marxist thought so identifies it but also because hatred of capitalism is an essential condition of the new religious fervor, the embodiment of evil in an age which disbelieves in Satan and, ultimately, disbelieves also in the moral culpability of any individual person. The religious mission has now transformed itself but still expresses itself in evangelistic ways, as by the former Benedictine abbot who tours Italy under Communist sponsorship urging Catholic support for the Party;[30] the Uruguayan priest-theologian who tells audiences that, even where oppressive, Marxism offers more hope than capitalism (its apparent oppressiveness is often the result of capitalist distortions, he adds);[31] or the American bishop who insists indignantly that "liberation theology" can be criticized only by its own proponents.[32]

Just as a certain type of traditional Catholic felt it necessary, no matter what the subject of conversation, to inject a religious message, so it has become acceptable, in much contemporary discourse, to inject diatribes about the status of women or the Third World or the evils of capitalism into discussions having little to do with them. Once orthodoxy has been assimilated, it furnishes the mind with a ready-made set of ideas which can be invoked automatically in every situation, an example of what George Orwell, one of the bravest and most acute leftist thinkers of the twentieth century, called "the gramophone mind." The following is by an officer of an association of Spanish-American priests:

> . . . you falsely identify the dominant class of petty bourgeoisie in the middle-class suburbs with the whole of the U.S. church, thus omitting the working class.

> . . . We Latin Americans, within and outside the United States' frontiers, are quite capable of liberating ourselves from oppression by the class whose interests you defend.[33]

The rise of a fanatical Christian political line is in many cases the result of the desperation of sincere and high-minded liberal Christians whose religion has reduced itself, by a series of almost imperceptible steps, to a vague ethical seriousness, a well-meaning humanitarianism which lacks an adequate objective outlet for its intensity. The prospect of making a better world, joining in the common struggle for a terrestrial utopia, is now the only enterprise capable of summoning up, from many people, a truly religious response, the only system with sufficient authority to enforce personal devotion and self-sacrifice. The appeal of Marxism, now and in the past, relies heavily on the invitation it offers to join in the world-wide struggle of a triumphant cause, of being on the victorious side of the march of history. Numerous analysts have observed how this is the secularization of a traditional Christian belief. The triumphalism of avant-garde Christians, their willingness to assert the moral superiority of their cause, the often fanatical sense of zeal and mission by which they are carried along, are directly related to this historical sense, a particularly powerful instance of the need to be carried along by the force of history.

Gregory Baum offers a particularly forthright proposal for the divinization of political action. The reinterpretation of the Scriptures, in order to support social change, is pronounced necessary, while those who refuse this task "actually show themselves willing to walk with their society, with its economic system, and its dominant cultural forms." Christians are urged to align themselves with "the re-creation of social life in greater accord with the future promises," and the Church's teachings are said to point to "a revealed utopia." Private confession is condemned because "This practice has created the imagination among Catholic peoples that sin is always a conscious and free decision to violate a divine commandment," a view which has "dangerous political consequences."

The entire idea of personal conversion to Jesus is likewise deemed to have "reactionary political implications. . . . The stress of Jesus as personal savior is always linked, therefore, to the defense of the political status quo." Most importantly, Baum demands an *a priori* and finally unquestioning commitment to "liberation" movements:

> To remain aloof, to seek a neutral place (which does not exist), to examine these movements simply from the outside without identification with their aims, will not provide the historical standpoint from which these movements and their interrelationship can be understood. . . . Conversion . . . precedes the critical reflection on policy and strategy. . . .

The important modern sociologists are then evaluated by Baum in terms of how well they support "the ineluctable continuity of the upward movement," and their orthodoxy or heresy, from a Catholic point of view, is thereby determined.[34] It is of more than idle interest to recall that, only a few years ago, this kind of unthinking self-surrender was the conception which many Catholics had of their own religious faith and that Gregory Baum was among those most eloquent in his insistence on the need for honesty and questioning in faith.

Christian radicals now speak of "utopia" without embarrassment, which is an index of how swift the change in political fashions has been. However, the usual criticism of utopianism—that it is vague and dreamy, without reference to reality—misses the most important point, which is that, however unlikely of actual achievement utopia may be, serious efforts to achieve it will nonetheless still be made, and these efforts sometimes carry with them enormous costs. In brief, the struggle to achieve utopia almost always leads to totalitarianism, because the immense displacements in social arrangements which are necessary even to approximate utopia are not likely to take place through the voluntary cooperation of those caught up in them. In a prosperous society like the United States most people are unlikely to welcome radical social change. Even in societies where it is welcomed there is unlikely to be agreement as to what kind of changes there should be. The achievement of utopia can only occur under authoritarian regimes, which, historically, have never voluntarily liberalized themselves to any significant degree. Many Christian advocates of utopia seem unaware of this elementary historical fact. Others, perhaps, are only too well aware of it, and also of how imprudent it would be to talk about it in public.

The unflinching "future-orientedness" of so many Christians itself tends towards totalitarianism. The late R. C. Zaehner, distinguished student of mysticism, noted how frequently Father Teilhard de Chardin, the patron saint of Christian futurists, expressed sympathy with a totalitarian world vision.[35] In practice being open to the future often means guessing accurately what the future may bring, putting oneself right with future regimes. The great totalitarian movements of the twentieth century—Communism and Fascism—have both claimed the authority of the future and denied the right of any individual to stand in its way, although Fascism also plays on popular feelings of nostalgia for the past.

The religious spirit of the new social consciousness naturally expresses itself in a holistic approach to politics in which ordinary, piecemeal, democratic solutions to social problems are judged inadequate or useless. Since the entire social system is at bottom corrupt and oppressive, only a complete and revolutionary assault on that system will suffice. The political quest takes on an aura of holiness, since it demands the individual's total donation of self and a wrenching break with the existing society, comparable to the kind of break once required upon entering religious life. Thus the Jesuit paper calling for a "neo-Marxist and Maoist" posture denied that orderly attempts to reform capitalism were even possible.[36]

A society like Mao's China therefore appeals to radical Western Christians not merely in spite of its totalitarian aspects but almost because of them. The methods employed by the Chinese—their utter contempt for individual preferences, their unyielding discipline, their adherence to an overall plan which promises a radically transformed future society—are all pledges of their profound seriousness, their total devotion to their cause, in comparison with which Western democratic reformism looks flabby and indecisive, devoid of all religious significance. The Jesuit paper urged the Society to identify itself totally with the Chinese cultural revolution.[37]

The most interesting of these responses has perhaps been that of the Maryknoll community from America—priests and religious who for decades did heroic missionary work in many parts of the world. Their promising missions in China were forcibly closed after the Communist victory of 1949, and many of the society's own members, as well as innumerable of its native converts, were killed, imprisoned, or exiled. Yet consistently, in its official magazine, the society has given highly favorable publicity to the Maoist "experiment." One priest referred admiringly to its "dictatorial regime that combines power with a sense of purpose and continual communication with the masses." Another writer found the austerity of the mainland Chinese a pleasing spiritual contrast to the gaudiness of Hong Kong and, since signs of extreme poverty were not visible, concluded that it was no longer a serious problem. The cultural revolution was praised as a necessary struggle against "vested interests." Another priest reported that refugees fled China mainly because they wanted "freedom, fancy clothes, etc." Chinese economic and technical aid to African countries was praised as a form of disinterested charity. A Chinese propaganda photograph was captioned "Two Chinese girls learn to experience trust in one another similar to that trust Christians place in Christ."[38]

The effusiveness of the Maryknoll Sinophilia might almost be suspected of being a deliberate ploy to ingratiate the society with the Communist government in the hope of being asked to return. Yet there is perhaps something more involved—a frank admiration for a creed whose members finally showed a level of dedication, obedience, fidelity to dogma, and intolerance of dissent superior to that of the Catholics who tried to convert them. In that sense the phenomenon of Maryknollers becoming Marxists follows the classic pattern of religious conversion—from the easier to the harder sect. A Maryknoll priest in Hong Kong has approvingly quoted Henry Kissinger: "China has a *Weltanschauung,* while the rest of us have all lost our way."[39]

Maryknoll's book-publishing arm has issued a work by a Swiss priest which reads as though written by the Chinese ministry of propaganda. Slogan-bearing wall posters are praised for the enthusiasm which they spontaneously arouse in the people, and the absence of vulgar consumerism is offered as a sign of the country's moral superiority over the West. The destruction of works of art is justified "in order to make clear that the treasures of the past must be put in the service of the revolution." Every twist and turn of official policy is blandly explained in accordance with the most recent government line, and the Red Army is glorified as embodying the spirit of the people. Criticism of official policies, "even when not expressed," is said to be taken more seriously than in the Western democracies, while at the same time the thoughts of Mao are treated as infallible and profound, even for the practice of medicine.[40]

The largely unspoken dirty little secret concerning "progressive" forces of social change is the degree to which their success in fact depends on the naked use of violence and other means of coercion, which liberal Christians are prepared to justify up to a point but which still makes them uneasy. Few of the effusive accounts of Mao's China, for example, even those which express cautious reservations as to how well the system is working, dwell on the fact that the discipline and dedication of the present citizenry has been achieved in part because of mass slaughters in earlier times, which eliminated those most likely to resist the new order and provided a dramatic warning for the rest. There has been little inquiry into the possibility of concentration camps in the remoter parts of China's vastness, where even now potential dissidents may be kept away from tourists.

There is much bad conscience on the subject because, for largely tactical reasons in opposing the American war in Vietnam, many Western

Christians eloquently espoused a pacifist rhetoric in which the traditional notion of the just war was questioned or rejected and in which the horrors of violence were dramatized in such a way as to force the conclusion that the deliberate harming of another human being was never justified. Yet, even while they were taken as pacifists by many, the Berrigan brothers, for example, remained admiring of Ho Chi Minh and others whose spirit was far from pacifistic. Philip Berrigan privately expressed reserved admiration for the Tupamaros guerrillas in Uruguay and said, "When I refer to murder it is not to prohibit it absolutely (violence versus non-violence bag) it is merely to observe that one has set a precedent. . . ." Daniel Berrigan declined to have his position characterized as non-violent and said, "I would prefer to say that our part in the resistance has never had violence attached to it," subsequently adding, ". . . especially in America, it is necessary to take a very clear and austere line on this question of war and violence. And I would go much farther in the direction of being *rigid* on these points than I would, say, if I were in the Third World." He did not think it possible to "transplant" moral judgments about the violence employed by Third World revolutionaries and was prepared to trust the promises of the North Vietnamese in view of their "humane" treatment of American prisoners of war.[41]

Within a very brief period of time violence perpetrated in a revolutionary cause has taken on a privileged status for many Western Christians, who are indisposed to examine its moral implications very closely. It is simply one more possibly traumatic necessity which history imposes on those who do its bidding, one more traditional inhibition which must be overcome for the sake of human progress. The Jesuit Gustavo Gutierrez, a Latin American exponent of "liberation" whose writings are very popular in North America, was once asked if, after a successful revolution, the oppressed would not simply become the oppressors. He replied, "But then at least we will take turns! Maybe it will be worse, but at least it will be different. What is more, it would be the majority oppressing the minority. Now the minority oppresses the majority."[42] In Rhodesia, governed by a racist white minority government, black guerrilla fighters have murdered at least fourteen Catholic missionaries, including some sympathetic to the black cause, as well as a number of other innocent persons (including other blacks). Yet in 1977 an American nun spent four months in the country and made rapturous comments about the guerrillas, whom she said she would join if she were black. She stated publicly that "I do not call them terrorists. I call them freedom fighters. They may in the course of their struggles commit terrorism." After her expulsion from Rhodesia she was given a heroine's welcome by members of her order in the United States.[43]

The reality of terrorism was brought to the United States itself in the

1960s and continued, somewhat abated, into the 1970s. Once again the ambiguity of Christian radicals manifested itself. Despite his dictum that it was necessary to be "rigid" in opposing violence in America itself Daniel Berrigan found it difficult to articulate a position towards the Weathermen, for example, a left-wing group which advocated and practiced terrorist acts. Regretting that "I can't walk with them" and hoping that he might sometime persuade them that their course was mistaken, he could nonetheless not bring himself to express outright condemnation of their acts. Asked whether they deserved punishment, he responded that too much emphasis was put on the deeds of the oppressed, not enough on those of the oppressors. Asked if their lawlessness was any different from the Ku Klux Klan's, he replied that their spirit was different and their violence was largely forced on them by society. "They were involved in trashing in Chicago . . . and later when there were those other explosions going on, too . . ." was the closest he was willing to come to discussing candidly the Weathermen's activities, the term "explosions" used so offhandedly that the unwary might assume he was speaking metaphorically rather than talking about real explosions.[44] One young American terrorist planted a bomb at the University of Wisconsin which killed a student who was a husband and father. The bomber fled to Canada and when he was later apprehended complained indignantly to the press that he was being treated like a criminal rather than an idealist. Philip Berrigan was among the witnesses appearing on his behalf at his trial, and among those protesting the "injustice" of the bomber's prison sentence.[45]

The Symbionese Liberation Army was a group in California which carried out the murder of the black school superintendent of the city of Oakland and perpetrated other acts of terrorism. Its most famous deed was kidnapping Patricia Hearst. (The group was largely decimated in several battles with the police.) One member of the S.L.A., killed in a gun fight, was the daughter of a Lutheran minister, who told the press that she had engaged in acts of terrorism for the highest of idealistic motives and was in fact a martyr, although not in a religious sense. Another of those killed was a Catholic, and at her funeral Mass the priest called her "a dear, honest, sincere girl" who was like Christ because "he died for what he believed in. So did Angela." She was, he said, "following Christian vocation." A former president of the Leadership Conference of Women Religious regretted that the media chose to emphasize the negative aspects of the S.L.A.'s activity rather than their concern for the poor. After Patricia Hearst had been convicted of criminal activity, the National Coalition of American Nuns protested that she had been examined only by male psychologists, while a prominent priest-journalist in

England thought she was being persecuted because, although well-born, she had sided with the poor.[46]

In 1975 violence erupted near a small Wisconsin town, where an unused novitiate of the Alexian Brothers was forcibly seized by a group of militant Menominee Indians. Many people in the area—both Indians and whites—reported being terrorized for refusal to support the seizure, and the elected head of the official Menominees' tribal organization, which opposed the seizure, had to hire a full-time bodyguard because of threats directed against her. A priest who had been a missionary to the Indians for over twenty years had earlier been murdered, allegedly in connection with these same internal conflicts. The Alexian Brothers donated the novitiate to the Indians, although legal complications as to who among them would own it eventually cancelled the transfer. Upon visiting the site, an Alexian official from Chicago noticed only "the cold way the white people treated us" and asked, "What kind of Christianity have we been teaching that they could feel that much hate and feel comfortable with it?" The National Coalition of American Nuns telegraphed praise to the Alexians because of their "compassion."[47]

The episode, except for the doubtlessly very real terror experienced by those involved in it, had about it the character of farce, in that the Alexians' actions illustrated certain rather trite themes in contemporary political life—the willingness of certain people in authority to bow to naked force, afterwards finding a moral gloss to pour over it; their sanctimonious inability to sympathize with people who were being asked to pay the price for someone else's high-minded moralism; the willful bypassing of elected spokesmen for the aggrieved group in order to respond to those who claimed to be its true representatives; and the fact that those who are most skilled at dramatizing their positions in fashionable media terms tend to be victorious in most such moral conflicts. In connection with the Alexian episode a distinguished political scientist wrote:

> That a Catholic religious order now in happy guilt should pay penance for historical misdeeds of official 19th-century renegades like Custer and his boys, mostly good Protestants, says something about the diminished rigor of theological training these days as well as a more widespread and general decline in our secular modes of reasoning.[48]

A former British ambassador to Uruguay, a Catholic who is sympathetic to social change in Latin America but who was nonetheless kidnapped by the Tupamaros, noted ruefully the double standard concerning violence that many socially concerned Christians seem to invoke, depending on whether it is used in a progressive cause. He raised the sensitive question of whether, for some of these people, the revolutionary commitment does not serve as a justification for personal hatreds which their Christianity would otherwise prohibit.[49] Despite their talk of institutionalized violence, radical Christians do not understand, or do not want to understand, how revolutions based on terrorism have always made terrorism a permanent feature of political life even after they succeed, or how the victors in violent revolutions are likely to be the most ruthless individuals, who have no particular motive for mitigating their ruthlessness after they have succeeded.

The point here is not that revolutionary violence is necessarily immoral, since classical Catholic just-war theory would justify it under certain conditions, or that new revolutionary regimes may not indeed be improvements on what they replaced, but the willingness of so many "prophetic" Christians to look away from what is actually involved in revolution, and in effect serve as apologists for terrorism.

Yet revolutionary violence is, finally, not merely a romantic act engaged in by exotic guerrillas in far-off countries. For the committed revolutionary, the act of violence comes to have a sacred character, something which the most advanced theorists of revolution have understood very well. Its evil undertones, its moral questionability, are the source of its spiritual power. For Christians who have accustomed themselves to breaking all kinds of moral taboos, the bold "statement" of the terrorist act has irresistible appeal. Few will engage in it themselves, but many will be attracted in the way that a devout Catholic businessman might be attracted to becoming a monk—it is the final test of commitment, the final proof of one's seriousness, the point beyond which there is no turning back.

The greatest moral and spiritual problem posed by radical politics is not its espousal of violence, however misguided and hypocritical this may be in many instances. It is rather the totalitarian nature of such a politics even prior to the establishment of a totalitarian state, a danger which threatens nothing less than the very survival of Christianity wherever such politics are taken seriously.

Liberal idealists fail to understand how much of what goes on in the world is a struggle for power and dominance in which one side wins and the other side loses. The pleasant ecumenical spirit which characterizes religious discussion in the West does not apply in much of the larger world. The politicizing of the Christian conscience is widely perceived, and correctly for the most part, as evidence of the bankruptcy of traditional religion and its willingness now to allow itself simply to be used for political purposes. The new radical Christianity is in essence a form of Integralism, a mirror image of the traditional alliances of throne and altar in which the Church was supposed to provide the spiritual mortar to hold the social order together. In both cases religion is seen merely as part of the social order, not as transcending it.

A well-publicized Christian-Marxist "dialogue" has been set up in recent years, although it has been pointed out that few Marxists show much interest in Christianity except those at one time themselves Christians, and even those who have entered into dialogue have shown little propensity to accept Christian doctrine. At best they have rather grudgingly admitted that religion need not be dogmatically excluded from participation in the class struggle.[50] The most ecumenical of the Marxists, the French philosopher Roger Garaudy, was expelled from the Communist Party for his heterodox views. However, even Garaudy rules out the possibility of thinking in terms of "body and soul, of time and eternity, of a human earth and a heavenly 'world of forms.'" He rejects the "myth—here in the pejorative sense—of the immortality of the soul" and insists that eternal life can only mean a new dimension of the present life.[51] Despite the fact that there are contemporary theologians who might agree with him, such an understanding of Christianity marks a radical repudiation of historical Roman Catholicism.

Some radical Christians appear to see one of their own principal tasks in the revolution as preventing any manifestation of piety which might conceivably interfere with a revolutionary commitment. A North American visitor asks a Cuban bishop how he conceives the task of the Church:

"To save souls," he answered.

My colleagues exhaled a deep sigh. The embargo had preserved the traditional ecclesiastical rhetoric in Cuba, whereas the language of the theology of liberation is dynamically operative in other Latin countries.

The bishop is pressed further as to how the saving of souls can be translated into the terms of the revolution. He fails to give a satisfactory answer, but a seminary professor reassuringly says that he is training "missionaries to the church to conscienticize Christians to the good the revolution has accomplished, that they may find their roles in it."[52] Sometimes this censoriousness against traditional piety takes extreme form, as in the proposal of a former Maryknoll missionary that, because American Catholics "do not think for themselves" and still believe traditional ideas about personal salvation, they should be deprived of the sacraments for six months by episcopal decree but be obliged to attend church each Sunday in order to be propagandized as to their true obligations. At the end of that time all parishes which still remain unconverted should be "placed under interdict" and recalcitrant individuals excommunicated.[53] A Paulist priest (who has since left the priesthood) visiting Colombia reported:

> . . . I discovered there is a hell. It will be occupied with great numbers of Pentecostals, charismatics, and guttural spiritualists with ample room left for patrons of such movements: The CIA, corporate entities, and right-wing political groupings.[54]

A leading Brazilian theologian of "liberation" has defined truth as "the name given by the historical community to those actions which were, are, and will be effective for the liberation of men." All discussion of Catholic doctrine, such as transubstantiation, are therefore merely distractions from the important questions and are seen as serving a reactionary social function. Attempts to understand love according to consciously Christian criteria are equally condemned as negative, and theologians are obliged to place themselves "at the service of groups recognized as being in the vanguard in the process of liberation."[55] (Typically, he does not seek to answer the question, "Recognized by whom?") Another prominent theologian, a Jesuit, frankly admits that the New Testament does not lend itself readily to liberationist themes and that the Old Testament is therefore to be preferred, since little can be known about the historical Jesus in any case.[56]

In extreme form this kind of "theology" simply becomes a way of using the Church, with its vast network of people and institutions and its large reservoir of moral idealism, for wholly political purposes. The socialist Michael Harrington, a former Catholic, has not hesitated to speak of a certain type of "shame-faced, hypocritical Catholic atheism" which he has encountered in radical political circles.[57] However, the implications go even deeper and end with a denial of the legitimacy of all specifically religious concerns which are not overtly political. Daniel Berrigan, for example, has said that he and his brother regard any interest in parochial schools, clerical celibacy, etc., as "retarded questions."[58] Philip Berrigan has expounded the theory that the only significant moral issue is nuclear war and that people are unfortunately always being "drawn off into lesser issues, minor or major distractions. . . ." When asked if abortion is one of these, he replied, "Oh, yeah!"[59]

Although the Berrigans are far from desiring it, the roots of totalitarianism are found precisely here, in that totalitarianism is the demand that people abandon all their "private" concerns and values in order to give full allegiance to the political task, whatever that may be. Although Christian moralists are now urging that this be done voluntarily, there are those who will see to it that it is done by coercion if necessary.

In the new dispensation no private moral beliefs will be allowed, no individual conceded the right to make moral judgments which are not related to those issues which have been identified as of overriding social importance, whether these be the latest preoccupations of bourgeois intellectuals or the officially proclaimed goals of a totalitarian society like China. All religion is "civil religion" in the most literal sense of the term, different from more familiar forms of civil religion only in being oriented towards the future rather than the past. There are no insurmountable barriers to Christians participating in socialist movements on a pragmatic basis. However, there is an ultimate moral conflict between true Christianity and true socialism because the purest kind of socialism has no time for religion and must always regard it as a distraction from a wholly mundane commitment. In this connection it is also significant that Christians who are drawn to socialism rarely even pay attention to the various forms of democratic socialism but seem inexorably attracted by the totalitarian varieties.

Virtually all the earlier generations of Catholicism, stretching back to the time of the Apostles, would have found incomprehensible the currently fashionable idea that it is impossible (or morally wrong) to preach religion to people while they are still hungry and poor. As an empirical-historical fact it is not true that the poor will not listen to such preaching, as the life of the Latin American peasants makes abundantly clear. Some missionaries, in fact, have devoted themselves to making the peasants less religious. Had the Church in its earliest years embarked on the policy of not seeking converts until all crying social injustices had been righted, Christianity would now be a mere footnote to the history of late Judaism. Virtually no major Catholic figure until quite recent times—not a Francis of Assisi, a Catherine of Siena, or a Damien of Molokai—ever said that the alleviation of bodily suffering was the primary purpose of the Church, taking precedence over all spiritual concerns. All insisted on integrating these two ministries closely, while giving pride of place to the spiritual. Ironically, by their decision to emphasize the material needs of the poor at the expense of their spiritual needs, secularizing Christians deprive the poor of something precious and make religion another monopoly possession of the affluent.

Another of the dirty little secrets in the radical Christian closet is religious persecution, the fact that, in those regimes which they most admire, not only can religion not be practiced freely but countless numbers of individuals have suffered and are suffering for the crime of putting God before Caesar. Yet almost nowhere in the literature of Christian "concern" will anything more than oblique, embarrassed, evasive references to this fact be found. In their often proclaimed solidarity with Third World peoples, they manifest little interest in those inhabitants of the Third World who are orthodox Christians and have, often enough, endured much hardship to preserve their faith. Such "backward" individuals are tacitly consigned to the scrap heap of history.

The issue of religious persecution appears to be, for many avant-garde Christians, merely another of those "retarded" questions which distract from the central political issues. For what in fact would modern Christians be willing to die? What doctrines or practices do they regard as so sacred as to be undeniable? Their public statements provide few clues, and it is difficult not to infer that for many of them an infinite amount of adjusting to the demands of the state would be acceptable, so long as the regime is properly "progressive." A case in point has been the reaction of the Maryknoll community to the release in 1970 of one of its bishops, James E. Walsh, after twenty years in a Chinese prison. Bishop Walsh was a heroic, possibly saintly man who was praised by his Maryknoll brothers for still maintaining a loving attitude towards the Chinese people. Yet that reaction, coupled with the prevailing Maryknoll admiration for the Chinese regime, could not explain why the bishop had been imprisoned in the first place. His twenty years of suffering have been turned into an inexplicable misfortune for which no one is to blame.[60] A Jesuit theologian has expressed condescending embarrassment at the writings of Jesuit missionaries persecuted in China by the Communists and charges that an interest in individual martyrs distracts Catholics from social injustice.[61] Christians who are constantly apologizing for the Crusades or the Inquisition seldom seem to realize that in the twentieth century by far the greatest mass slaughters have occurred in the name of political orthodoxies of one kind or another, many of them for the sake of "progress."

Oddly, Christians who begin by proclaiming that there is no authentic religion which is not politically involved, and who condemn the Church for its passive complicity with existing regimes, end by blandly praising nations (Cuba, China, Vietnam) where, if it is allowed to exist at all, the Church is permitted no political role other than that of supporting the regime. A wholly "privatized" Christianity, passive in the face of officially perpetrated injustices, becomes an acceptable model.

The Second Vatican Council proclaimed a theology of social concern in certain ways almost the precise opposite of that which now prevails in advanced Catholic circles. In *Gaudium et Spes* the Council Father praised "the dynamic movements of today by which these rights [of man] are everywhere fostered" but added that "these movements must be penetrated by the spirit of the gospel and protected against any kind of false autonomy." Christ was said not to have given the Church a properly political or economic mission but rather a religious mission out of which worldly concerns might properly develop. No particular social order was said to enjoy the Church's full approval, and a wide variety of social arrangements were given its blessing. A warning was issued against those whose entire mentality seemed to be dominated by economics, a phenomenon which the Council found prevalent in collectivist as well as in other kinds of societies. Both the philosophy of rampant individualism and others which "subordinate the basic rights of individual persons and groups to the collective organization of production" were condemned. The right of private property, and its virtual necessity as a guarantee of freedom, was reaffirmed. "Earthly progress" was carefully distinguished from "the growth of Christ's kingdom," although said to be relevant to it. In its decree on the priesthood the Council warned priests "never to put themselves at the service of any ideology or human faction."[62]

Philip Berrigan has said that he came to value priestly celibacy when he found it to be "an essential tool for revolution" (a statement which remains confusing in view of his later declaration that he and his wife considered themselves already married several years before they announced that fact).[63] Yet a true understanding of freedom would surely find ways to validate the various elements of the Christian tradition in its own terms, not as "tools" of some political purpose. A zealous politics which threatens to suck up the total energies of some of the most religious people of the age requires an equally strong antidote, which a fervent and unashamed Christian piety is eminently suited to be. However, many influential Christians, as previously noted, seem to prefer a bland and weak kind of religion. Proponents of the social gospel are under moral requirement at present to reassure the Church that they do regard religion as a valid thing in and of itself, an assurance which many of them seem by no means prepared to give.

The final connection between a zealous politics, religiously motivated, and the advent of totalitarianism is a passive link. As people are systematically deprived of their religious heritage, as their roots in their tradition are cut, they become maximally susceptible to manipulation and propaganda by dominant political movements. They no longer have a spiritual space independent of the public and political space they are required to occupy. They no longer possess beliefs which they believe can never be surrendered, and they are thus more easily molded into new social identities.

In the twentieth century the work of remolding has often been carried out by tyrannical governments armed with the full technological panoply of the modern state. But when so many Christians seem eager to do the same work voluntarily, as their proffered contribution to the cause, why need force be used at all? The journey to utopia can be a painless one, if only people will let it.

CHAPTER 8

The Kingdom of Politics

WHEN supported by the mass media, modern intellectual revolutions occur with such speed and pervasiveness that their very newness is soon forgotten. Before the Second Vatican Council, those who argued that being a Catholic implied involvement in political and social questions found themselves on the defensive, despite a body of papal teachings which seemed to support this view. Most Catholics thought rather eccentric the proposition that their faith somehow encompassed direct political action and by instinct sought to preserve a wall of separation between piety and citizenship. From arguing that Christian political activity on behalf of justice was permissible, Catholic liberals have, however, moved in an amazingly short period of time to the position that it is mandatory.

In America the question of racial integration marked the last great exercise of the Church's interdictory power—in the early 1960s excommunication or the threat of it was employed against outspokenly recalcitrant Catholic segregationists in Louisiana, and appeared to have an effect. Almost at that very moment, however, the thrust of liberal impulses at the Second Vatican Council was seeking to undermine the concept of ecclesiastical authority which underlay such interdicts. The use of religious authority to change beliefs saw its last great manifestation in the segregationist battles and was a major element in the process by which massive resistance to racial integration swiftly declined in the United States. A few years later, when Catholic liberals called for a similar use of Church authority against the Vietnamese War, it was not forthcoming. They blamed this failure on the timidity of the bishops. In reality the liberals themselves, in the birth-control controversy and other episodes, had effectively undermined that authority and rendered it impotent. American Catholics are now accustomed to the fact that Church agencies, sometimes speaking in the name of the bishops, regularly take official positions on everything from industrial strikes to the Panama Canal Treaty, but few any longer pay much attention.

Both liberals and conservatives have exaggerated the strength of the social gospel, however. Liberals sometimes celebrate a postconciliar Church vastly improved by the awakened moral sensitivity of Catholics to all forms of social injustice, while conservatives regret the substitution of political for religious interests. In reality, however, this new social awareness has not penetrated very deeply into the church and is not likely to. Among the laity, the decline of traditional piety has been to the benefit of an easy-going worldliness, the therapeutic mentality delineated in Chapter Three, which is unashamedly self-centered. It has been primarily among religious professionals and a relatively few "professional layman" that the new social consciousness has caught hold, but the most dedicated and enduring Catholic social apostolates—Francis of Assisi, Vincent de Paul, Mother Teresa of Calcutta—were always built on a basis of strong asceticism.

It has caught hold in a special way that requires close examination, since the point is not that Catholics have somehow become more sensitive to human suffering than they formerly were, although this self-serving version of events is often put forward, but that their new social concern has taken certain approved forms which bring Catholic liberals close to the mainstream of prevailing secular currents.

At least until World War II, Catholics in America were hardly insensitive to human suffering, since they were themselves so often the passive bearers of it. They had a deep and mute comprehension of its harsh realities which they seem not to have passed on to their children because they wished a brighter and happier life for those children. Although it verges on heresy to say so, there was probably more genuine awareness of suffering and injustice, and more really sacrificial action to alleviate it, on the part of the generations of American Catholics prior to 1940 than by their descendants who talk about suffering as though it has been newly invented. A church now often glibly and routinely accused of never having done anything to improve the lot of humanity in fact built and maintained a great network of hospitals, orphanages, homes for the aged and for unwed mothers, and asylums for the insane and the incurably ill. This network was put up quite literally with the nickels and dimes of people who were themselves poor and for whom any contribution to charity was a real sacrifice.

These same people's response to human need was, furthermore, often personally sacrificial. Religious, especially religious women, were servants in the literal sense. They did not expect nor allow their own desires to enter into their choice of assignments but went where they were sent, to perform whatever work was deemed necessary. Their food, clothing, and lodging were usually of the plainest, their recreations almost nonexistent. Most lay people followed a long and hard daily round of work, and whatever time they gave to others was from their few precious hours of rest. Despite that, they nursed the sick and cared for the aged. Often they performed such unpleasant tasks as preparing bodies for burial.

The feeling of some postconciliar Catholics that they are the first generation in the Church to break out of a pattern of narcissistic, privatized piety is historically unwarranted and is similar in nature to the satisfactions that rich young heirs sometimes take in being able to live so much more "cultivated" and "humane" lives than their money-grubbing ancestors, never stopping to reflect that it was precisely the exertions of these uncouth forebears that made such modern refinements possible.

There is perhaps more widespread social concern in the contemporary world than at any time in the past, compounded from the ability of the mass media to dramatize varieties of human need hitherto not even recognized and from a sustained prosperity that has placed the majority of Americans far above the level of subsistence and given them the material security and leisure which make systematic social action possible. There is another important ingredient as well—fashion, in the broadest sense of a cultural expectation so pervasive as almost to be unspoken, a badge of social belonging that increasing numbers of people are loath to be seen in public without.

One of the great ironies of current social awareness is that, while its most eloquent spokesmen decry the materialistic consumer society of late capitalism, this social awareness is precisely a product of that same society, a predictable historical development among people many of whom are surfeited with materialistic striving, guilty about their prosperity—and bored. Perhaps most importantly, this is a society which emphasizes being "sensitive"—delicacy of feeling as contrasted with the grossness of earlier generations—and properly liberal attitudes on a range of social questions are a sign of this sensitivity. An acute British observer has captured the quality of so much American Catholic social consciousness.

> The things that are wrong are clearly and fully expressed, with the well-developed jargon of political and philosophical analysis, which everyone seems to have at his or her fingertips.
>
> . . . . there is a tremendous spiritual power in American Christianity, much of it muted and even turning sour because of an odd pervasive type of what I can only call radical smugness.

I think it happens as a direct result of the communal breast-beating and sackcloth-and-ash distributing which is such a marked feature of the American Catholic scene. The constant discussion and elaboration of such self-accusations becomes, after a time, a kind of formula, the repetition of which is easily equated with the experience of real humility.

There was a nice little sister . . . who talked for half an hour about her need for fulfillment, and how the new freedom from hypocritical submission to superiors meant that she could use her God-given talents as a witness to the Word. But it was apparently necessary for her self-respect that her talents should find a cash value in competition with other women, and that she should prove this by the quality of her clothes and possessions. She had all the right phrases but what they amounted to was a rehash of the values of commercial society, with a frosting of radical theological-cum-psychological jargon. And there was the group of young married couples, buoyantly dismissing the entire Catholic past in favor of a free, informal community style. . . .

they talked a lot about the moribund condition of the Church and how great they had felt last week when someone read a passage from Isaiah, about the suffering of God's servant. Only there was not much suffering going on, everyone being comfortably incomed, with good quality carpets and well-fed children. . . .[1]

The new social consciousness has been revealed, in many cases, by an attitude which unconsciously parodies the prayer of the Pharisee in the Gospel: "Thank God I am not like the rest of men—racists, war-mongers, male chauvinists. I am on the mailing lists of a dozen liberal organizations. I campaign for the right political candidates. I have walked picket lines and written letters to newspapers." As one analyst observed, becoming politically involved is for many people not merely based on the desire to help the downtrodden; it is a "trip" in itself, appealing to bored middle-class people who find the routine of daily jobs unfulfilling and unexciting.[2] In the Church the new social gospel especially attracts priests and religious dissatisfied with what they consider the dull routine of parish work or teaching. They have chosen to forgo the undeniable if limited opportunities for good which such work affords in favor of a grand commitment to remaking society. Whether this new commitment is in fact more productive than the old remains to be seen.

Robert Nisbet has pointed out that affluence tends to breed amonie in those who enjoy its benefits and eventually gives rise to feelings of guilt. But it is a guilt which is often divorced from religious roots.[3] As a consequence, fashionable gestures of "concern" replace genuine repentance. Many comfortable middle-class Catholics are quite capable of using the rhetoric of renunciation without renouncing anything at all. A nun-theologian, for instance, suggests that a truly Christian spirit of simplicity is found in the contemporary taste for "natural" substances—in food, furniture, and decoration—over what is "artificial."[4] Such tastes are in reality usually expensive. The gospel of "making a better world," in any case, appeals mainly to the young, the educated, and the affluent.

The desire to bear moral witness in society, although it involves much that is noble and genuine, is part of the general process of middle-class "liberation" by which certain people, consciously or unconsciously, learn to transcend the narrow boundaries of their culture in order to take "enlightened" and "advanced" positions on controversial questions, positions on which they are certain history will vindicate them. This means, among other things, that only certain kinds of social injustice are recognized and responded to. In 1976, for example, a staff member of the United States Catholic Conference told a committee of the United States Senate that the Senate should reject a proposed American treaty with Spain lest it be construed as "an accolade of legitimacy" for the Spanish government of King Juan Carlos. Only when substantial reforms had been instituted, he insisted, should the treaty be approved. A year later the same priest turned a deaf ear to Hungarian-Americans agitated over the United States government's intention of returning the Crown of St. Stephen, most sacred of Hungarian symbols, to the Communist government of Hungary.[5] This choice example of ecclesiastical Newspeak reflected a habit, widespread in religious circles (the World Council of Churches is notorious in the matter), of protesting injustice only in Western nations, never behind the Iron Curtain, and in effect distinguishing "good" dictatorships from "bad" ones. The episode also demonstrated the general unwillingness of avant-garde clergy to respond to anything that might be construed as narrowly Catholic interests and their desire to place a certain distance between themselves and the mass of ordinary Catholics burdened with too provincial an outlook.

Avant-garde religious have, for nearly two decades, chipped away at the dogmatic certitude of ordinary believers with regard to traditional doctrines, hoping to replace it with a commitment to social justice. What they have apparently succeeded in doing, in many cases, is merely inducing a scepticism about all moral and doctrinal questions, including those involving social justice. The therapeutic mind first becomes unreachable through appeals to authority and finally even through appeals to conscience. It can be roused to concern on behalf of others only to the degree that this prospect can be made to seem either self-gratifying or fashionable, preferably both. (A national poll of high-school students in 1977 found the majority to be "liberal" on questions like the use of marijuana and premarital sex, "conservative" on matters of foreign policy and military expenditures, and unabashedly "money-oriented.")[6]

The revived social gospel, in so many ways an inevitable mutant of late capitalism, is virtually by definition an avant-garde movement. Like all avant-garde movements, therefore, it depends for its energy and its appeal on its continuing minority status, the aura of daring which surrounds it. For nearly two decades, socially aware Catholics have castigated the mainstream of believers for their lack of sensitivity to, and complicity with, social injustice. Catholics whose ancestors were either peasants in Europe or exploited laborers in the United States have been urged to bear the moral burden of slavery and to atone for it. Yet the avant-garde have failed to acknowledge, even to themselves, how their own positions depend on this mainstream's continuing to be "insensitive." If a keen social conscience were distributed evenly throughout the Church the avant-garde would lose their own positions of leadership. Since the secular agenda is largely accepted, the Church also remains by definition always "behind" the world.

The transition which so many clergy and religious have made from strictly religious to quasi-political roles has come about through a variety of factors. Among them is the recognition, made early in the Kennedy years by some, much later by others, that the kind of authority which could be wielded in strictly ecclesiastical roles was very limited and narrow in contrast to the authority provided by the government or various social agencies. While carefully employing an antiauthoritarian rhetoric and insisting always on the necessity of "service," the "new breed" of religious unerringly gravitated towards what they correctly perceived were centers of power far more important than the Church.

The old model of ecclesiastical leadership, in which lay people instinctively deferred to and obeyed the clergy, was obviously becoming obsolete. Social justice was perceived as the only area in which the forthright and uncompromising exercise of moral authority was still possible. If priests could no longer lecture their people about birth control, they could lecture them on racism. If the pastor could no longer claim to have the answers to questions of sexual morality, he could claim to have the answers on questions of current political controversy. The embracing of the social gospel was for many religious (and some lay people) a way of salvaging a prophetic, even an authoritarian, role. If the educational gap between clergy and laity was no longer as wide as it once had been, those clergy who affiliated themselves with avant-garde political movements had no trouble keeping it open. Holding the correct political opinions came to be yet another important index of having entered the enlightened segment of the great middle class, another measure of the distance travelled from one's own parochial roots.

Despite the fact that many of their own fathers probably belonged to labor unions, members of the Catholic Committee on Urban Ministry in 1977 rejected a proposal that they seek closer ties with the labor movement. Comments included, "It's hard to see unions as a hopeful force" and, "The labor movement doesn't really concern me." A nun walked out of the meeting in the middle of the presentation, exclaiming, "What a waste; as if we hadn't heard all that stuff before!"[7]

Influential persons in the Church now seek to make social action, or at least the correct beliefs concerning social problems, the only basis of unity in the midst of an endless process of liturgical, doctrinal, and moral change. Since the historical symbols of Catholicism, especially its liturgy, have been so severely weakened in recent years (the liturgy is now often a source of division rather than of unity), the social gospel is offered as a common bond through which unity is possible without symbols. Social action becomes a kind of sacrament, far more sacred in the minds of some people than the established rituals of the Church. Devotees of the social gospel are frequently suspicious and uneasy at the prospect that a more traditional kind of sacramentalism might reassert itself, especially in liturgical style, thus providing something else to fill those empty places in the human soul which the social gospel would like to claim as exclusively its own domain.

The extraordinary importance which attaches to gestures of informality in the postconciliar Church—priests appearing in sport clothes, public speakers ostentatiously removing their coats and ties, nuns in shorts, the compulsory use of first names even to people one scarcely knows, exaggeratedly warm greetings—reflect that same cultural style. They serve as rituals which, consciously or not, attempt to substitute for the Church's now discarded sacramental rituals. The high point of their religious life is for many the "greeting of peace" at Mass, entered into with such gusto and for such ever-lengthening stretches of time that it becomes the emotional climax of their worship. There is a strong tendency to confuse these quintessentially American cultural excrescences, which have obvious affinities with certain well-advertised aspects of the consumer society (the "Pepsi Generation"), with genuine charity and to assume that those who engage in them are thereby revealed as more open, more loving, and more sensitive than those who do not.

Ironically, a Church so many of whose leaders strive to make it relevant to worldly concerns is probably, in many ways, less relevant now than it was twenty years ago, precisely because it has no distinctive voice with which it speaks, no special wisdom to contribute to the common fund. Despite a great quantitative increase in social involvement in the postconciliar Church, there has also occurred a decrease in the quality of involvement. The familiar figure of the labor priest, for example, who became an expert in industrial disputes and was called upon to arbitrate strikes, is rapidly disappearing. Replacing him are priests and religious who, mainly on the basis of certain general theological principles, achieve instant expertise on a wide range of questions and issue moralistic pontifications. After a flying two-week visit to the Paris peace talks in 1971, the president of the National Coalition of American Nuns pronounced on why the negotiations were not going well—the American ambassador failed to take "tea breaks" with the Vietnamese delegates.[8]

Contemporary Catholicism fails to make a crucial contribution to the needs of society because it often contents itself with merely echoing what is being said, and usually said better, elsewhere. Specifically, despite their intensely moralistic rhetoric, many Catholics now have no properly moral approach to social problems, merely a sociological approach dressed up in moralistic clothes. Catholic social thought has always been simultaneously compassionate and tough-minded, willing to look at society in realistic terms and not through the sentimental lenses of idealism. As a result, Catholic social thinkers (and ordinary Catholics, on an instinctive level) have had an acute sense of what is or is not possible. They have not been hypnotized by the ultimately destructive myth of a wholly good and infinitely improvable human nature. They have recognized how large a role tradition, authority, law and interdict play in inculcating moral values. They have undertood how crucial the family is to any kind of healthy society and have not willingly surrendered its prerogatives to governmental and educational bureaucracy.

By contrast the prevailing modes of social analysis—composed of approximately one part vulgar Marxism, one part sociological behaviorism, and one part the empty clichés of the human potential movement—are irredeemably shallow, unable to come to terms with moral evil except in the most trivial ways and consequently doomed forever to treating symptoms rather than causes. Every social evil is responded to, with almost mathematical predictability, in four ways: hortatory castigations designed to make the middle classes feel guilty, "educational" programs (called propaganda in other contexts) in schools and the media, the establishment of new bureaucracies, and the appropriation of large sums of money (which, however, never turn out to be quite enough). A few of the purer souls dissociate themselves from all these modes of response by explaining that the problem in question will not be solved short of a total revolution.

The works of Jacques Maritain, to mention only a single name, contain far more insights into the nature of modern society and the root causes of social malaise than almost anything produced by the present generation of self-consciously secular-minded Catholics. Almost because of that, Maritain has, within the few years since his death, been in effect declared a nonperson, his books not read, his name scarcely mentioned. To the degree that the substance of Catholic social thought is still being kept alive it is maintained by thinkers who are for the most part not Catholics—Daniel Bell, Robert Nisbet, James Q. Wilson, Jacques Ellul, and others. Those whose thinking about social questions has the Catholic label specifically attached to it are all too likely to be of the mentality that reads Dostoevsky's *Crime and Punishment* as a fearless exposé of the exploitation of elderly female pawnbrokers and who regret that the novel obscures its central message with too much mystical talk about evil.

The Jesuit John Courtney Murray, probably the most influential theologian American Catholicism has produced, delineated, to the satisfaction of most people, the relationship which ought to exist between church and state.[9] It was an appealing and balanced theory, but it suffered from the fact that certain of Father Murray's assumptions about American society, especially his concept of civility, were ceasing to be valid even as he was making them. The climate of culture was far more hospitable to traditional Christian values when he wrote, and during the euphoric conciliar years, than it would perhaps ever be again.

In particular many Catholics fail to understand the modern process whereby what is first secularized, that is, declared autonomous and independent of all religious influence, is eventually deified, that is, declared to be sovereign and authoritative in all areas of life. The balance of independence between religion and politics has proven discouragingly difficult to maintain in reality, and the loss of momentum sustained by organized religion in recent times has made possible a rapid expansion of the moral authority of the state.

In a less intense but equally pervasive way, the social gospel as preached in liberal Western societies demands allegiance from its followers just as insistently as the totalitarian forms of it discussed in the previous chapter. For the first time in the history of the Church a frank interest in things spiritual has been rendered suspect in the eyes of many who consider themselves Catholics, and those who uphold this spirituality have been placed on the defensive, forced continually to justify what has traditionally been the heart of a devout Catholic life. Gregory Baum, for example, has warned that a revived interest in spirituality might be "a political move to the past." St. Thérèse of Lisieux, he has pointed out, failed to take a critical stance toward "the economic system or the colonial policy of France," while her pious parents made money selling jewelry and lace. "They lived from the bourgeois desire for luxury."[10] (Professor Baum does not consider the case of those who live from the bourgeois hunger for trendy ideas.) A Carmelite nun announces that the contemplative convent life "can no longer be seen as a valid Christian vocation at all." Any regimen involving solitude and recollection is declared an "aberration," and only a life involved in service to others is said to be legitimately Christian.[11]

The point is not that humanitarian concerns are themselves illegitimate but that they have become a procrustean bed into which all other aspects of the Christian life are ruthlessly fitted, no matter how much they are damaged in the process. In the contemporary Church a Pelagian humanitarianism is in fact the quintessential heresy, in the original sense of a part of the truth exalted into the whole and driving out other aspects of the truth as it expands. Christopher Dawson posited that in most battles of ideas, the simplest and crudest notions usually triumph.[12] A reductionist, humanitarian version of Christianity, in which the ideas of helping others or making a better world are paramount, has appeal not only because it fits in with certain prevailing cultural fashions but also because such ideas are the easiest to grasp in the whole great panoply of Christian theology.

Throughout its history the Church has usually served whatever human, even secular, needs were required of it, generally needs which no other institution of the time was capable of filling. The most notable example would perhaps be the monks of the Dark Ages who preserved the light of learning and maintained places of refuge from a brutal society in addition to observing their own daily religious rounds. Yet these same monks would doubtlessly have been astounded to hear that their secular services, no matter how valuable, were more important than the *Opus Dei*—the divine liturgy, and attendant private prayer. They would have been shocked at the suggestion that the many hours they spent in church constituted a kind of escapism from their real Christian duties.

Devotees of the social gospel, once themselves on the defensive, are now established as arbiters who can demand an accounting from those who do not wholeheartedly embrace their particular concerns. For instance, a Dominican purporting to write on spirituality in fact seems determined to forestall outbreaks of spirituality which might impede political involvement. Anyone who decries the absence of mysticism in the Church is dismissed as merely nostalgic for his own lost social privileges, and classical mysticism is described as merely a way of "keeping the nigger down, the nigger defined as all who pray differently from us (meaning our class)." Mysticism is defined as "dangerous" to prophecy and therefore to be kept in strict subordination to it.[13] In 1977 the Inter-American Conference of Major Religious Superiors, representing the governing officials of religious orders in the Western hemisphere, solemnly announced that the aim of religious life is to "achieve justice for the poor and oppressed." The past president of the group, a nun, explained that while these orders had previously seen their principal task as to defend or preach the faith, they no longer regarded that as primary.[14]

T. S. Eliot, writing in a historical context similar to the present one, quoted Samuel Johnson saying of a man that "Politics did not, however, so much engage him as to withhold his thoughts from things of more importance,"[15] which is perhaps the principal objection that can be made to the latest reincarnation of the social gospel. The pity of it is that often Catholics who have been converted to this gospel become merely ideologues, endlessly repeating the latest clichés on fashionable topics but with little that is original or penetrating to add to them. (The 1976 Call to Action Conference was like a giant sausage machine grinding out "correct" positions.) A well-known priest-leader in the charismatic movement, for instance, feels called upon to make the compulsory remark that "the United States has had a devastating effect on the rest of the world in the last thirty years" and that it will require "a real educational effort" to bring charismatics to the point of seeing it.[16] A Jesuit theologian, writing for an audience of religious, identifies multinational corporations in America as the principal villains on the international scene. Those who oppose the compulsory busing of school children for purposes of racial integration are identified as those who have "just made it" and are insecure in their own social positions. Violence on behalf of the poor, while not condoned, is "understood." Christians are obliged to "identify" with the poor and work for the conversion of the rich.[17] The point, here as elsewhere, is not that such opinions are necessarily wrong as that they are songs sung by rote by tone-deaf people, religious attempting to establish their credentials of relevancy in areas where they have no expertise and little insight, mouthing political clichés without apparently realizing that it is possible even to offer intelligent arguments on the other side. They are people whose gifts would be far more usefully employed in areas of spiritual concern.

Religion, according to St. Paul, has to do with things unseen. But the social gospel is impatient with the intangible, since there are so many quite tangible problems waiting to be solved. In its more extreme form it has become quite literally materialistic, convinced that the material needs of humanity come first on the modern Christian's agenda, and more than a little suspicious that those who talk about the spiritual are deliberately seeking to fob off opium. As the novelist Muriel Spark describes a modern nun,

> Felicity wants everyone to be liberated by her vision and to acknowledge it. She wants a stamped receipt from Almighty God for every word she spends, every action, as if she can later deduct it from her income-tax returns. Felicity never sees the point of faith unless it visibly benefits mankind.[18]

Throughout the history of the Church there was always confusion between faith and culture. Rarely, however, has culture been more forthrightly invoked as normative than at present. A Christian Brother, for example, argues that since American culture is optimistic and does not recognize the reality of evil (a debatable proposition, historically), the Church should avoid "picturing Christ mythically as the savior who descends from heaven" and emphasize instead the divinity in all men. Predictably, this leads back to the familiar terrain on which the contemporary liberal intelligentsia already live—the human potential movement and rhetorical opposition to war, capitalism, nationalism, and racism.[19] What begins with brave words about prophecy turns out to be the most completely culture-bound religion of all, and quite deliberately so.

Jacques Ellul has pointed out how, in the absence of a vital sense of transcendence, physical suffering becomes the greatest imaginable evil. What follows is almost inevitably totalitarian politics:

> Everything is political. Politics is the only serious activity. The fate of humanity depends on politics, and classic philosophical or religious truth takes on meaning only as it is incarnated in political action. Christians are typical in this connection. . . . As Christianity collapses as a religion, they look about them in bewilderment. . . . Since they are religious, they are drawn automatically into a political sphere, like iron filings to a magnet.

As religion is demythologized, the culture is proportionately divinized.[20]

As with the movements of Third World revolution, the meliorist political movements in the West establish standards of unquestionable orthodoxy. A nun, for instance, argues that society now knows how to abolish poverty and other kinds of suffering and merely requires the will to do so. Consequently she advocates a philosophy of pragmatism, in which Christians will "find out our identity in the action itself, not by first reflecting and theorizing and then acting. . . ." God is said to be speaking through the "signs of the times," and "our culture" is calling to Christians to put aside their outmoded beliefs and practices.[21]

In many cases the new Catholic social gospel appears to be merely the desire to use the Church, and whatever authority and prestige it still enjoys, to achieve political goals. For example, although secular clothes have become *de rigueur* among advanced clergy and religious, in 1977 a group of priests wore full Mass vestments to march on behalf of the Equal Rights Amendment in Washington[22] A prominent member of the Catholic Peace Fellowship has argued that, although many in the movement do not marry within the Church or attend Sunday Mass, they still call themselves Catholic, "as one might call himself American, or a Minneapolitan, or an Atlantan. . . ."[23]

The new Catholic political awareness came to fruition through a fortuitous combination of factors—certain of the documents of the Second Vatican Council, the sense of liberation towards the world which many priests and religious experienced in the wake of the Council, the election of the first Catholic to the American presidency, and the unparalleled glamour which surrounded that presidency: the Camelot myth that intelligent, benign, idealistic, and attractive people·were going to solve all the world's problems. The magnet effect to which Jacques Ellul refers was maximally operative in the heady atmosphere of the early 1960s, and its after-effects are not as yet completely spent.

Liberal Catholics in the postconciliar era have shown a consistent preference for political candidates whose style is religious. John F. Kennedy, when it was still possible to think of him as a committed Catholic, was a comforting symbol because he suggested that the layman of the future would express his religious beliefs in essentially secular and political ways, piety left unobtrusively in the background. Those who came afterwards—Eugene McCarthy, George McGovern, Jerry Brown, Walter Mondale—were men who seemed to have redirected their youthful piety into quasi-messianic political channels (McCarthy a former Benedictine novice, Brown a Jesuit scholastic, McGovern the son of a minister, Mondale the half-brother of a minister and husband of a minister's daughter). Jimmy Carter remains a perplexing and suspicious figure in the eyes of many precisely because he appears to have a strong residue of personal piety which has not been safely tamed within political boundaries.

For many Christians political activity now has sacramental value and serves as a surrogate religion. In 1972, for example, a former Jesuit priest, writing in the Catholic press, asserted that the Democratic Party convention in Miami Beach was a true gathering of the people of God, more so than any church. The convention's orators were compared to biblical prophets and their orations characterized as "the power of the sermon momentarily revived." The coming November election was then assessed as a choice confronting the American people between good and evil. The same author became personally involved in Senator

McGovern's campaign and described the experience (working with "obviously selfless" people) as a "quest for personal and communal transcendence." The McGovern campaign was seen as pointing to "social reconciliation and social redemption." Senator McGovern's speeches were again characterized as "prophetic" ("when such chords are struck, politics interlaces with religious passion"). When the Senator lost overwhelmingly in the November elections (most observers thought because of his own mistakes), the same former Jesuit attributed his defeat to the inherent evil of the voters ("the victorious majority also depicts a punishing demand to conform coupled with a willingness to sacrifice civil liberties in order to curtail deviance").[24] A nun wrote that the McGovernites were the only hope of the country, the only alternative to despair,[25] while another nun claimed that even to speak publicly in favor of the Senator was an act of high courage.[26]

Liberal Catholics have justified their attraction to politics by the rationale, true in itself, that moral issues of great consequence are often decided through the political process and that people of deep moral commitment must therefore involve themselves in that process. But their approach to politics has often been naive. Not only have its complexities eluded them and they have been attracted to romantic lost causes like McGovernism but also they have failed to realize how the political process, and participation in it, soon becomes an end in itself, a kind of drug which enables people to live at such a level of glamour and artificial excitement that they become unfit to function in ordinary situations. They come to be cut off from their own roots (for instance, "Potomac fever" makes many politicians, after leaving office, prefer to continue living in Washington to returning home).

Catholic political participation would be more promising if it seemed to involve a genuine desire to insure that Catholic moral principles were represented in the political process and Catholic voices heard on questions where they had something distinctive to say. Such would be true pluralism. But the internal weaknesses of the Church, already discussed, and the desire of so many avant-garde Catholics to fit into the prevailing liberal consensus prevent this from happening. Everything which has a distinctively Catholic look about it raises the specters of parochialism and divisiveness. Catholics who do involve themselves in politics often find that they can function only in accordance with someone else's rules. They are welcomed to the degree that they are willing to offer Catholic support to the enlightened liberal consensus. To the degree that they appear to chart an independent course, they are ostracized. The Berrigan brothers, for instance, amassed an immense amount of moral capital with secular liberals because of their actions against the Vietnam War, and it has been an intriguing question how they would spend that capital to force these same liberals to take seriously certain questions to which they are insensitive. To date, however, the Berrigans have chosen to leave their capital in the bank and failed to confront issues not already firmly within the secular liberal orbit.

Abortion is naturally the single most significant issue in terms of the divergence between Catholic and secular political perceptions, and it is instructive to follow the fate of that issue among Catholic liberals over a period of years. That the abortion issue might sever a developing coalition of Catholic and secular liberals was obvious from the time it became a national political issue in the early 1970s, due mainly to the determination of various organized groups to repeal all existing abortion laws. Catholics caught in that dilemma had two possibilities open to them— either to remain in the coalition on the liberals' own terms or to attempt to force some accommodation to the Catholic position. Almost without exception, those who were prominent in the coalition chose the first course. Willfully allowing themselves to become politically naive, they solemnly warned their fellow Catholics against being "single-issue" voters, overlooking the fact—obvious to anyone who claimed even a cursory acquaintance with the democratic process—that only when a movement has shown that it is effective with regard to a single issue is it respected enough to be included in political coalitions.[27] Certain strategically placed Catholics were in fact willing to give up the struggle before it even began.

As early as 1972, for example, a Jesuit on the staff of the National Council of Churches characterized the Catholic position on abortion as "uniformly unecumenical and therefore disastrous." Most members of the N.C.C., he said, "deplore abortion" and permit it only as "the lesser of two evils."[28] The next year the Supreme Court in effect permitted abortion on demand, and most of the member churches of the N.C.C. applauded the decision. Many Protestant and Jewish resources have gone into the struggle to widen the scope of abortion rights. When the president of the N.C.C. (herself in favor of legalized abortion) deplored the "catastrophic" effect the issue was having on ecumenical relations, another Jesuit obligingly suggested that Catholic doctrine need not uphold the humanity of the fetus.[29]

Gregory Baum called on Catholics to respect the pro-abortion opinions of many Protestants, noting that the Protestant churches often espoused advanced moral positions "at a time when the Catholic Church continued to teach moral norms from the cultural experience of the premodern age." He urged Catholics to move very cautiously on the issue and not to assume that they had right on their side.[30] It was the precise opposite of the advice he had given Catholics with regard to the question of war and which he would later offer with regard to the achievement of a just, socialistic society.

During the 1972 presidential election campaign Senator McGovern's Washington headquarters mailed sermon outlines to priests and nuns throughout the United States, in conjunction with the Respect Life Week proclaimed by the American bishops. The sermon outlines were sent by the president of the Liturgical Conference, who was on leave from that post to work in the McGovern campaign. He declined to comment on reports that they were sent in order to counteract a possible "over-emphasis" on abortion which might harm Senator McGovern's candidacy.[31] (The Senator was proabortion.) The Supreme Court's decision the following year, and the announced intention of many people to reverse it, immediately catapulted abortion into a prominent place in the 1976 presidential campaign.

A year before the campaign, before there was more than a vague notion who the Democratic Party's candidate might be, certain Catholic journalists were already attempting to discredit the anti-abortion movement in the interests of the party's future standard-bearer. "Xavier Rynne" blamed the bishops "for encouraging the less stable among the faithful to adopt a fanatical stand."[32] There was already a strong probability that the 1976 Democratic candidate, whoever he might be, would be proabortion. Many prominent Catholic politicians—Edward Kennedy, the Jesuit Congressman Robert Drinan, Eugene McCarthy, and Governor Hugh Carey of New York—had already developed a ritualistic position on the question: "I am personally opposed to abortion but I do not favor legislation to regulate it." It had become a litmus test imposed on Catholic politicians as proof of their political reliability.

One journalist (an employee of the official National Catholic News), having already planted in the Catholic press the seed of an idea—that Catholics ought not to take abortion too seriously as a campaign issue—continued to work to undermine the anti-abortion movement as the campaign progressed. Governor Jimmy Carter of Georgia was not the first choice of most liberal idealists, and his own position on abortion was confused and inconsistent. But as it became clear that he would win the party's nomination, his agents inserted into the official party platform a clause opposing any constitutional restrictions on abortion, an act which was a direct and deliberate slap at anti-abortion Catholics. The N.C. News reporter gave the governor's campaign highly favorable coverage. After the governor's victory the reporter explained that abortion had scarcely influenced the election at all and that candidates were safe in ignoring it. He congratulated Catholics on not allowing their narrow religious perspectives to influence their votes.[33]

At the Democratic convention outspoken Catholics, including a number of priests, were highly visible, but few appear even to have raised the abortion question. There were numerous complaints that Governor Carter ignored urban Catholics in the Northern cities, but such complaints were mainly cast in terms of ethnicity and social identity, not of religion or morals.[34] The lieutenant governor of New York, a Catholic, spoke from the convention platform and urged the delegates to remember pickets gathered outside the auditorium and to "remain open to the wrongs addressed." But she was referring to militant homosexual organizations, not to antiabortion pickets.[35] A leading Catholic journal pronounced the anti-abortion movement "intransigent," said its demands were "impossible in a pluralistic society" and congratulated Governor Carter on not having made any futile gestures in that direction.[36]

After the conventions of the two major parties, a delegation of American bishops met with both Governor Carter and President Gerald Ford and questioned them, among other things, about abortion. Afterwards they said they were "encouraged" at the president's stand, "disappointed" at the governor's. These rather mild remarks were met with a savage crescendo of abuse, some of it from Catholic circles. A Catholic member of the *New York Times* editorial board lectured the bishops on the danger that they would stir up the "more fervent outriders of the right-to-life movement," which would result in "an offense against that spirit of mutual charity and tolerance that should prevail in political discourse." He explained loftily that the Church's teaching on abortion merely aimed to proclaim a "message of hope" and did not require that abortions actually be prevented.[37] The *Times* also reported that several (unnamed) staff members of the United States Catholic Conference had threatened to resign if the bishops did not back down from their stand. The president of the National Federation of Priests' Councils appeared on national television to express "deep concern" at the overemphasis being placed on abortion.[38]

The National Conference of Catholic Charities refused to support the antiabortion amendment, to which the Democratic platform was also opposed, because, according to one of its officers, the group was "turned off by the way that abortion has intruded itself into the presidential campaign." (He was the same man who sent out the McGovernite sermon outlines for the 1972 Respect Life Week.) Governor Carter appeared before the convention and was frequently applauded; he was not asked about his position on abortion.[39] A former president of the Catholic Theological Society of America expressed fear that the abortion question would become a "single-issue test for public office," obscuring the fact that the Democratic platform reflected Catholic moral teachings on many issues.[40] The media gave maximum exposure to those Catholics willing to censure the anti-abortion movement for reasons of partisan politics, and there was a report that Governor Carter had decided to appeal "over the heads of the bishops" and directly to the Catholic people.[41]

Part of his strategy involved securing the cooperation of certain influential Catholics who in effect ceased being servants of the Church and became servants of the Carter candidacy. A staff member of the National Council of Catholic Bishops was won over, as was a staff member of the Liturgical Conference and a nun. All obligingly announced their opposition to an anti-abortion amendment. Asked if he thought he had a "Catholic problem," Governor Carter said he was appointing one of the Catholics on his staff to oversee relations with Catholics. The appointee, although he bore an Irish name, turned out to be a Protestant minister.[42]

Meanwhile the vice-president of the National Federation of Priests' Councils wrote a letter, given national circulation, in which he attacked the anti-abortion movement as "myopic." An Indianapolis priest, he was particularly concerned to defend Senator Birch Bayh of Indiana who, he said, was unfairly stigmatized as having "joined the camp of the abortionists" merely because he opposed an anti-abortion amendment. The priest described himself as pastor of a "progressive community" where people had little interest in the anti-abortion campaign.[43] A few months later, Senator Bayh was given a special award by the National Abortion Rights Action League, the nation's largest pro-abortion organization. He expressed himself as deeply grateful for the award and in his acceptance speech referred to anti-abortionists as "our opponents."[44] Earlier the Network, an organization of nuns lobbying on behalf of social justice, had ranked Senator Bayh as their favored candidate for the presidency.[45]

Having enjoyed a love affair with romantic radicalism in the 1960s, many avant-garde Catholics returned to electoral politics with a vengeance and virtually sacralized it. Supporting the right party, the right party platform, and the right candidate became religious duties, and those who appeared to obstruct the progress of the anointed leader were cast in the role of enemies. Many clergy, having with some trauma turned themselves into orthodox liberals, are now unable to serve also as critics of this new orthodoxy.

The irony was that those who entered politics because of a proclaimed necessity to bring religious and moral principles to bear, to use politics for the promotion of social justice, ended in 1976 by exerting every ounce of their influence against the proper discussion of one of the major moral issues of the age, and one which has close ties to a number of other crucial moral questions. Since the chosen party, and the chosen candidate, did not wish to discuss abortion and found it an embarrassment, their Catholic supporters turned to attack those other Catholics who insisted on raising the question. In the name of morality, morality was suppressed. Partisan orthodoxy took precedence over religious convictions, and those who voted the straight party ticket were praised for their "independence," while those who sought to follow their consciences on the abortion question were called myopic and narrow. Catholics were urged, even by some of their own priests, to disregard the moral leadership of their bishops and turn instead for guidance to the duly elected head of a major political party.

This strange episode demonstrated once again the existence of rigid political orthodoxies in progressive religious circles, violations of which are not tolerated. Liberal Catholics, while purporting to be themselves opposed to abortion, argued that legislation was not possible or appropriate to solve the problem. They also accused the anti-abortionists of being rigid, fanatical, uncharitable, and narrow. The second charge, to the degree that it has truth, is equally applicable to every other social movement of recent times—civil rights, opposition to war, feminism, or environmentalism—and has never been perceived by these same liberals as therefore disqualifying the movement from their support. The first objection, it may be recalled, is precisely the one made by many people against civil rights legislation in the 1950s and early 1960s—that it did not have broad popular support and that "education" was preferable to legislation. In truth, because abortion is an unfashionable moral issue, many liberal Catholics would prefer that the Church content itself with an occasional formal statement of opposition, while otherwise remaining wholly passive. Those who proclaim that they are opposed to abortion but do not regard legislation as germane would seem thereby to incur a special obligation to use vigorous moral suasion to win over those who fail to recognize the seriousness of the issue. Few, however, have done so. Only those issues which are on the approved list of the enlightened consensus are deemed worthy of attention and energy. A "prophetic" social role is possible only so long as it does not threaten to disrupt the enlightened consensus.

This preferring of political to religious orthodoxy now seems to be a permanent feature of life in the American Church, and is graphically illustrated in the growing involvement of so many nuns in the feminist movement. Since the mainstream of feminism is fanatically and uncompromisingly in favor of abortion, such involvement creates moral dilemmas which, however, turn out to be easily solved.

When a pro-abortion Congressman-doctor was defeated in an election for the Senate from Kansas, a nun accused anti-abortionists of being "rabid and hate-filled." Noting that he had supported the approved positions of the Network organization in over eighty per cent of cases, she accused anti-abortionists of using the abortion issue as a "political tool."[46]

The president of the National Assembly of Women Religious then publicly criticized the American bishops for supporting an anti-abortion amendment to the Constitution, which she said "is neither winnable nor enforceable in this pluralistic society. . . ." Referring to some members of the organization, another nun complained that "As soon as you even whisper the word abortion, they turn red."[47]

Having affirmed the principle that "divisive" constitutional amendments ought not to be supported, the N.A.W.R. then reaffirmed its unwavering support for the Equal Rights Amendment and announced that it would refuse to hold its meetings in any state which failed to ratify the amendment. A nun, addressing the convention, called on her fellow sisters to counteract the "takeover" of the planned International Women's Year meeting in Houston by "well-schooled, well-disciplined groups of Catholic and Protestant women" who opposed the amendment. Passage of the Equal Rights Amendment was termed the only way to decrease the number of abortions, since it would give women a sense of dignity and responsibility.[48]

A few months later the National Conference of Catholic Women voted to support the anti-abortion amendment and to oppose the Equal Rights Amendment. Earlier the N.A.W.R. had declined to cooperate with the N.C.C.W.[49]

Also in 1977 the Leadership Conference of Women Religious, the official organization of major superiors, declared that any anti-abortion amendment to the Constitution was unsatisfactory because "it will be looked upon as an imposition of one view on the rest of society." (By this reasoning, of course, no controversial legislation would ever be passed.) While acknowledging that abortion involved the taking of human life, the conference advised that nuns not support legislation designed to prohibit it. However, on other issues it urged that nuns become politically involved and make use of the tactics of political persuasion.[50]

A former president of the National Coalition of American Nuns publicly attacked the Illinois Congressman who sponsored legislation to prohibit the financing of abortions through Federal taxes. She chided him for "pontificating over women's bodies" and said that "women must make their own decisions, according to their own educated consciences." The same nun also said that religious groups which opposed the Equal Rights Amendment were guilty of "sacrilege." She called for a total economic boycott of those states which had not ratified the E.R.A.[51]

At the International Women's Year Conference in Houston, also in 1977, delegates voted overwhelmingly to approve legalized abortion financed through taxes. Anti-abortionists were largely prevented from expressing their views; by a special concession of the presiding officer they were allowed four minutes to make their case on the floor of the convention. (Advocates of lesbians' rights, also approved by the convention, were given more than an hour.) Nuns were in evidence at the meeting, and few apparently supported the anti-abortion cause. The former president of the National Coalition of American Nuns was a delegate and endorsed all the convention's positions, proclaiming that at the group's approval of the Equal Rights Amendment "I was moved . . . to a point I haven't been moved by a liturgical ritual in ten years." (The convention did not allow debate on the E.R.A.) Several nun-delegates told the press that they supported the conference position on abortion, and several criticized what they termed the "obstructionist tactics" of the anti-abortionists.[52]

As an issue abortion is so sensitive because it has many ramifications beyond the immediate question of the rights of the unborn, a fact at least dimly sensed by people on both sides of the question. Already it has led into the issues of infanticide and euthanasia, which in turn are resurrecting long-forgotten theories of eugenics. On another level, abortion is a key expression of the therapeutic mentality, the assertion that the imperial self need tolerate no restraint from the outside. As a consequence, the humanity of the unborn child must be denied in favor of the unlimited rights of the mother. Those who say abortion is immoral but ought not to be forbidden by law are thus in the position of saying that the law should permit the killing of helpless persons. The act of self-assertiveness which is abortion, the claim to unlimited personal freedom which underlies it, becomes something sacred, and the moral questionability which surrounds it merely adds to its charism. The therapeutic personality cannot rest until every taboo has been broken, of which the relationship of mother and child is one of the most sacred.

Abortion is also so sensitive because it is the issue chosen by the enlightened consensus to use as the entering wedge in its final campaign against the survival of a distinctly Christian world view. Christian values will be allowed to survive only to the degree that they have been encompassed by this enlightened consensus and their religious content largely filtered out. Catholics who wish to play an influential role on the national scene soon discover that their repudiation of the Catholic position on abortion is almost the first thing required of them.

A particularly interesting example of this is the career of the last nun-president of Manhattanville College, once considered the most prestigious Catholic women's college in America. At first indignantly denying that her "reforms" of the college were having the effect of secularizing it, she eventually resigned the presidency, left the Sacred Heart Order, and set in motion the process by which the college legally gave up its religious identity. A few years later, in her capacity as "philanthropic advisor to the Rockefeller Brothers," she publicly attacked the anti-abortion movement and urged the American bishops to abandon the campaign because it was unsuccessful.[53] (Shortly thereafter the anti-abortion movement in fact won several important judicial and legislative victories.) The Rockefeller brothers have for years given massive financial support to a variety of population-control programs, including abortion. The priest-president of Notre Dame University was in 1977 elected chairman of the board of the Rockefeller Foundation, which also gives money to abortion projects.[54]

This eagerness on the part of some Catholics to join the liberal consensus on its own terms is merely symptomatic, however, of a far more serious threat facing the Church, namely, neo-Erastianism, eventually a kind of totalitarianism. It advocates that the needs and interests of the state dominate all aspects of life and the doctrine of the separation of church and state relegates religion to a purely private affair, permitted to have no public voice.

At first such a possibility may seem so far-fetched as to be fantastic, especially since avant-garde Catholics have been highly critical of certain government policies, even (as in the case of the Berrigan brothers) to the point of disobeying the law and suffering the consequences. But the positions which avant-garde Catholicism have taken in recent years have been, even when antistate, so heavily political that political considerations almost totally dominate, submerging properly religious considerations. Whether as supporters or critics of the government in power, progressive Catholics allow that government in effect to establish the rules of discourse, and they look towards the state for the eventual solution of all social problems.

With unforeseen speed, due largely to a 1973 Supreme Court decision, the United States adopted official encouragement of abortion as one of its policies. The right to have an abortion was suddenly enshrined in the Constitution alongside freedom of speech and the press. Tax money is, despite certain restrictions, used to pay for abortions. Government agencies officially favor them as a method of birth control.

In a pluralistic society with no fundamental moral principles shared by everyone, official government policy comes to define morality for many people. When the Supreme Court decreed in 1973 that abortions would henceforth be legal, that the Constitution guaranteed the "right" to have an abortion, for many Americans this was tantamount to proclaiming that abortions were moral. The thought that the Federal government might guarantee a "right" which was in fact an immorality was unthinkable. There were strong psychological pressures to defend the practice of abortion.

Thus despite the opinion of several highly respected secular scholars that the Supreme Court's 1973 abortion decision was bad constitutional law,[55] a priest who was an associate dean of a Catholic law school hailed *Roe* v. *Wade* as "Christian" and said that the Vatican Council's decree on religious liberty would prohibit Catholics from "imposing" their moral principles on others. Hence attempts to amend the Constitution to prohibit abortion were declared to be "reprehensible" and Catholics were told that they should praise the Court's "pro-life" stand.[56]

Once abortion had come to be enshrined in the Constitution, to oppose it seemed almost a sacrilege—progressive Catholics are likely to have far more reverence for that document than for the creeds of their Church. Thus the Jesuit Congressman Robert Drinan first refused to support any anti-abortion legislation, then became a firm supporter of bills to fund abortion through tax money ("we have no right to go against the Supreme Court"), and finally rejoiced that in agreeing to finance abortions through government medical payments Congress had staved off a threat to a "basic constitutional right." Father Drinan in effect proclaimed moral and religious principles to be divisive and excluded them from the realm of politics. A journalist for National Catholic News rejoiced that Catholics in Congress had demonstrated their "independence" from hierarchical control by the refusal of a number of them to support anti-abortion legislation. But in this as in other matters, independence is defined only with respect to Catholic orthodoxy, not to other kinds. Father Drinan, for example, received a perfect rating from Americans for Democratic Action, a liberal, largely secular lobbying group, and won approval from the Friends' Committee on National Legislation (a Quaker group) on twelve of thirteen Congressional votes.[57]

The willingness to allow the state to define the permissible limits of Catholic moral behavior is a growing tendency in the American Church:

> A leading moral theologian, a priest, has argued that, since many people do not think abortion is wrong, it ought not to be prohibited by law. (By this reasoning slavery would never have been outlawed.) He also posits the "independence" of the secular world from all religious authority and that Catholic hospitals can permit sterilizations if this is a condition of receiving public aid.[58]

> A Jesuit moralist, also on the issue of sterilization, has postulated a dilemma between hospital guidelines "generated by the hierarchy" and "the pressing demands of service to the people in a pluralistic society" and also predictably concludes that Catholic hospitals have no right to be "rigid" on the question. Significantly, the "needs" of the people are here equated with official government policy. A committee of the Catholic Theological Society of America has designated Catholic hospitals as "quasi-public" institutions which ought to permit medical procedures forbidden by Catholic doctrine, and the United States Catholic Conference has submitted a proposed pastoral letter on health care to the scrutiny of, among others, the president of

the Rockefeller Foundation, John Knowles, who seeks to force Catholic hospitals to perform abortions.[59]

The California Catholic Conference declined to lobby for anti-abortion legislation on the grounds that it was unlikely to be approved. After first opposing a "death with dignity" bill, the Conference withdrew its objections and allowed the bill to pass. Subsequently the majority floor leader of the legislature stated that the bill, which he characterized as permitting euthanasia, passed because the C.C.C. allowed its "neutrality" to be construed as approval. The legislator charged that the law as passed left elderly people at the mercy of those who might try to pressure them into signing a "living will."[60]

The myth that, on questions like abortion and sterilization, the state is merely neutral, neither forbidding nor denying particular human actions, has understandable appeal for those Christians who face the problem of becoming good citizens of the secular city. However, it has little basis in reality. The modern liberal state is, for better or for worse, an active organ which is never neutral, constantly employing its power, its money, its influence, and its personnel for or against particular social policies. Avant-garde Catholics are caught in a mesh of hopeless contradictions, simultaneously urging that politics partakes of a moral and religious significance but deploring attempts to "intrude" religion into politics, and insisting that Christians must "witness" to justice and truth but that they must also not "impose" their values on other people.

The result is to deny any distinctively Christian influence over the political process at the very time that important moral decisions are made through that process. The moral tone of society for the next quarter-century is being set largely as a result of certain judicial and legislative decisions towards which progressive Catholics are either benignly favorable or naively indifferent. There is no more striking contrast in contemporary society than that between the confident and aggressive social reformer and the diffident Christian afraid to be thought fanatical.

The fact that contraception was the issue on which the avant-garde chose to demonstrate its independence from ecclesiastical dictation is highly significant, because it is also the issue which serves as the means to exchange the dominance of the church for the dominance of the state. The modern liberal state is committed to a policy of population control, both within its own borders and in the Third World, where it distributes contraception, abortion, and sterilization information and equipment at the expense of the American taxpayers. Voluntary limitation of family size has so far been effective in the United States, but the more outspoken advocates of zero population growth have made it clear that coercive measures will be taken if necessary. The coming together of several factors—environmentalism, the threat of excess population, the corresponding fear over diminishing resources, and the feminist demand for liberation from motherhood—make it not at all unrealistic that totalitarian government will be introduced into the West, if it is, under the rationale of human survival, an overarching necessity which "irresponsible" individuals cannot be permitted to endanger. The fact that an acceptance of the contraceptive mentality has been made a badge of Catholic emancipation will permit many Catholics to be servants of this totalitarianism, knowingly or not. In 1977 a group of American family-planning experts toured Communist China and applauded the Chinese success in regulating population, under a system whereby women report their methods of birth control to government authorities and receive quotas as to the number and spacing of children they are permitted to bear.[61] A leading American Catholic newspaper published an anonymous article calling for "realism" in population control. "Contrary to popular belief," the author asserts, freedom means "freedom from instinctive control." "Unguided behavior" and society's need for survival dictate that restraints be imposed on those who refuse to restrain themselves.[62] Those who began by rejecting papal "interference" with their sex lives may well end by passively allowing the state to regulate human reproduction by law, just as some Protestant churches which began by affirming a right to use contraceptives have moved virtually to the point of requiring it as a condition of being "responsible."

There is in fact a long tradition in Catholicism whereby those who are dissatisfied with the Church's failure to reform itself turn instead to the state as an instrument for forcible reform. Marsilius of Padua, John Wyclif, Martin Luther, Henry VIII, Joseph II of Austria, and many others fall into this category, the religious "liberals" of each age willingly acquiescing in the extension of state power in order to achieve the desired "updated" church. Those Catholics who have, historically, regarded papal authority as an illegitimate usurpation, or have sought to diminish its scope in the interest of an independent "local church," have particularly fallen prey to dominance by the state, since the papacy has for many centuries been a bulwark of protection behind which the church in each nation has been able to assert at least a measure of independence against the state.

The English historian Lord Acton, for instance, a hero to many modern liberal Catholics, not only opposed the definition of papal infallibility at the First Vatican Council but entered into an alliance with representatives of the English and German governments to hinder its proclamation. He shared a view, common among many liberal Catholics of the time, that the appointment of bishops by the state was a proper thing.[63] It is significant in this connection that while many Catholic ecumenists, in their dealings with the Church of England, have lamented that the papal office is a stumbling block to unity, few have suggested that the anomaly whereby Anglican bishops are appointed by the state is at least an equal stumbling block. (One prominent modern Anglican ecumenist, a bishop, favored continuation of that system because it permitted political and social radicals to attain episcopal office.[64])

The prospect of state control of religion may seem remote because of the American tradition of separation between the two, the constitutional guarantee of religious freedom, and the fact that many avant-garde Christians have taken a stance of resistance to the state in recent years. But the tradition of looking to a benign and "enlightened" state to remedy the deficiencies of the church remains, even in the United States:

A Pennsylvania nun flew to Florida to oppose anti-abortion legislation on the grounds that "Catholic doctrine is changing" and permissive laws about abortion would facilitate that change. Her testimony included the bizarre assertion that, as celibates, nuns could be more "objective" about abortion than could mothers.[65]

Although the courts have consistently refused to permit tax assistance to Catholic schools on the grounds of the doctrine of the separation of church and state, various government agencies have been asked on several occasions to intervene to force these schools to rehire teachers who had been dismissed for various reasons, some having to do with Catholic doctrine and discipline. How the courts will eventually rule on these demands is still unclear. However, a Catholic newspaper has thunderingly called on the National Labor Relations Board to administer "the cold douche of the law" to the Church and ridiculed the idea that any question of religious liberty is at stake.[66] Catholic liberals commonly invest the state with powers of coercion they deny the Church, thus leaving the Church always dependent on the state's good will.

The director of human relations for the city of Detroit, a former priest of the Detroit archdiocese, threatened the archdiocesan agencies with the loss of all government contracts unless half of their staff members were black. The archdiocese's defense—that the twenty per cent of its staff that was black was more than twice the percentage of black Catholics in the city—was disallowed.[67]

When the city of Wichita passed a homosexual rights' law, the bishop announced that, despite the law, the diocese would not permit known homosexuals to teach in Catholic schools. The director of the city's human-rights commission then announced that he would welcome the opportunity to force the diocese to conform. There were vicious attacks on the bishops in some segments of the Catholic press. Meanwhile, in St. Paul, suit was brought to force a Catholic parish to hire a militantly homosexual teacher.[68]

The vice-chariman of the Democratic Party in California, a former nun, publicly attacked the Vatican's choice as bishop of a new California diocese and proposed her own candidate.[69]

Also in California, a state official warned churches that they would lose their tax exemptions if they encouraged their members to sign a petition to repeal a homosexuals'-rights law.[70]

The question of the moral orientation of the schools and, more broadly, the moral philosophy embodied in all programs supported by the law and by taxes, is obviously crucial to the future of society, and it is an issue to which progressive Christians have made themselves willfully insensitive. A former attorney for the American Jewish Committee, one of the principal architects of a series of court decisions whereby, over a period of years, religion was banned from the American public schools and all forms of public aid were denied to religious schools, has announced "the triumph of secular humanism." In his analysis the churches have, over the years, suffered a series of political defeats on matters like prayer in the schools, contraception, abortion, divorce, and pornography, to the point where religion is all but banned from public life. As a result, even church members have gradually come to accept the general secularist consensus on most issues. Catholic colleges, he predicts, will inevitably become secular, and the Catholic Church will be forced, sooner or later, to accept the morality of abortion. There will be no alternative to "secular humanism" as the prevailing philosophy.[71] Ironically this analysis, sung as a hymn of triumph, is rejected by most "enlightened" Catholics when it comes to them from alarmed fellow Catholics. (At the University of San Francisco, a Jesuit has filed a complaint with the National Labor Relations Board demanding to be allowed to teach a course in Catholic spirituality. In the future, government agencies may have the power to determine who is or is not qualified to teach courses in Catholic theology.[72])

In order to qualify for public assistance in New York State, colleges and universities are required to explain and justify to the state any religious affiliation they may have, including whether they teach "any denominational tenet or doctrine." The state may, if it wishes, send a team of inspectors to the college to investigate its departments of philosophy and theology and to judge whether its library has a disproportionate number of "denominational" books.[73] The irony of this situation, to which most Catholic colleges in New York have conformed, is that Catholic educators who for so long proudly proclaimed their independence from the Church and its hierarchy have for the most part supinely accepted whatever conditions the state chooses to impose as the price of survival.

The state alone is now conceded the right to teach with authority. Catholics who have rejected ecclesiastical authority are sometimes attracted to the power of the state as a substitute. For example, a Catholic moral theologian, a former priest who by his writings did much to promote the "emancipation" of Catholics from ecclesiastical authority, argues vigorously for the intervention of government bureaucracies to promote "equality" and "justice" and ridicules the "invidious" notion of individual liberty. ("He who wills the end of justice must will the necessary means to that end.")[74] After President Carter's election one of his aides, a former Catholic three of whose sisters are nuns, told the press that "the Catholic Church does a better job of screwing people than any other institution around." A few months later he proposed that children be encouraged to report to the government whether their parents were consuming too much energy in their homes.[75]

There was a generally unperceived symbolic significance in the large numbers of priests and religious who abandoned their sacred callings in the age of *aggiornamento* in order to take positions in government bureaucracies or bureaucracies of private or semipublic social agencies closely linked to government. In its early centuries the Church was able to attract men like Ambrose and Augustine away from governmental careers and into its own service; now the reverse is true—government is perceived to be the center of power and authority in a way the Church no longer is. In 1972 a Boston archdiocesan priest joined the staff of Mayor John Lindsay of New York, in a job paying $30,000 per year. He publicly supported the mayor's stand in favor of legalized abortion and, when he was subsequently recalled to do parish work in Boston, resigned from the priesthood.[76] Although in the Church they boldly proclaimed the right of dissent, they often find that in these bureaucracies conformity to established policies is expected and required.

In all ages the structure of the Church has inevitably been affected by the prevailing political systems. Perhaps never in its history, however, has the obligation of the Church to conform to the dominant models of secular government—in this case democracy—been asserted more insistently, to the point where the democratization of the Church has become for many people a goal in itself, without reference to what the Church's underlying purpose is. With the corresponding decline of a vital sense of the transcendent, the Church is in danger of merely becoming another ingredient in the general enlightened consensus, without distinctive voice or authority of its own. This seems already to have happened to certain Protestant churches.

What avant-garde Catholics perhaps do not understand, or do not want to understand, is how the forms of democracy are being effectively manipulated to create a worldly utopia, a humanistic consensus which will encompass the entire Western world and a good part of the East as well. In this consensus the "enlightened" state (or, more ambitiously, an enlightened superstate transcending conventional political boundaries) will be the focus of all human energies, the machine whereby progress is achieved, and whatever seems to retard that consensus will be harassed and eventually outlawed. At the 1975 International Women's Year forum in Mexico City, sponsored by the United Nations, one of the moderators refused to allow any argument against abortion and proclaimed that "religion is a disease of the world."[77] At a 1976 UN conference in Canada a staff member made a speech ridiculing Mother Teresa of Calcutta; it was reprinted in a Catholic newspaper.[78]

The World Health Organization has defined health as "a state of complete physical, mental, and social well-being and not merely the absence of disease or infirmity."[79] Another United Nations study urges a campaign to promote a "positive" attitude towards sexuality all over the world. Children are to be taught that sex for pleasure is valid and are not to be taught that sex is sinful.[80] One commentator notes that "official sanctions of a paradisical ideal" encourage bureaucratic action and asks, "Once started, where will they stop of their own accord?"[81]

The totalitarian state of the future, whether national or international, is less likely to arise from crudely "fascistic" and militaristic sources, against which many people are now on their guard, than from seemingly benign and freedom-loving agencies promising health, happiness, self-fulfillment, and—the trump card—survival. Sex education is a far more potent device than liberal Catholics can allow themselves to imagine, because it often seeks to break the authority which religion and family have over the private lives of children, seeks to make their moral education solely the function of the enlightened secular consensus. The concept of "fit parenthood," already recognized by the law, may prove indefinitely expandable, to exclude those parents whose attitudes are deemed too rigid, negative, dogmatic, and backward to be allowed to raise children.

Ordinarily the Catholic Church would be considered a major bulwark against such a development, because of its traditional strong emphasis on family autonomy. But that emphasis has weakened considerably. It is ironic that the most impassioned recent defense of the family has come not from a Catholic but from a secular-minded socialist.[82] It is also likely that in the years ahead the Church's own institutions—its schools and hospitals, especially—will be squeezed out of existence by the state so that the state enjoys a monopoly in all sensitive areas of life.

Some Catholics in fact seem already to have conceded the battle in advance. Daniel Berrigan, for example, has been strongly critical of families and enamored of communal methods of child-raising.[83] At one of the regional hearings of the 1976 Call to Action Conference the invited "experts" included a sociologist who announced that he was "not personally disposed toward the conservative, moralistic position about the role of the family in American society" and proceeded to give an essentially negative assessment of marriage and motherhood. He ended by calling for public policy that would impose "constraints" on the freedom of action of individuals ("I am not advocating the traditional family and individual freedom at the same time") and called attention to styles of communal child-raising available in other cultures. Following his talk a bishop congratulated him on his "excellent and provocative presentation" and asked whether, in order "to get the national commitment reversed, do we not need a more authoritarian government than we now have. . . ?" The sociologist responded that such might indeed be necessary.[84]

Many postconciliar Catholics have in reality already had an experience of benign totalitarianism, without realizing it. This has been particularly the case with certain religious communities whose quest for renewal has been through encounter groups and other exercises in group dynamics in which, in the name of greater "openness" and "growth," long-held values have been turned topsy-turvy and changes of belief of global proportions have been introduced amazingly rapidly. A concern with process for its own sake and the idea that human nature is capable of limitless remolding leaves the individual finally without a core of stable being.

Philip Reiff points out how the totalitarian state is maximally able to use empty people, especially people who have been rendered empty by an unstinting embrace of the therapeutic spirit. The state will, in fact, encourage therapy, which ultimately proves to be compatible with totalitarianism. The totalitarian spirit, he insists, is not fanatical, and he cites Hannah Arendt's observation that "the aim of totalitarian education has never been to instill convictions but to destroy the capacity to form any."[85]

CHAPTER 9

The Coming World Religion

THERE has been a curious double thrust to much of contemporary Catholicism, a thrust which on first appearance seems to be contradictory. On the one hand there is an unusual emphasis on local communities, to the point where many Catholics seem to have become fervent congregationalists. They treasure their own liturgies and their own religious experiences, and demonstrate indifference or even hostility to the liturgy and doctrines of the whole Church. Episcopal authority is all but denied, papal authority routinely sneered at. Yet on the other hand there is an equally fervent desire to overcome all manifestations of narrowness and provinciality. The people who seem to believe that their own small corner of the Church can best flourish without external "interference" are often the very people who wish to reach out to all mankind, convinced that the religious experiences of the human race are ultimately one.

This double thrust is merely paradoxical, however, not contradictory, and in fact is quite logical, reflecting one of the most ominous, if largely unnoticed, trends in contemporary society. For what it reflects is simply the desire to abolish all intermediate communities, of which churches and families are the most vulnerable. Nation-states are equally disliked but are not likely to crumble in the foreseeable future. The withdrawal into localism, and even into a solipsistic individualism, is first of all a personal declaration of independence, an act of freeing oneself from that community which at the moment seems most oppressive. The particular liturgical community, occasionally an actual canonical parish, declares itself in effect free of the "tyranny" of its bishop, free to go wherever it thinks the Spirit is moving it. (Certain religious communities do the same thing.) The national Church is declared best able to solve its problems without "Roman interference." However, the simultaneous proclamation of a sense of solidarity with the whole human race, and particularly with those segments of the human race whose cultures are most remote from one's own, is also intended as an act of liberation. What is being proclaimed is that the individual has no culture to which he or she must remain faithful, that family, religion, and nationality are mere accidents of birth that can and must be discarded.

Involved here is a cultural process which parallels the totalitarian political process already described. The contemporary political radical often asserts his personal freedom in a fanatical way, only to end by just as fervently becoming the servant of the totalitarian state. The fanatical drive for freedom masks a yearning for unwavering authority. So also those most inclined to deify their own experiences often end by willingly submerging those experiences in some version or other of a new universal culture.

In Christianity a number of factors have helped to promote this condition, which is much more clearly visible in liberal Protestantism than it is in Catholicism and seems hardly visible at all in conservative Protestantism. The demythologizing first of dogma, then of Scripture; the tendency to see ethical behavior as the only genuine criterion of real Christianity; the habit of continually reformulating Christian teaching to get rid of its "outmoded" elements; the instinctive acceptance of prevailing cultural assumptions as normative for faith; and the willingness to regard good will and sincerity among men as all that ultimately matters combine to encourage the slow disappearance of anything like a distinctive Christianity in visible continuity with the church over two thousand years and thereby render Christians vulnerable to any religious movement which seems to possess the aggressive vitality their own church lacks.

The statements of the Second Vatican Council regarding ecumenical relationships are in many ways conservative, a fact predictably glossed over by the media in their eagerness to explain the "true" meaning of the Council, and popular ignorance of what the Council really said has sometimes been knowingly exploited by people within the Church who wish it had said something different. Among the Council's actual sayings, in its decree on ecumenism, is:

> For it is through Christ's Catholic Church alone, which is the all-embracing means of salvation, that the fullness of the means of salvation can be obtained. It was to the apostolic college alone, of which Peter is the head, that we believe our Lord entrusted all the blessings of the New Covenant, in order to establish on earth the one Body of Christ into which all those should be fully incorporated who already belong in any way to God's People. [1]

The Council noted defects in those churches "separated from us," said that all people are called to belong to the Church, and urged the necessity of evangelistic activity towards conversion. Even in its declaration on religious freedom, the Council asserted that there was one true Church, made known to men by God.

Departing from the kind of ecumenism mandated in these conciliar documents, many Catholics came to regard the "scandal of disunity" as so great that it was to be overcome by any means possible. The most effective means, it was soon discovered, was large doses of modern cultural relativism. Since all beliefs mainly reflect the culture in which they were formulated, an essential unity could be assumed to underlie apparent differences. The various churches could in different ways abandon or radically redefine their own distinctive doctrines in the interests of a unity which finally came to depend only on good will. In what was falsely termed "grass-roots ecumenism" (it was actually quite elitist), cooperative eucharists and other manifestations of interdenominational unity were made to depend precisely on the assertion that doctrines did not matter, all doctrines being more or less equally false.

But to apply such attitudes merely to ecumenism within Christian boundaries was always arbitrary and, once formulated, such ideas were bound to extend the ecumenical horizon to the entire world. An ecumenism which began by asserting proudly that fidelity to Christ was alone the test of the true Christian, not adherence to the doctrines of a particular church, would end by finding Christ merely one more sectarian obstacle to unity. A good will embracing the entire human race would emerge as the only necessary common denominator. Although few Catholics have formally developed a theory of the eventual merging of world religions, certain ideas and actions seem to be based on that assumption.

The process of renewal in the Church has (as discussed in Chapter Two) been for some people essentially a denial of the historical nature of Christianity, an attempt to eradicate by fiat certain historical developments of the Church which are deemed to be unfortunate, in the interests of recovering a "pure" church uncorrupted by history. Ecumenism provided the excuse for abolishing the Reformation and the Counter Reformation, the former now interpreted as merely a series of unfortunate misunderstandings, the latter a reactionary deformation which should now be undone.

But the movement backwards through history to find pure Christianity was bound, given the nature of the momentum which sustained it, to continue beyond the supposed purity of early Christianity. Having first, in their own minds, successfully collapsed Protestantism and

Catholicism together in a spiritual union independent of historical developments, the reformers now seek nothing less than to collapse Christianity back into Judaism, to wipe out all two thousand years of Christian history. It is a movement supported by some Christians of good will because of their overwhelming sense of guilt at the slaughter of the European Jews during World War II.

The most extreme statement of this position, in which Christianity's historical right to exist is virtually denied, comes from Rosemary Ruether.[2] A priest-theologian has also suggested cautiously:

> What these theologians are generally saying is that Christianity must re-examine its belief that the Messianic age, the time of fulfillment, took place at the coming of Christ. However we may eventually come to explain the uniqueness of the Christ event (something we must maintain if we are to avoid emasculating Christianity), we can no longer simply say that the Jewish idea of the Messianic age, far more important to Judaism than the idea of a personal Messiah, was realized in the Death-Resurrection of Christ. We may still call Jesus the Messiah but we are going to have to radically reshape our definition of this term.

The same priest urges abandonment of the term *Old Testament* in the interest of a concept of "equality between the two faith communities."[3]

The assertion of equality of faiths falls soothingly on modern ears, but is impossible if each faith is to be taken seriously. A Christianity in which Christ is denied to be the Messiah is not really Christianity, and thus "equality" is achieved by one faith repudiating its identity. A leading Jewish spokesman has declared that such equality is "quite unacceptable—on Jewish grounds," because Judaism claims to be the "truest" religion and expects that claim to be taken seriously. Hence Judaism is not offended by the claim of other faiths that they are the "truest" religions. To deny Christians the right to make such a claim would, he argues, be in effect to deny Judaism the same right. Judaism rejects Christian theology and thus cannot demand that such theology be reformulated to make it acceptable to Judaism.[4] Another leading Jewish scholar points out that while a weakening of Christian self-confidence may lead to a diminution of Christian forms of anti-Semitism, it also leads to an increase in non-Christian or pagan anti-Semitism. This new anti-Semitism, more intellectually respectable than the old, is especially manifest in Christians who have exchanged their religious orthodoxies for political orthodoxies. He detects in some apparent Christian philo-Semitism "manifestations of Christian self-hatred," in which Judaism is merely used by people interested in striking a blow against the Christian Church.[5]

Just as the basis of Christian ecumenism was supposed to be a devotion to Christ which would overcome all sectarian differences, so the new attempt at Jewish-Christian reunification is supposed to be the sharing of a common Scripture and the worship of the same God. But just as Christ had to be denied central importance in order to achieve rapprochement with Judaism, so also the unique importance of God's dealing with the Jews is (predictably) denied so as to permit both Christianity and Judaism to be assimilated in the other great world religions. If the Jewishness of Jesus can be emphasized to the point where there is no longer even a distinct movement called Christianity, so the elements which Judaism allegedly shares with other religions can be emphasized to the point where the existence of Judaism, and of Christianity as an offshoot from it, comes to be seen as merely a historical and cultural accident.

A Benedictine monk who has spent some years in India has led the way in relativizing both Christian and Jewish beliefs so as to give them no more than a status of equality with Hinduism. He first denies that a genuinely revealed religion is found only within Judaism and Christianity, and differences between Hebrew and Hindu religion are reduced simply to "different experiences of God." In the end, he asserts, "'God' is a name which we give to that ultimate mystery of existence which cannot properly be named," and whatever names have been employed by the various religions of the world can be taken as rough equivalents. Hinduism is then conceded a certain superiority to Christianity in its refusal to "impose" doctrines on its followers. In traditional Christianity, he insists, "There is nothing . . . whether it is its dogmatic formulas or its sacramental system or its hierarchical organization, which is not subject to change." The only changeless thing is "the voice of the Spirit in every Scripture."[6] Another Benedictine monk has written about the translation into English of an anthology of Vedic sayings, "A decade or so ago the *Jerusalem Bible* inaugurated a new phase in community prayer. Now the time is ripe to add a second volume: the Bible of the gentiles," which would, he says, stand next to the Jewish-Christian Bible "as its companion volume." Christians are invited to integrate Vedic prayer and doctrine fully into their own worship.[7]

The author was once present at a talk by a Trappist monk, a former abbot, who told his mostly Catholic listeners that, if they paid attention to religious experience only, they would discover that all these experiences of mankind are identical and differences between religions therefore illusory. "Do not worry about theology; it will only confuse you," was his convenient advice. In his talk the name of Jesus Christ was not mentioned even once, and when a member of the audience asked whether Christian religious experience was not centered on the person of Christ, the monk evaded the question and treated it as though it were the expression of a hopelessly narrow and underdeveloped mind.

Much contemporary Catholic theology has so emphasized the concept of religious experience that the idea of a divine revelation which transcends human experience, a faith which requires people to believe precisely in things unseen, is in danger of being lost. The emergence of this dominant idea of experience is no historical accident. It feeds directly the contemporary cultural hunger for total self-sufficiency, the instinctive rejection of anything which is imposed on the individual from the outside. Conveniently, it provides the basis for a religion which is endlessly malleable and manipulable, because it has no objective weight and is purely a function of personal experiences.

Despite the Second Vatican Council's uncompromising assertion of the unique and dominating importance of Jesus Christ,[8] He has in fact been treated with remarkable cavalierness by some postconciliar Catholics. The search for a "human Jesus" has gone far beyond a salutary reminder that He was indeed fully human and has reached a point where certain people are embarrassed at any remnants of Christ's divinity. "You can't identify with Superman," says the editor of a diocesan newspaper, and adds, "Jesus the wonder-worker may be the average Christian's biggest stumbling block to mature faith."[9] A popularizing theologian denies to Jesus the title of redeemer and sees in Him merely an example or inspiration. Furthermore, "one reason why divinity [of Christ] would seem not to be an issue, to start with, is that apparently everything is somehow divine." The author, a Christian Brother, complains that "I had lived through a phase of the American Catholic Church when St. Paul's enthusiastic exclamations about Jesus were held up as a mark of authentic faith and when parish practices were a kind of Jesus religion."[10] A popular Dominican author blandly asks "how history has been altered by the deaths of Jesus; of Lenin's brother; of John Kennedy; of Martin Luther King Jr.,"[11] as though all four were moral and theological equivalents. Another priest casually insists that the historical truth of New Testament narratives about Jesus is of no interest or importance, the question based on a "Western misunderstanding."[12]

Certain questions concerning the identity of Jesus, supposedly closed since the fourth century, have been reopened in the last quarter of the twentieth not, as it is sometimes asserted, merely in the interests of scholarly honesty but because the culture demands a Jesus cut down to human size. Two purposes are thereby served, an individual and a social one. On the individual level it serves the needs of those people who cannot bear the thought that there is something greater in the universe than themselves, something or someone to whom they must submit. Socially it helps make possible the great fusion of all religions which is the desire of some of the most "progressive" people in the various churches, people whose ambitions have already gone far beyond schemes for the reunion only of Christianity. The greatest single obstacle to such world unity is the looming figure of Jesus Christ the Lord, calling all people to Himself. But a demythologized Jesus no longer constitutes such an obstacle.

A priest-theologian has expressed "impatience" at efforts towards Christian unity based on historical theology and biblical studies and postulates an inevitable convergence of world religions which individual faiths will be powerless to resist. He offers as a salient example the inability of Asian countries to resist the triumph of European Marxism.[13] At one point the Berrigan brothers were willing to extend the Eucharist to one of their associates who was a Moslem, and Elizabeth McAlister (the nun who later married Philip Berrigan) explained that to receive the Eucharist it was not necessary to believe in Christ but merely "to believe in this as a sacred and important act to engage in." After conversation, members of the group noted striking parallels between their own Christianity and the Moslem faith of their companion.[14] The companion, Eqbal Ahmad, repaid this confidence by publicly criticizing the piety of the Berrigans, while admitting its strategic political usefulness.[15]

However, the most significant, if perhaps extreme, insight into the syncretistic nature of avant-garde Christianity is provided by Rosemary Ruether. Her achievement in decimating historical Christianity in favor of a return to Judaism might be thought sufficient for one person in one lifetime. However, her ambitions extend a good deal further:

> Through him [an anti-Christian college professor] I discovered the meaning of religious symbols not as extrinsic doctrines but as living metaphors of human existence.
>
> . . . I knew that Ba'al was a real god, the revelation of the mystery of life, the expressions of the depths of being which had broken through into the lives of the people and gave them a key to the mystery of death and rebirth. . . . As for the defects of Ba'al, were they more spectacular than the defects of the biblical God or Messiah, or perhaps less so? . . .
>
> . . . I could not give allegiance to any "jealous god" on the level of historical particularity. . . .
>
> I could not tell her [a nun] that my devotion to Mary was somewhat less than my devotion to some more powerful females that I knew: Isis, Athena, Artemis.[16]

Professor Ruether relates that she formed these opinions while still an undergraduate, and thus held them throughout the period when she had a public identity as an orthodox Catholic theologian.

It may be objected that such ideas are indeed extreme and that few contemporary Christians, of any denomination, are consciously advocating a synthesis of world religions in this fashion. However, the objection has validity only to about the same degree as the objection that relatively few Christians are conscious devotees of political totalitarianism. The point in both cases is that many people who would stop short of advocating either a totalitarian state or a great world religion nonetheless serve the ends of either, or both, unwittingly. In particular they do so by systematically weakening organized Christianity in such a way that it is easily usable by those who do advocate such things, and they succeed in creating conditions which make it difficult if not impossible for the Church to resist being used.

The demythologizing of Christianity, as argued in Chapter Two, means primarily its dehistoricizing. It is the attempt to reduce Christianity to a set of ideas, metaphors, or symbols which in some way reflect human realities. The elements which make up Christianity, including finally the "symbol" of Christ Himself, are deemed capable of being endlessly relativized and adjusted to suit the presumed needs of a particular time and place, or even the presumed needs of particular individuals. A priest-theologian, for example, says

> They [the Christian churches] must resist with all their strength the literalist spirit that is destructive of the meaning of the Bible and preserve the poetic imagery that alone conveys its meaning. . . . The Scriptures are meant by God to allay madness, not to induce it.

> A healthy culture cannot endure large segments of its population out of touch with reality. The Christian churches that know the Bible as something God has given them for use, not as the oracular pronouncements of a printed deity, must in the next quarter century instruct . . . with a special view to their members and others who would wrest these books to their own (and others') destruction. [17]

The new "liberated" style of Catholicism is a weightless Catholicism in which individuals are free to make use of its various elements in whatever way they choose. An American bishop, for instance, ridicules the notion of credal orthodoxy and the idea that "in the lives of the saints you find true orthodoxy," relentlessly warns his people against "nostalgia," and urges constant "progress" in religion. [18] A theologian denies that the Church has access to any "divine information" and proposes "contemporary experience" and "the human race church" as the normative criteria for change. The Bible is characterized as "a collection of human documents . . . the word of man," and the idea is denied that Christianity is founded on the direct words of Jesus. Men have no ability to talk about God, and all such talk is said to be merely "a God fashioned wholly by human tools to serve human needs. . . ."[19] A Jesuit theologian writes that "both dogma and liturgy are roadmap and vehicle for a journey into experience which simplifies the self," and the Church has no unique resources for this spiritual quest. "The Jesus-symbol often becomes a substitute rather than a vehicle for attuning us to the unfathomable mystery of our being. . . . If any of this generation decide to take seriously the spiritual journey, they are virtually forced to renounce the church's 'Christ.' "[20]

What is thereby produced is a virtual supermarket religion, in which shoppers (no longer worshipers or believers in the traditional sense of either word) pick and choose what they find attractive, hurry home with their purchases, and try them out in infinite varieties of combinations. The most forthright expression of this spirit has come from the most fashionable theologian of the 1960s, Harvey Cox, a Baptist with much influence in Catholic circles:

> I will not let the Catholics keep St. Teresa or the Unitarians have Michael Servetus or the Jews have Martin Buber or the Hindus have Lord Krishna all for themselves. . . . Within a span of weeks I have sensed the presence of the holy at an Apollo temple at Delphi, a Toltec pyramid in Xochicalco, and a Moslem mosque on the island of Rhodes. What would an anthropologist from Mars make of our family's rituals and the cultic objects in our house? We celebrate the Seder at Passover. We often attend Catholic Masses, never missing on Christmas Eve. A straw Mexican Indian crucifix blesses our living room, and a Jewish *mazuzah* enclosing a text from the Torah stands watch at our doorway. A serene Buddha gazes down from just over the inside windowsill of our front room. Nearby stands Ganesha, the elephant god, who is the Hindu patron of sagacity and worldly wisdom.[21]

Such an approach to religion purports, among other things, to be more open-minded towards other faiths, less arrogant and exclusive. But its openness is bought at the high price noted above by the Jewish scholar—none can be taken seriously, none can be respected in their own terms. The liberal-minded Westerner's arrogance merely deepens as he ceases to believe in his own faith. His conviction grows that he can relativize the faiths of others just as he has relativized his own, and that this culture-bound process, so characteristic of the Western academic mind, has universal validity. The tolerant liberal mind is open to all faiths in the same way that a blender is open to all foods. Harvey Cox, for example, receiving a blessing from an Eastern Orthodox bishop, "explains" the blessing's meaning, which the bishop himself cannot be expected to understand.[22]

This new taste for supermarket religion is another inevitable product of late capitalism, because the habit of consumption eventually extends itself to spiritual as well as material things. As the classical Epicureans recognized, purely material habits of consumption—real hedonism—are ultimately unsatisfying and self-defeating. The spirit also has needs and desires and, properly fed, these desires can lead to experiences far more exquisite and pleasurable than purely bodily ones. A great industry has grown up to cater to this taste—Esalen and its many imitators, the human potential movement, the various schools of meditation, uncountable varieties of religious sects, etc.

It is often said that this proliferation of religious or quasi-religious movements, most of them unheard of twenty years ago, is evidence of people's search for meaning and of their spiritual anguish. But just as certainly it is a search for pleasure of a high order. People who have accustomed themselves over a period of years to the gratification of their every material desire gradually come to assume that their spiritual desires, once they discover that such exist, will also be gratified. Although he seeks wherever possible to "identify" with the poor, Harvey Cox seems not to recognize that the religious life-style which he extols depends on the opportunity to fly all over the world in order to pluck the choicest fruits of each religious tradition. Its viability depends either on personal wealth or skill in obtaining grants. The widow of Episcopal Bishop James A. Pike now guides a quasi-religious movement called The Love Project. She explains that when she travels, "Accommodations are always first class so unnecessary material annoyances do not slow down spiritual growth."[23]

Such an approach to religion must break radically with the past of Christianity not only in doctrines, rituals, and ecclesiastical structures but, most importantly, in the basic attitudes and assumptions which underlie that historical Christianity, particularly the belief that Christ summons men to discipleship, that this summons is issued with authority, and that no one can refuse it without peril to his soul. The most offensive text in Scripture, therefore rarely alluded to, is Christ's awesome statement, "You have not chosen Me. I have chosen you." Devotees of the new religiosity wish to remain free to be secularizers one year, would-be mystics the next. They will aspire to the austere simplicities of New Testament discipleship in certain of their moods, reverting to the mentality of sophisticated modern sceptics at other times. They will be Christians, but only so long as Christianity does not interfere with other ways of living which they may, at certain times, find equally attractive. This new religious Epicureanism is, not surprisingly, especially strong in California, the home of sophisticated pleasure-seeking at its best, where the worship of nature entwines with other pagan cults and where Christianity is inevitably sucked into the mixture.

Ordinary materialism has always been highly vulnerable to Christian criticism, and the eventual surfeits of a wholly materialistic way of life have historically been the occasions for some notable religious conversions. The new Epicureanism, precisely by including spiritual pleasures among its wares, seeks to make itself immune from such attacks. Religious conversions will no longer have relevance, both because the idea of repentance for sins has been declared unhealthy and because the would-be convert is told that whatever spiritual benefits he might have derived from a formal affiliation with Christianity are more easily obtainable in other ways. The fruit can be plucked without the need to prepare and till the soil, or even to understand how it is prepared and tilled.

The new religiosity is the ultimate self-centeredness, the final expression of the conviction that the universe owes the individual its full range of pleasures. A revived interest in mysticism, far from being a sign of a genuine renewed spirituality, is precisely the opposite—it is a search for the elusive but presumably exquisite mystical experience, the mentality which the great Christian mystics like St. Teresa constantly warned against. A Dominican spiritual writer urges drug-taking as a way of "democratizing" the mystical experience by obviating the need for many years of religious discipline. He also thinks that the popularity of taverns shows how common these experiences really are.[24] With the central idea of penitence amputated, what passes for the contemplative life becomes simply a self-gratifying interiority, the enjoyment of the pleasures associated with spirituality.

Philip Rieff diagnoses this phenomenon as the therapeutic ability to use all commitments while giving loyalty to none.

> . . . men will have ceased to seek any salvation other than amplitude in living itself. Faith can then grow respectable again, as one entertainable and passing pastoral experience among others, to enhance the interest of living freed from communal purpose.
>
> Psychological man, in his independence from all gods, can feel free to use all god-terms; I imagine he will be a hedger against his own bets, a user of any faith that lends itself to therapeutic use.
>
> The more the material satisfactions will be taken for granted, the more important would grow the spiritual satisfactions. What the consolations of religion and philosophy were to the millenial cultures of scarcity, the consolations of psychology would be to the culture of plenitude.
>
> Each god-toy is stamped for the user's mind-blowing: "This product has no compelling or directing element in it and need not be disbelieved."
>
> Among Western mystics there was no nonsense about getting high. Experienced timelessness was anything but a radical contemporaneity: that latter rejects the authority of the past, which mysticism accepts.[25]

It is important to note how the adoption of the therapeutic mentality imposes itself not only as a right but as a historical obligation. The Dominican spiritual writer who advocates drugs also sternly warns his readers against self-denial, since "enough evils and crosses exist in our lives without making up new ones." He is willing to permit it only for demonstrably self-enhancing purposes, such as to "heighten awareness and lower blood pressure."[26]

Perhaps the most eager devotees of the "new Church" are young people whose memories do not extend much beyond World War II, the formative period of whose conscious lives has been spent amidst the extraordinary and sustained prosperity of the postwar period. There is fixed, between them and many of the older generation of Catholics, a silent gulf of incomprehension, the nature of which is rarely alluded to. For most persons raised before 1940 life was accepted as involving deprivation, duty, and self-sacrifice. Religion was both a need and a duty and one of its principal purposes was to console those who suffered, to give meaning to lives which were in certain ways bleak. For many of the postwar generation, however, this sense of life is simply incomprehensible. Religion for them is neither a need nor a duty and has little to do with suffering. It is rather one more vehicle through which the individual seeks to expand his personal horizons as widely as possible, to summon for his own use the spiritual riches of the universe. Thus, while the modernizers of Catholicism have to some extent successfully adjusted it to the present cultural mood, they have also adjusted it to what may well be an aberrant and untypical phase of history, given the inevitable return to an economy of scarcity which many economists predict.

The process by which the firm and even rigid Catholicism of the preconciliar era has so easily been accommodated to this cultural phase took remarkably little time, proceeding through a number of identifiable stages: (1) The assertion that, while remaining faithful to its own dogmas, the Church could also render itself more open to other creeds and traditions. (2) The tendency to understand ecumenical agreement primarily in terms of good will and purity of intention. (3) A spirit of tolerance based less on strong-minded charity than on intellectual and moral flabbiness, a growing feeling that all doctrines and traditions are equally constricting. (4) The divorce of religion from its institutional matrix, so that the visible church comes to seem at best unnecessary to faith and possibly a hindrance. (5) The diminution of the sense of the universal church, with a corresponding emphasis on the autonomy of local churches, understood variously as national or ethnic entities or even as parishes and congregations. (6) An eclecticism which welcomes the prospect of taking from each religious tradition those elements which seem useful and relevant and ignoring those which do not. (7) The relativizing of all religious traditions so that none can be permitted to teach with authority. (8) An understanding of religion in which its sole purpose is to serve human needs. (9) The detaching of all religious symbols from their historical and especially their ecclesiastical matrices, so that each is made available for alien uses. (10) The tendency to understand religious symbols, and especially doctrinal formulations, as metaphorical only, means devised by the human intelligence to express its own deepest insights into the nature of reality. (11) The consequent willingness to accept human experience alone as the substance of religious belief and to exclude the possibility of a genuine divine revelation.

The divorce of religious belief from its institutional matrix would be quite fatal to anything even remotely resembling historical Catholicism, for if Catholic Christianity has meant anything it has meant a refusal to entertain the distinction between an expendable institutional church and a pure faith independent of that church. Such a distinction, however, has become part of the operative mentality of a good number of Catholics, who often accept it unthinkingly and without realizing how radical a departure it is from the entire Catholic tradition. In their fervent anti-institutionalism, Catholic congregationalists perceive the issue as merely one of control, the tendency of a bureaucratic organization to impose its structure wherever possible. In reality, however, the issue is one of belief, since historical experience demonstrates that the life of each local community is simply not rich or deep enough to preserve the fullness of the Catholic faith, a condition which is greatly exacerbated by the instinctive modern attitude of antiauthoritarianism.

In America this congregationalism has sometimes taken the form of unofficial or quasi-official communities, nonparochial in nature, which undertake to live their faith in experimental ways. The results, in terms of any viable continuity with the Catholic tradition, have not been reassuring. Perhaps the best known of these communities, which appropriated to itself the name of Pope John XXIII, was located in Oklahoma City. Its members were described as white, well educated, and economically comfortable, and after five years of existence had come to include self-described Buddhists and agnostics as well as Catholics. The priest who presided over the community came to believe that there was no essential difference among denominations and that the principal role of the Church was to support the struggle for social change. After a decade of existence one member said, "I don't feel a Catholic spirit running through the community. Mostly, it's intellectual stimulation and friendship." Every week the group conducted "a sort of ritual" involving bread and wine, although another member said, "Why we still do it no one knows."[27] In Wisconsin the priest-leader of a similar community defines the purpose of liturgy as "to give expression to a person's inner feelings in such a context and such a manner as to further his/her spiritual growth."[28]

The growing pressure in favor of autonomous national churches is likely to have similar effects, albeit perhaps more slowly, since the Church in a whole nation has intellectual and spiritual resources which the local congregation lacks. However, the history of autonomous national churches is not reassuring with respect to the continued preservation of genuine Catholicity. Those who point to the Church of England as an example of such a church forget that for nearly half of its existence, from about 1640 to 1840, the Catholic tradition within it was largely dormant. One author has been quite frank about the implications of such autonomy:

> Once set on this path, the Latin American theologian is going to find himself alone, almost devoid of links with the Christian reference points of the past, both on the level of essential doctrine and on that of the historical forms taken by the institution charged with mediating that doctrine in history.[29]

The chafing against papal authority which is now so marked a feature of Church life in various Catholic countries must be understood for what it is—the desire to be free of a universal, normative Catholicism which transcends cultural, social, and political contexts. The search for a new world religion is accompanied, as indicated earlier, by a willful provinciality, a desire to allow limited and relatively narrow experiences to serve as the foundation of the actual life of the Church. Theoretical questions of church government aside, it is obvious that at the present moment only the papacy has the ability and the will to preserve and develop the fullness of the Catholic tradition. If each national church, and even more each local church, is allowed to develop in its own way, in accord with its own cultural conditions, it is inevitable that some of these churches will cease to be Catholic and some, perhaps, will even cease to be identifiably Christian. The attack on the papacy, and the corresponding emphasis on regional and local autonomy, is a prelude to the breakup of the universal Church, which will then allow its various parts to be reabsorbed into some newly emergent world church.

The refusal to value the Church as institution also relates directly to the penchant of many contemporary people for using whatever they find valuable in every existing tradition, while rejecting each tradition as a whole. Historical Christianity is now treated by many people (including church members and even denominational officers) as a quarry from which valuable pieces can be extracted to become part of whatever new edifices they are busy constructing. They ruthlessly pick over what they regard as merely the debris of the historical Church, just as the early Christians, with equal lack of sentiment, took whatever they needed from the wreckage of late antique paganism.

The most important of the treasures which are being stolen from the Church is Jesus Christ, and irenic, optimistic Christians who take heart from the evident resurgence of popular interest in Jesus fail utterly to comprehend what is involved in this popularity—the desire to detach Christ from Christianity and to leave the Church on the roadside of history, even as the figure of Christ is then employed for various new cultural and political experiments.

In fact, however, it is impossible to separate Christ from His Church since the Church is His Body. Even on a purely historical plane, nothing is known about Jesus Christ except through the Scriptures and the traditions of the Church, and the Scriptures themselves were formed and gathered by the Church. Ironically, the less reliable the Scriptures are deemed to be as narrative history, the harder it becomes to separate Christ and Church, because the figure of Christ then does not exist apart from what the Church has claimed Him to be.

Those Christians so eager to approve *Godspell* and *Jesus Christ Superstar* were pathetically grateful for some recognition of Christ on the part of the powerful and deeply pagan entertainment industry, without realizing how much they were being made to give up in return for this recognition. It is a process similar to the one by which, for many years, the cinema has produced "biographies" of historical characters only at the price of distorting those characters' lives beyond all recognition. Gregory Baum was among those extravagant in praise of *Godspell,* noting with apparent approval that the messianic and miracle-working dimensions of Christ's life were omitted and that He was presented merely as a clown, able to speak to children but confounding those (presumably the Pauls, Augustines, and Aquinases of history) who sought to "weave a whole philosophical or theological system" out of his teachings.[30]

A distinguished classical scholar, writing about the last pagan Roman emperor, Julian the Apostate, observed that Julian sought to construct "a grandiose syncretism which is to include even Jehovah if only Jehovah will make up his mind to come in."[31] It was a fact of the highest significance that, almost alone among the religions of late antiquity, Judaism and Christianity refused to be party to any such syncretic venture, a fact which made the adherents of these two faiths seem to the cosmopolitan Romans like fanatics or worse. The willingness of so many Christians to cooperate now in activities which are syncretic in tendency is a sign of their belief, conscious or not, that Christianity is now fit to be absorbed into some greater religious synthesis, even as two milennia ago it was

Christianity which stubbornly resisted such absorptions and which ended by absorbing all existing creeds.

Other elements of Catholicism are also deemed fit candidates for absorption, especially the rich and complex symbolism which the Church has generated over the centuries. A common if largely unrecognized contemporary cultural process is operative here, by which the powerful symbols of Catholicism—the liturgy, the saints, the Virgin Mary—are first denied and suppressed, then, after banishment from public life has largely broken their power and rendered them unfamiliar and exotic, are summoned back in weakened condition. The purpose of this process, perhaps only dimly understood even by many of those who employ it, is to insure that the symbols are weak enough to be controlled and manipulated by the individual or the society. At all costs they cannot be allowed to dominate either the individual or society, which was their earlier historical reality. There thus emerges the kind of Catholic who has more veneration for a monstrance as an antique or a certified work of art than as a repository for the Body of Christ. The Blessed Virgin is no longer sought out as a refuge and a mother but is taken as an example of the possible roles women might play in history. As monks refuse to sing Gregorian Chant, paid choirs of unbelievers are happy to undertake the responsibility, and in this way one more religious treasure is preserved, devoid now of inconvenient religious meanings.

Since politics exercises such a strong hold over the imaginations of avant-garde Christians, it is especially in the arena of fashionable politics that some of the most significant expressions of this the new nonecclesial Christianity have manifested themselves. Not only did the Berrigan circle find it appropriate to include a Moslem in their Eucharist, it is also reported that Daniel Berrigan "celebrated liturgies in Sargent Shriver's living room which participants described as 'fit to knock out your right eye,'"[32] Sargent Shriver being the brother-in-law of the Kennedy family, a central figure in fashionable Washington circles, and at one time an aspirant to the office of the presidency. (Obligingly, he announced his opposition to anti-abortion legislation during that campaign.)

The significance of Leonard Bernstein's composition *Mass* eluded many Catholics in the same way that the real importance of the popular musical plays about Jesus eluded them. That so noted a figure from the secular world would bestow his attention on the Catholic liturgy was to many people a cause for immense rejoicing. A priest from the Liturgical Conference was deliriously enthusiastic over the work ("profoundly correct instincts and intuition") and gratuitously claimed that the great composers of the past were like slaves who only hypocritically and dishonestly pretended to believe in the doctrines of the Church.[33]

But Bernstein himself had in fact written a Mass designed precisely to show the impossibility of Church-centered belief in modern times. The symbolism of the liturgy was murky (the celebrant, for example, used a sacred vessel which was unidentifiable but which most closely resembled a monstrance), and as the "Mass" moved towards the climatic moment of consecration a rising chorus of murmurs from the congregation, along with the celebrant's own doubts, forced a halt to the ritual. The ceremony was finally completed, but not as a Catholic Eucharist. The peaceful words of dismissal, "Go, the Mass is ended," were ambiguous, giving rise to the thought that it would no longer be possible to celebrate the Mass: it was finished. A Jew who had been Bernstein's assistant for eight years saw the performance much more clearly than did the naive Catholics. The work was not a Mass at all, he wrote. Bernstein had simply used the Latin missal because it afforded him "the doctrinal targets for doubts, questions, and even ridicule."[34] What was being celebrated in Bernstein's *Mass* was the process by which Catholics had ceased maintaining a powerful and coherent tradition and had entered into the general existential doubt and anguish of contemporary culture.

It was therefore eminently fitting that the work should be written for the opening of the Kennedy Center in Washington, named for the American Catholic who most effectively symbolizes the secularization of the American Church. The première was an event which gave new life to the liturgy in the sense that this liturgy, now so weakened as the result of nearly a decade of "reform," took life from the excitement and glamour of political Washington. In itself deemed insignificant, the Mass could be revitalized through its connection with the one sacrosanct religion of contemporary America— the religion of politics. (A few days before the performance, Bernstein is reported to have had qualms about his use of Catholic doctrine in the work. A Jesuit theologian quickly flew to Washington to reassure him. Their meeting took place in the Watergate apartments, soon to bask in a different kind of political glamour.)[35]

Catholics also fail to comprehend how the attention which has been bestowed on their Church since the time of Pope John XXIII often amounts to a subtle attack on their beliefs, even when that interest appears to be complimentary. For example, a Dutch artist who did much to publicize Pope John in the pope's own lifetime later wrote that John "had far transcended being a pope" and that "to me he was proof that enlightenment can be reached through any spiritual discipline, in his case a very conventional Catholic one,"[36] as though there was something disreputable about being a pope and as though Catholic spirituality were suspect.

Modern unbelief is often no longer overtly antagonistic to religion and may even give the appearance of approving and welcoming it. But, in the manner of Harvey Cox, this approval is entirely on the unbeliever's own terms. It rests on the assumption that "enlightened" modern man, armed with the resources of the social sciences, actually understands religion better than simple souls who profess it wholeheartedly. Modern unbelievers have discovered that the therapeutic mentality frees them from the need to regard any creed, institution, or symbol as antagonistic to themselves. Rather the skills of therapy enable their users to enter into every alien mentality in an imaginative fashion and extract from it whatever seems vital or relevant. The thoroughly contemporary individual may actually prefer that pockets of traditionalism—ethnic, technological, or architectural—be preserved as reserves to which the jaded modernist can return periodically for refreshment.

Many Catholics wittingly or unwittingly serve this purpose, often because they are flattered that the world pays them any attention at all. Virtually anything in the Catholic tradition is liable to be, at any given moment, either rejected as pernicious and irrelevant or recovered and proclaimed to have hitherto unrecognized depths of meaning. The elements of Catholic faith are handed over for secular use because no element is deemed to have validity unless it can first be given meaning in secular terms. Religion is put on the defensive and must constantly struggle to prove itself in secular eyes. Doctrine is rarely denied outright, but a deliberate vagueness is cultivated which is ultimately even more destructive of real belief; enormous energy is expended seeking verbal formulas which will offend or exclude none but the most uncompromising. As the Jesuit theologian Avery Dulles has pointed out, "Many of the unspoken assumptions of our culture are out of harmony with Christian faith. Thus we imbibe from our environment a kind of latent or implicit heresy."[37]

A number of Christian theologians now operate in the manner of the enlightened pagans of late antiquity, treating the "myths" and traditions of their religion essentially as metaphors for the human condition, drawing from them whatever inspiration or instruction they can find but not believing in them in any ultimate way. A "pluralistic" approach to religion, that is, one which contents itself with presenting, virtually side by side, the various religions of mankind (or the various conflicting versions of the same religion), renders all these religions inherently incredible, which is in fact the purpose of certain modern approaches to religious education. To speak of "sharing diverse faith experiences" is already to rob those experiences of their power and authority and to reduce them merely to expendable episodes in an unfolding drama. People now talk knowingly of finding their "religious roots," but the search is often no more than a diversion, like tracing one's family tree or indulging a nostalgia for ethnic customs. This synthetic Christianity also fits in with the therapeutic mentality in its tendency to take from each religious tradition whatever is most permissive, for example, the Eastern Orthodox practice on divorce but not its view on the ordination of women, the Methodist indifference to doctrine but not its puritanical attitudes towards alcohol.

But the sole thing which the genial and open-minded modernist cannot accept or even tolerate is precisely dogma, the claim to truth, the insistence that what is taught is to be accepted and understood on its own terms and not simply as metaphor. It is for this reason that successful propaganda attempts have been made to give the very words *dogma* and *authority* sinister connotations, and it is why popes and bishops who take their teaching offices seriously are subjected to so much abuse. The enormous interest the Protestant and secular worlds have taken in conciliar and postconciliar Catholicism derives in great part from the fact that the Roman Catholic Church was the largest Christian body still resisting an approach to doctrine which rendered it metaphorical only. The drama of the past twenty years has been the drama of such an institution, its teachings remarkably stable over twenty centuries, enduring the agonies of relativization. Many observers probably believed that, if Rome fell away from orthodoxy, no other church could continue to stand. Instead the spread of the modernist mentality in the Catholic Church seems to have been an important condition for the aggressive resurgence of evangelical Protestantism.

The word *catholic,* as applied to the Church, means a condition in which the entire truth permeates the life of the Church in all its fullness. It is the antithesis of heresy, meaning a selectivity about the truth.[38] However, many contemporary Catholics prefer the derivative, secular understanding of the word in which catholicity means "all-embracing." Understood this way, the Church has never been catholic and has never sought to be. It has always been highly selective about what it will include and embrace (although not about whom it will embrace), accepting some ideas and movements, repulsing others, subjecting all to the rigorous judgment of orthodoxy.

The claim that a truly catholic Church would open itself wide to all other faiths and all the secular movements of the age is therefore a profound misunderstanding. Roman Catholicism has always been a religion of boundaries, and the history of the Church could be written in terms of the great struggles over precisely where the boundaries should be drawn. The modernist mentality is hostile to boundaries (pseudomysticism and drug-taking are in great part techniques for dissolving all boundaries), and in the guise of friendliness towards Catholicism it often seeks to persuade the Church to let down its boundaries one by one. The irenic modern Catholic finds himself quickly backed into a corner—it is not merely this or that secular idea that he is asked to accept, this or that religious tradition he is asked to jettison, but all secular ideas and all religious traditions. The secular world, abetted by influential people within the Church, is constantly devising tests to determine how far the Church will accommodate itself to secularity. Every apparent new accommodation is applauded; every hesitation or refusal is stridently condemned.

Many contemporary Catholics affirm the unity of the Church but also insist that it does not subsist primarily in doctrinal uniformity. Having said this, however, they are usually unprepared to say in what it does subsist. They allow a doctrinal pluralism which involves fundamental antitheses (concerning the identity of Jesus Christ, for example, or the papal office). A unity in worship is rendered dubious by the extremely wide latitude permitted in liturgical practices, some of which also seem fundamentally antithetical to one another. If the unity of the Church is its faith in Christ, this is immediately undermined by a deliberate vagueness as to who Christ is and by a growing willingness to entertain the possibility that He was not the unique incarnation of the Godhead. In the end what is left is a Church held together merely by good will and historical accident.

It should again be stressed that the process by which Catholicism is systematically stripped of its uniqueness and rendered fit to be absorbed into some new religious synthesis is not, for most Catholics, a conscious one. It is rather carried forward by well-meaning, often fundamentally orthodox people who nonetheless treat the various elements of their tradition as though they were endlessly malleable. A liturgical journal, for example, presents a rite of baptism which seems essentially a celebration of the natural powers of water ("a series of slides . . . showing the place of water in the family's life . . . ," followed by a baptism performed with water brought from home).[39] In another ritual a staff member of the Liturgical Conference celebrates "scents"—fresh-baked bread, roses, new paint, essence of skunk—and participants are given paper cups of cologne, anointed on the forehead, and commissioned to "spread the fragrance of God's love to everyone you meet."[40] A professor of religious education proposes a concept of ministry within the Church which has no connection with ordination or formal calling and is even antagonistic to it. ("I'm afraid that if I get ordained I'll lose my priesthood.")[41] Meanwhile a priest charged with the training of future priests looks forward to the disappearance of "the whole clerical priesthood."[42]

What is conspicuously absent is the willingness even to ask the question what connection these things have with the historic Catholic faith.

Rather, this faith is treated merely as a starting point, a location where the individual finds himself by historical accident and which he then endeavors to make use of in some new way. Doctrines are treated as metaphors for the human condition, rituals as means to celebrate life, ecclesiastical structures merely as oppressive burdens. There remains finally no compelling reason why the doctrines and rituals of Catholicism are of any more merit than those of Methodism or Buddhism, or why they should be respected at all if they seem to hinder the unification of the human race.

Avant-garde Catholic thinkers argue that religious meaning already exists in the secular milieu and merely needs to be celebrated. Secular readings at Mass are often more meaningful than Scripture, according to a former president of the Federation of Diocesan Liturgical Commissions,[43] and a Jesuit theologian proclaims that "What the feast of Christmas calls us to attend to is . . . that contemporary pagans have a keener sense of these [human] values, and that one need not be an explicit Christian to promote them." Christmas is, therefore, a properly secular feast.[44] However, such pieties ignore, among other things, the symbolic impoverishment of modern Western man and his consequent failure, often enough, to catch even a glimpse of the deepest truths of existence. What is objectionable about much of what passes for creativity in modern religion is not its contemporaneity, nor even primarily its casualness about the traditions of the Church, but its shallowness. What begins with a sometimes justified criticism of rationalism in religion and a determination to respect the mystery at the heart of faith, often ends by making the mystery even less mysterious, merely a metaphorical way of expressing certain familiar human insights.[45]

The logical end of this kind of religion is the process of celebrating everything which seems meaningful or good in life, a task in which religion is really superfluous and intrusive and in which, ironically, it fails to respect the human ability to celebrate quite independent of religious categories. Far more important is humanity's need for religion as a deliverance from evil, a task for which human beings in themselves are wholly unfit. The need to hold a baptism, a eucharist, or a sacramental wedding to celebrate one of the milestones of life is likely to be felt only by those raised in a strong tradition. For the next generation it will seem at best like an expendable luxury.

Many Catholics are already reduced to this. For example, a Benedictine abbey offers a range of Christmas cards only a minority of which explicitly advert to the birth of Christ. The others variously proclaim "peace, love, and joy," "a new day," and "hopes and dreams."[46] A group of priest-musicians reflect that the experience of baptism is supposed to be like a rock singer establishing a mystical and "oceanic" rapport with his audience, revealing "an exhilarating sense of the largeness of life and the power that belonged to each one of us."[47]

Religion is in danger of being trivialized in contemporary culture in the same way that art is so endangered, and for the same reason—both are seen as almost the only remaining bastions of the nonscientific mind, and each is in danger of simply being used as a vehicle of expression for human feelings and beliefs which are thought to be either unverifiable in any rigorous way or else ought to be kept free from rationalistic contamination. In this capacity religion and art are liable to attract all kinds of cultural hangers-on who merely use these vehicles for their own purposes.

The parallels between religion and art are so obvious that one of the great temptations of contemporary Christianity is to confuse artistic insight and expression with religious insight and expression, the unexpected because belated victory of the Romantic heresy which sacralized all art and deified the artist.

A priest-liturgist is perfectly content, for instance, to have the Mass used by artists as "a symbol of ultimacy," because Western civilization has no better symbol for this purpose. He is also willing to turn churches into centers for artistic celebration.[48] A Dominican spiritual writer regards the great musicians of history as the true saints. "Mozart's spiritual influence on the West has exceeded that of all the saints canonized since the Renaissance."[49] A novice of the Sisters of Loretto proposes the rock-music star Bob Dylan as the highest expression of religious faith in modern America. ". . . I realized his work largely reflected the lives of the Hebrew prophets."[50]

In the end the churches may simply become convenient centers for whatever activities the enlightened bourgeoisie find meaningful at any given moment, the refuge for activities which no other institution currently exists to foster. A prominent Catholic architect, for example, says that "Churches are a thing of the past" and, "It's not the church that's needed, it's the community center."[51] Churches in fact harbor a wide variety of secular activities, from Boy Scouts to Alcoholics Anonymous, and this is not improper. What would be improper would be a situation, which seems already to have come about in some Protestant parishes, in which these secular activities are seen as the church's sufficient reason for existence and worship is treated as merely one among many activities.

There is a tendency on the part of modern Christians to deify secular activities and give them a spurious religious significance, a tendency which certain fashionable theological ideas render almost inevitable. A Jesuit editor, for example, suggests that journalists are apt candidates to replace the clergy as the moral leaders of society.[52] A lay Catholic editor reassures nonbelievers that there is really no need to attend church so long as they are "out in front on civil liberties and other issues."[53] A former priest turned stockbroker finds total continuity between those two vocations, because, like religion, the stock market is based on "the establishment of trust." He chose the life of a broker in order to implement his philosophy of "bringing a message of real love to the heart of the people," a task in which the Church contrived to frustrate him.[54]

By logical, and perhaps almost inevitable, historical development, the Church's existence ceases to have any necessary connection with its past and becomes simply a vehicle for human service. "Xavier Rynne," for instance, now the rector of a major seminary, asserts that a concern for doctrinal orthodoxy "is a luxury which only the leisured class of Christians have time to indulge."[55] A prominent English Catholic journalist argues that there is no difference between being a "practicing" and a "lapsed" Catholic and that the Church has no boundaries. Many persons belong to it without knowing it.[56]

Catholicism, despite its rigorous insistence on doctrinal orthodoxy and its strong system of discipline, is potentially more vulnerable to being used as a secular convenience than some of the Protestant churches, because the richness of its symbolic life appeals to the sophisticated modern mind which, if it is interested in religion at all, desires a religion rich in myth and symbol. Langdon Gilkey's advice to Catholics on how to "update" their church[57] is a remarkably frank plea that the Church simply abandon its historical identity and give itself over to secular uses. The Church, after all, is valuable property, not primarily in the material sense but in the sense that its long history, its immense membership, and its spiritual authority make it a highly useful institution for anyone able to capture it for his own ends.

The Anglican Church is even more vulnerable than Roman Catholicism, because in addition to the richness of its symbolic life it also has a relatively weak governmental structure and a concern for doctrine which has been steadily weakening in recent times. Unless Anglicanism takes vigorous steps to guard itself against this process, it may end as a church replete with symbols which people manipulate and redefine at will. It will be guided almost entirely by the therapeutic spirit which offers people no more than they feel comfortable in swallowing and never disturbs the prevailing assumptions of enlightened bourgeois culture. Despite its recent large membership losses, the Episcopal Church in America may be the church of the future, attracting all those people who feel a vague desire for religion but do not wish to commit themselves to any particular creed. It will simply be a useful agency for expressing all the varied aspirations of the human spirit.

However, there is still more at stake than the prospect of a church which will drift in a pleasant and euphoric haze until it is painlessly absorbed into some new cultural synthesis. Many people now surmise that the death of historical Christianity is occurring (a death which has been falsely reported more than once previously), and they aim at nothing less than to repeal as much as possible of the Christianity which dominated Western civilization for nearly two millenia. The modern Christian's benign, trusting outlook on his culture occurs at precisely the moment when that culture is characterized by a resurgent paganism perhaps bolder and more hostile to genuine faith than at any time in nearly two centuries.

Among the pernicious manifestations of this paganism is a resurgence of the worship of nature, at the heart of most historical paganism, which Judaism and Christianity did so much to root out of genuine religion. Both rightly and wrongly, the ecology movement charges that Christianity bears major responsibility for the notion, so fundamental to Western culture for so many centuries, that man dominates and uses nature in accordance with the divine plan. But the ecological movement goes far beyond mere conservationism or, where animals are concerned, mere humaneness. It aims at nothing less than collapsing man back into nature, erasing the radical distinction between the two which is fundamental to biblical religion. Ecological concerns tend to represent a whole cultural nexus which, while still claiming the title of humanism, rapidly depreciates human worth in the interest of exalting nature. The movement also represents one of the respectable forms of potential totalitarianism—draconian measures may be imposed by governments in areas where a threat to some natural resource is alleged.

A report on the religious life of the Pacific Northwest of the United States finds that less than forty per cent of the population is affiliated with any church and surmises that "the outdoors, it seems, is worshiped instead." The reporter finds this a hopeful sign, along with the fact that Catholics are a small minority of even the church-going population. The result is a situation in which people are not "hung up" on doctrine, do not take their religion too seriously.[58] This regional condition, to the extent that it is true, may well be an advanced example of what will prevail in other parts of the country as the leisure society—the therapeutic mind at its quintessence—continues to spread. This new paganism is for the most part an unreflecting, well-meaning, instinctual kind of thing, difficult to dislike but a breeder of attitudes fatal to any meaningful kind of Christianity. The worship of nature, linked with certain geographical areas whose cultures are "free," is part of the conscious process whereby some American Catholics have thrown off their religion, "finding God" on the seashore or the ski slopes.[59]

This benign new paganism inevitably gravitates towards avant-garde politics, the excitement of each stimulating the other. Governor "Jerry" Brown of California, for example, former Jesuit and aspirant to the American presidency, visits Zen centers and tells the press of the "fundamental essence" which the major religious traditions of the world share. At various times he designates himself according to the nature of his audience, either a "Catholic" or a "catholic." One of his aides, a former Christian Brother, points out triumphantly that the governor refuses to oppose legal and tax-supported abortions but has found a useful issue in the crusade to save the whales.[60] Despite strong evidence that Governor Brown only occasionally attends Mass, "Xavier Rynne" told English readers that the governor's "credentials as a Catholic are unimpeachable."[61]

Modern popular culture (which is not genuinely popular but rather the creation of a popular-culture industry) has perhaps always been pagan, but until recently attempts were made to conceal this fact behind a hypocritical facade of piety and traditionalism, the tribute vice paid to virtue. Now, however, popular music, the films, the press, and television have thrown off all pretense. Religion is rarely dealt with sympathetically and is routinely treated as a cause and a result of neurosis. The entire weight of a multi-billion-dollar industry is thrown behind the continued celebration of the experiences of the moment and the belief that such experiences alone have validity for human life. The stars created by this industry use their prestige to demonstrate contempt for Christian virtues like humility, chastity, or poverty and to glorify drug-taking and sexual adventuring.

Although virtually no even minimally alert Christian of earlier times would have had any difficulty recognizing the rank and destructive paganism which now permeates popular culture, many contemporary Christians remain impervious to it when they do not actually embrace it. *Hair*—a musical play which deliberately exploited sex and blasphemy on stage—won a ringing endorsement from a priest in an archdiocesan newspaper. He delighted "in the warm, free, exciting atmosphere of this genuine experience in community" and sternly warned that those who judged it obscene were really judging themselves. Was the play irreverent towards religion? Only to the degree that religion deserved such irreverence, he insisted. The play, he concluded, "left me a little more hopeful that the Son does shine in. . . . And that is Good News." The management of *Hair* published his encomium as an advertisement for the road company.[62]

Two British commentators have summed up the situation very perceptively:

Coinciding, as it does, with the decay of traditional Christian belief, and the rejection of a large part of traditional Christian ethics, pop culture and the worship of pop stars cannot be dismissed as a trifling phenomenon. However banal its actual content, it is full of menace for civilization and has to be taken seriously.[63]

"Do you dig Mick Jagger?," somebody once asked me, "do you like the Stones?" "No," I replied, "I'm a Roman Catholic." That wasn't a joke: there's a real dividing line there, a "disparity of cult."[64]

To criticize the consumerist mentality and popular materialism is extremely easy from a Christian point of view and has been the stuff of sermons for centuries, long before capitalism was even thought of. By constantly decrying consumerism, the modern religious critics seriously underestimate the degree to which pagan values run deep in American culture and infect even many of its critics. Similarly, the emphasis on social justice, valid in itself, tends often to imply that the material deprivations suffered by some Americans are the only important moral evils. It is possible now, by taking a stance of stern condemnation towards social injustice, to become a "prophetic" Christian while failing to notice evidence of un-Christian moral values present everywhere. An Anglican scholar has diagnosed the condition:

> By cultural liberalism I mean a value structure rooted in the imperative to gratify one's senses and appetites immediately. . . . It is simply that modern liberalism is known for demanding self-control in social rather than personal conduct. . . . It is the disciplines of family life—including parental and patriarchal authority, and the commitment to remain faithful until death—as well as the disciplines of chastity and sobriety in general that earn the special animus of the cultural liberal.[65]

The volcanic energy generated by popular culture in the past twenty years obviously has its roots in sexuality and the deliberate, flaunting denial of the sexual ethics that have governed Western civilization for two millennia. It is the final shattering of that icon, so often hammered at in the twentieth century, which has provided the exhilaration, the sometimes manic energy, the sense of being special and exempt which characterize the leaders of that culture and make possible the consciously demonic stance of Mick Jagger, Alice Cooper, and (it is not unfair to posit a connection) Charles Manson.

Earnest Christians, aware of the rapid decline of religious belief, attempt to respond by entering into high-minded dialogue with the leading philosophers of secular modernity. Only belatedly do they realize (some still do not realize) that the principal vehicle of secularization is less Marx, Nietzsche, or Sartre than *Playboy* magazine. In particular the alienation of youth from religion is based on the rapid rise of a youthful subculture (imitated by many adults) which is hostile to Christian values in certain very fundamental ways, despite its employment of reassuring words like *love* and *compassion.*

Sexuality has been the battering ram chosen by neopaganism to assault the remaining fortresses of Christianity, and the assault is strategically brilliant because it succeeds at least partially no matter what the Christian response. Resistance by the Church to the new sexual freedom occasions the desertion of many of its members and the projection of a public image of rigidity and anachronism. But acceptance has even more disastrous results, because in giving up its sexual doctrines the Church gives up a good part of itself (sexual morality not being related merely accidentally to fundamental dogmas) and also signals its willingness to let the new paganism dictate the terms on which the Church itself is permitted to exist.

Avant-garde Catholics have been trapped by their own rhetoric of "man making himself" and their unthinking willingness to believe in the essential goodness of human nature, and they will be forced thereby to accept a great deal of the new paganism, even when they find it distasteful. The sexual revolution is a movement which is now reaching gale force, and its deafening roar easily drowns the "responsible" and measured distinctions by which advanced Catholics try to come to terms with it. Sexual emancipation is in fact a process which has been occurring since World War I, and its prophets insist, even as illegitimacy, venereal disease, abortion, divorce, and impotency increase almost geometrically, that the sexual promised land lies just over the next horizon.

The classical Christian view of sexuality, including the positive value of chastity, is scarcely ever presented in the mass media, and Christians do not even request that it should be. Chastity, if it is dealt with at all, is treated as either hypocrisy or a timid conformity to respectable mores. Prominent Christians, meanwhile, are required to make repeated public denunciations of the "rigid" traditions of their church and are applauded for their courage when they do so. Catholics who are successful in public life—John F. and Edward Kennedy, Eugene McCarthy, Jerry Brown, as well as assorted journalists and authors—frequently emit signals to the alert secular public that they are not "trapped" in the Catholic pattern of monogamous family life.

Catholics have especially not understood the significance of the homosexual-rights movement. If the sexual revolution is in general the deliberate invocation of pagan patterns of behavior—a new barbarism in which there is no higher law than the "need" of the individual to gratify his desires—homosexuality is the most obvious instance of the conscious desire to repeal two thousand years of Christian history, by reverting to pre-Christian practices.

There are few subjects on which there is greater consistency of teaching within historical Christianity than sexual behavior. Until virtually the twentieth century (and for the most part until about the last decade), Christian leaders insisted that there could be no legitimate sexual activity outside marriage. The ancient world had tolerated homosexuality and even sometimes exalted it, and there are few more striking signs of the social revolution wrought by the triumph of Christianity than its uncompromising rejection of all homosexual behavior. (Abortion is a somewhat similar case. Properly understood, abortion, which has been condemned in Christianity since at least the time of the *Didache* in the early second century, does not pose an ecumenical problem. Its recent acceptance by some Christian churches marks their repudiation of their own authentic traditions and their acquiescence in secular values.)

Catholics have been readily enlisted in the cause of gay liberation, and are already (and predictably) prepared to accept whatever that movement requires them to accept. At a meeting of Catholic homosexuals in Chicago, for example, after a Mass concelebrated by fifty priests there was a dance in which "the marvellously good-humored but never indecorous jollification went on until past midnight."[66] In England, when a magazine published a poem portraying Christ as having a homosexual relationship with a Roman centurion (the editors were convicted of blasphemy), a Catholic journal defended it on the grounds that the author was a certified scholar and that each person has only a "private image" of Christ, of which the poet's might be construed as valid as anyone's.[67]

Beginning at least as early as Victorian and Edwardian litterateurs like John Addington Symonds and E. M. Forster, intellectualized homosexuality in the modern West has consciously repudiated Christianity as a distorted, inhumane religion which snuffed out the joyous, guilt-free paganism of ancient times. The intent of this homophilia has been to recreate as far as possible the conditions of that ancient paganism, for which the destruction of Christianity as a cultural influence has been seen as an essential prerequisite. Such a view of history, which from the homosexual viewpoint is to a great extent correct, is continued into the present by, among others, Gore Vidal, the admirer of Julian the Apostate, who manifests both the obsessive anti-Christian sentiment and the contempt and hostility towards heterosexual values which seems characteristic of much of the homosexual subculture.[68] That Christian defenders of homosexuality do not necessarily share this perspective, and that in fact they seek to synthesize Christianity and homophilia, does not lessen the fact that, objectively, they serve the purposes of those who would, if they could, repeal two millennia of Christian history. They attempt to gain full moral and social respectability for homophilia, including the right to present the gay life-style to young people as a legitimate alternative to heterosexuality.

Despite their concern to enter as fully as possible into the dynamics of the secular world, many modern Catholics are naive (something quite different from religious innocence). They essentially fail to comprehend the degree to which such worldly dynamics is not communal but competititive, based not on the irenic desire to encompass all points of view but on the aim of one creed to vanquish or eviscerate another.[69] This does not necessarily involve organizational conflicts, although it often does, but it always involves competing systems of symbols—alternative ways of understanding the world which are ultimately not compatible with one another. At present Catholicism in America does not face its primary rivalry from other religions, with the possible exception of evangelical Protestantism. Rather the primary threat comes, as already suggested, from a pervasive paganism. Comparing the "Humanist Manifestos" of 1933 and 1973, for example, reveals that secularism has not had its Second Vatican Council. It is still militantly antireligious, triumphalistic, and unecumenical. Traditional religion is proclaimed to "do a disservice to the human species," and attempts to redefine these religions in humanistic ways are treated as fraught with the danger of "escapism."[70] Despite such strong sentiments, one of the leading American humanists dared to attack Pope Paul VI as "intolerant and divisive" because the pontiff had declared that humanism of itself is insufficient.[71] The British humanists insist that the inculcation of religious faith in children is "immoral" and want to suppress all denominational schools, using state schools as a vehicle for counteracting parental religious influences.[72]

The new aggressiveness of unbelievers derives in large measure from their perception that organized religion is on the decline, that it has become a beleaguered minority position which should be harassed until it becomes socially impotent. Far from being open-minded towards religious faith, these secularists are utterly persuaded that such faith is a psychic aberration to be tolerated only in the barest legal sense. Many Christians find it impossible to recognize the depth and strength of anti-Christian feeling in the Western world and console themselves that, where it does exist, it is based upon disappointment with Christians who do not live up to their beliefs. In fact, however, the Church is hated not primarily because its members fall short of its teachings but precisely because it insists on being what it is supposed to be. It speaks of God, of eternity, of right and wrong. Its fidelities are despised, not its infidelities.

The dream of modernist Christians, since at least the time of the Enlightenment, has been that by showing themselves reasonable, open-minded, nondogmatic, and humble they will win the respect and even the acceptance of Christianity's "cultured despisers." In fact, however, there is scant evidence that such tactics have ever attracted any significant number of sceptics to take religion seriously. Rather they have served as stages of accommodation of those already in the Church but troubled by doubts, many of whom merely employ the various modernist strategies as means of easing themselves totally into the secular milieu.

One of the most basic and most clearly erroneous modernist assumptions is that the Church encounters problems in the world because it is authoritarian, rigid, and unbending, when the historical truth is often the opposite. For example, the Church was savagely attacked in the French Revolution because of its social privileges. However, as a distinguished historian has demonstrated, the attack was made possible by its prior loss of spiritual authority with much of the aristocracy and middle class, precisely because of the spread of scepticism and the spirit of compromise within its own ranks.

Much of this history has a strikingly contemporary ring.

> By and large, the religious did not believe in their doctrines with the intensity, the sense of personal discovery and conviction, with which the *philosophes* believed in theirs. . . . It made Catholics often more reasonable than *philosophes*, more willing to persuade, examine, or remonstrate, less given to sarcasm, mockery, and abuse.

In this context many people, including some of the clergy, regarded an enlightened and progressive state as the proper authority for ruling men, often in opposition to the Church. A spirit of "pleasure and civility" made such staples of Catholic piety as self-denial, meditation, and love of solitude seem "useless and morose." Students of theology, in their examinations "often showed themselves more familiar with the objections raised by unbelievers than with the correct reply to be made to them. . . ." The monks of a leading Benedictine abbey petitioned against wearing their habits (which they said made them look ridiculous) and the austere monastic regime, asserting that they wished to be known as scholars rather than monks. At the great Seminary of St. Sulpice seminarians rioted and attempted to burn the building after being forbidden their elaborate wigs.

Almost the only Catholics whose intensity and militancy of faith could match that of the *philosophes* were the reviled Jansenists. Since they were cut off from most of the centers of society and culture, the Christian virtues for which they stood, like strict personal piety and morality, could be ridiculed as merely the products of ignorance and lack of sophistication. Meanwhile

> the Jesuits, like all theorists who emphasize conscience and intention rather than fulfillment of objective standards, tended on the whole to make conscience less exacting, regarding an anxious conscience as a spiritual disease, which the confessor should do everything in his power to cure.

> The new ideas spread among people . . . who needed new subjects for sprightly conversation and saw in "philosophy" an exciting novelty of the day; persons for whom the Christian virtues of chastity and humility were usually remote. . . .

> Law, rational or divine, was not for them a rule to which men must force themselves; it was a cosmic authorization for them to do what gave them happiness in the world. . . .[73]

The high paganism of the Enlightenment remains a permanent element in Western civilization, and thus the Catholic response cited above remains a constant temptation to the churches. However, until the period following the Second Vatican Council the Catholic Church successfully resisted such temptations and avoided repeating the grievous mistakes of the eighteenth century. Contemporary paganism shares some of the attributes of Enlightenment Deism, including the willingness to believe that God exists but the equal tendency to deny Him any lively presence in human lives. Hence the preference for speaking of God as "the deepest ground of our being" and for dismissing the possibility of a genuine divine revelation.

The true unbeliever regards all liberalization as confirmation of his suspicion that Christianity is false and that its own adherents are coming to realize it. A leading American humanist, for instance, notes that Hans Küng's celebrated *On Being a Christian* is really a work of liberal Protestantism and judges that it fails to make a case even for its highly modified and attenuated Christianity.[74] A Russian Marxist journal offers the opinion that Küng's remedy for the ills of Christianity is so radical that it confirms that "the patient is incurably ill," and suggests that Küng is left with nothing of Christianity except the name.[75]

If the modern Church is to have anything to say which is woth listening to, it must be willing at least to risk offending nonbelievers and must cease behaving as though unbelief is ultimately a product of the Church's own deficiencies. The latter is reassuring to people whom the evangelical style makes uncomfortable and are content to spend endless hours in breast-beating. If the prophetic function of the Church requires that it sometimes speak harsh words to those who connive at injustice, it is surely also appropriate that the Church speak with equal bluntness about an entire range of moral values and the question of belief itself.

The historical situation in which the Church now finds itself is in many ways the mirror image of its situation in its first three centuries, especially its minority status in a hostile pagan world. The image is reversed, however, because the roles of Christians and pagans are reversed. Now Christians constitute a demoralized and declining establishment, pagans an aggressive rising movement. Whereas once the Church took from paganism whatever it found useful, confident of its ability to digest such borrowings without harm to itself, it now watches helplessly as neopaganism ransacks what it takes to be the ruins of the Church. The most notable conversions run from Christianity to paganism, not the other way, and the dominant theme is liberation, not humble submission. Just as the early Christians sometimes strained the truth in their propagandizing against pagan vices, so now every accusation directed against the Church is treated with great seriousness, even by Catholics themselves. Predictably, these accusations are often self-contradictory. For three centuries unbelieving rationalists pilloried the Church as the enemy of science. Now the new paganism accuses it of having fostered the Western technological world view.

The decline of the missionary impulse is of crucial importance, because Christianity is a fundamentally missionary religion. For example, a Benedictine monk in India suggests that, since Christ's admonition to His disciples to teach and baptize all nations is regarded by some biblical scholars as a late addition to the text, it need not be regarded as authoritative. Stories of Christians converting to Buddhism he finds more inspiring than the reverse and, he suspects, now more common.[76] The missionary impulse is a crucial touchstone of the health of the Church not only because it is an obedient response to the command of Christ but also because Christianity is a dynamic religion which must either grow or decline and cannot merely remain stable. (An exception may be the Eastern Orthodox and other Christian groups whose social basis is almost entirely ethnic.) The willingness or unwillingness of Christians to proselytize for their beliefs is an index of the firmness with which they hold those beliefs.

One of the open secrets of liberal Christianity is that, despite its talk of making the faith credible to nonbelievers, it has never been interested in conversions and is in fact made uneasy by them. Liberal Christianity is an inward-directed thing, seeking to assuage the anxieties of people who are already church members. It is in no sense dynamic. When the

Catholic Church, as a result of the Second Vatican Council, is said to have become less provincial and more concerned with the world, this might be reasonably supposed to imply an intensified missionary activity. Closer to the reverse has been true, however, as vastly disproportionate amounts of energy have been squandered in the postconciliar Church on essentially internal questions—liturgical change, updating of religious communities, celibacy, women priests. Instead of eagerly undertaking to bring the "good news" to unbelievers, many religious professionals have chosen to invest their efforts in a campaign to "purify" and "update" the religion of their fellow Catholics.

The claim that the revolution in thinking about missions merely represents the end of religious colonialism is a simplification which covers a multitude of severe problems. Compulsive breast-beating over the "imposition" of Christianity on Third World cultures begs many questions. There is rarely a corresponding anxiety expressed over the "imposition" of other Western creeds, for example, Marxism, which has often been imposed on Asian and African societies by force. The fact that Christianity is not a native European flower but was "imposed" on Europe from the Near East is never alluded to, and by the logic of some of the new mission theories Westerners should now seek to reclaim their rightful heritage of forgotten pagan gods. Finally, the proposal to "adapt" Christianity to native cultures is one which almost everyone can agree to in principle, but in practice it is fraught with the gravest difficulties. In practice many enthusiasts for an "indigenous" Christianity are indifferent to dogma and treat symbols as though they were endlessly manipulable. They would be quite willing to see develop a "Christianity" which had only the most oblique ties to what has historically gone by that name. Just as in the West the repeal of Christianity tends towards the recovery of a classic paganism, so outside the West it will tend towards a resurgence of those pagan religions over which Christianity had apparently triumphed.

The drama is played out most starkly in missionary lands, but it is a larger dynamic which has equally valid application in the West. There too, except among evangelicals, there is an absence of any vigorous and self-confident Christian presence in society and a willingness to bless the development of forms of Christianity which are heavily influenced by the surrounding pagan environment. A telling sign is the willingness of Catholics to concede the air waves to the secularists and the evangelicals. Catholic radio and television is confined largely either to the Sunday morning ghetto or to platitudinous, humanistic offerings like the brief radio vignettes "from the Franciscans."

The hope that modern culture can somehow be "neutral," hospitable to all creeds but committed to none, was dashed by T. S. Eliot many years ago.

> It is my contention that we have today a culture which is mainly negative, but which, so far as it is positive, is still Christian. I do not think that it can remain negative, because a negative culture has ceased to be efficient in a world where economic as well as spiritual forces are proving the efficiency of cultures which, even when pagan, are positive, and I believe that the choice before us is between the formation of a new Christian culture and the acceptance of a pagan one.[77]

The root of the problems analyzed in this chapter is a simple one—the conviction, held by some Catholics at a conscious level and many others only semiconsciously, that historical Roman Catholicism has had its day; its thread has at last run out, and it should gracefully allow itself to be used by history in whatever way the spirit of the age makes appropriate. There is, among many Catholics, a sometimes unrecognized death wish for their Church, along with a corresponding desire to have that Church taken up into some emerging and dynamic new world purpose. A prominent Catholic philosopher writes that the Catholic Church is "the single most effective hindrance to the evolution of man's religious consciousness."[78] A nun on the staff of the National Council of Churches dismisses the Bible as a "sexist" book and the Church as a "sexist" institution for proclaiming the Bible.[79] A prominent Catholic editor rejects the conciliar metaphor of the pilgrim Church and proposes a "wanderer church," its destination unknown, ready to follow the movement of history and welcoming secularization.[80] A theologian and former priest welcomes a humanism which does not take "religiosity" seriously and hopes that in the form of Marxism such a humanism will have a "cleansing" effect on the Church. Catholicism should accept its role as merely "a starting point for something other than itself" and should abandon any attempt to control even its own life.[81]

One of the unanticipated results of the Second Vatican Council is a spirit of defeatism in the Church, a result diametrically opposed to the Council's intentions but one which became inevitable as soon as the Council was viewed primarily in the "remissive mode," that is, as the Church systematically admitting its past mistakes and accommodating itself to modern culture. That this defeatism is often accompanied (especially in official statements) by a superficial optimism does not alter the situation, because it is so frequently the kind of optimism which stems from mental and moral laziness, the refusal to look closely at what is really happening in the world and especially the refusal to ponder the probable long-term consequences of present decisions. The chaos now infecting so much of Catholic institutional, doctrinal, and liturgical life is an expression of the intuition that the Church is now a weak and profoundly disordered community incapable of sustaining coherence at any of these levels. (The condition of liberal Protestantism is far worse.)

The final stage of the Church's history, were it to accept certain of the various formulas for "renewal" now urged on it, would be to render it so weak and anemic, so lacking in firmness of bone and muscle, its very skeleton no longer susceptible of articulation, that it would be easily assimilable by whatever stronger religious impulses happen to arise in the world. A British forecaster describes the church of the future:

> The Church of tomorrow will be a place for the celebration of life, and its characteristics will be spontaneity and acceptance; . . . It will be a place of colour, movement, and vitality where young and old will not only look at what men of past ages have painted, listen to what they have written and the music they have made, but where they will be themselves free to paint, dance, talk and express themselves in ways no longer easy in an age of automation . . . and leisure lostness. Few, if any, places in the new society will offer such arresting and beckoning horizons of human creativity. Political leaders will be glad to discover in the Churches centres where somehow man's place and dignity in the world is mysteriously maintained. . . .[82]

There is much unrecognized negative symbolism in contemporary Catholic life. Beautiful old churches are abandoned, for example, and schools of all kinds are closed not only because of population movements and the expense of maintenance but precisely because of the, spirit of defeat and the unwillingness to invest money and personnel in the future. Discomfort over the ownership of property by the Church stems not only from a spirit of Christian poverty but also from the implications of permanence implied in such ownership. New churches are built as multipurpose halls, and modern congregations prefer to worship on metal folding chairs, around portable altars, in the half-conscious expectation that in time the religious functions of the church will cease and it can then be adapted easily to general community needs.

Many modern Catholics are extremely naive about the implications of being open to the world. In citing the examples of early theologians who welcomed Platonism or St. Thomas Aquinas daring to assimilate Aristotle, they misperceive the spirit of those historical epochs. The great philosophical theologians could make use of pagan thought without fear because they were unshakably convinced of the superiority of their own creed and thus of their ability to dominate and tame alien creeds. As the novelist John Updike has written,

A religion will be intolerant of others as far as its own strength reaches. The destruction of rival icons is a rite of faith. Iconoclasm always seems barbaric to those who have no faith. . . .[83]

What now passes for ecumenism, in the broadest sense, is often an invitation to allow oneself and one's church to be taken up into the next great stage of the religious development of mankind, a process in which many Christians are eager to participate and a process for which the weakening of existing creeds is a necessary prerequisite. This kind of syncretism always signals the end of religion's vitality, the desire to receive new energy and dedication through an infusion of alien religious blood. On a global scale it is noteworthy that those who anticipate a convergence of Eastern and Western religions generally do so entirely on the East's terms. They welcome the opportunity to jettison Western doctrinal baggage, for example, and do not ask that the East try to enter more deeply into the spirit which has characterized Western ecclesiastical Christianity.

Daniel Bell has pointed out how the decline of formal faith and institutionalized religion leads to the multiplication of cults, each based on a supposed direct religious experience. As in modern art, the modern religious person feels free to "ransack the world storehouse and to engage any and every style it comes upon," precisely because there is ultimately no authority higher than the searching self.[84] One of the great neglected modern Catholic thinkers, Romano Guardini, observed even before the Second Vatican Council:

> When the believer no longer possesses any fundamental principles, but only an experience of faith as it affects him personally, the one solid and recognizable fact is no longer a body of dogma which can be handed on in tradition but the right action as the proof of the right spirit. . . . The relation with the supernatural and eternal order is thereby broken. The believer no longer stands in eternity, but in time, . . . Religion becomes increasingly turned towards the world, and cheerfully secular. It develops more and more into a consecration of temporal human existence in its various aspects. . . .[85]

To this might be added that a religion which has reached this state also becomes expendable. Its entire justification is in its usefulness, and where other social entities prove even more adapted to serving requisite needs, such a religion has no honorable course except to allow itself to fade into history.

CHAPTER 10

The Future of Roman Catholicism

CONVENTIONAL wisdom, especially as conveyed in the media, holds that traditional Catholicism is dead, and inevitably so. It could not withstand, so the argument runs, the pressures of a rapidly changing world, and the windows which were opened at the time of the Second Vatican Council were enough to blow away the accumulated dust and the brittle furniture underneath as well.

But, speaking of organized religious life, a Lutheran observer has offered the opinion that:

> . . . the older form need not have died . . . with its death the larger Christian community is the poorer for the loss. The times did not kill religious life. Rather, it killed itself by a studied, even if unintentional, form of slow suicide.[1]

The fact that the radical changes in Catholic life over the past two decades were not the result of popular demand, that to a great extent they were enforced against lay opposition or lack of enthusiasm, must be constantly recalled, along with the fact that this way of life is even now not dead. There survive many firm pockets of traditional Catholicism even in secular America.

Another point about traditional Catholicism which must be recalled is that, whatever else it was, it was a way of life. It was capable of defining a meaningful, coherent, self-reinforcing spiritual order in the lives of countless numbers of people, of all social classes and levels of sophistication. Despite many attempts to portray that life as narrow, mean, oppressive, and miserable, it bestowed peace on many people.

The Catholicism which exists now is, in the terms of analytic philosophy, not vulnerable to falsification, and therefore it cannot make claims to truth or credibility either. The spirit of liberation from old rigidities is so pervasive that many of those in a position to shape the present spirit which governs the Church seem determined to avoid at all costs anything specific, distinctive, or unique, anything which could delineate a Catholicism as a way of life. In doctrine now, a Catholic (including a Catholic priest) may be anything from a Tridentine rigorist to a Unitarian, in practice anything from a credulous peasant to a secular sceptic. The immense popularity of the charismatic movement, in origins and spirit clearly not Catholic, owes much to the fact that it does define a way of life for those who are religiously serious, at a time when practically nothing else in the Church does. As the distinguished philosopher Stuart Hampshire writes,

> There are rather precise grounds in experience and in history for the reasonable man to expect that certain virtues, which he admires and values, can only be attained at the cost of certain others, and that the virtues typical of several different ways of life cannot be freely combined, as he might wish. . . . He will reject those that seem likely in practice to conflict with others that seem more closely part of, or conditions of, the way of life that he values and admires, or that seem irrelevant to this way of life. We know that human nature naturally varies, and is deliberately variable, only within limits, and that not all theoretically compatible achievements and enjoyments are compatible in normal circumstances.[2]

Someone has observed that, although the Church is now able, as a result of strenuous and often traumatic efforts, to speak to everyone, to employ a language which the world will comprehend, it now finds that it no longer has anything to say. More accurately, it has nothing to say which the world does not already know.

There are at present four major forms which Catholicism takes among those whose adherence to it appears to be more than merely formal and customary.

The first is what might be called *Anti-Establishment Remissive.* It is the religion of those who were raised amidst the rigidities of the preconciliar Church (many of them entered the priesthood or religious life) and who are in a state of more or less permanent rebellion against those rigidities. Their religion has meaning (see Chapter Four) insofar as it permits progressive "breakthroughs" against things which were formerly forbidden or discouraged—in liturgy, in doctrine, in morals. For many, this stage of Catholicism has merely been a necessary psychological prelude to abandoning the Church altogether. For others it continues to have strong if diminishing appeal. However, in its negativity it is patently doomed to extinction.

The second form can be called *Sentimental Communalism,* and it is often a stage into which people pass after working their way out of the first (although the two are not necessarily incompatible). It is also, for many younger Catholics raised wholly in the postconciliar epoch, the only kind of Catholicism of which they have any knowledge. In essence it is the belief that religion is for the sake of "encountering God in other people." It is quintessentially therapeutic, in Philip Rieff's sense of the term, in that its goal is to facilitate maximum self-fulfillment in each person, for which the local church community is to serve as the nurturing matrix. Like the first, it seems doomed to eventual extinction, because there is little in this model which cannot be found better somewhere else and it is, ultimately, intellectually and emotionally impoverished.

The third and fourth forms which an animated Catholicism takes in the present cultural milieu are the *Charismatic* and the *Social Gospel,* neither of which requires additional description or definition. The former, whatever good it embodies, seems to exist in only a loose and ill-defined relationship with the sacramental and hierarchical life of the Church. It is private devotion elevated to a position of ecclesial centrality. The latter is a necessary part of any legitimate Catholicism but tends, imperialistically, to crowd out the other parts.

The great task of the Catholic Church, in the last two decades of the twentieth century, is to re-create conditions which will make a vital, compelling life of devotion possible in continuity and harmony with the authentic Catholic tradition. How can it be achieved? The dangers which the Church faces have been identified in the previous chapters. It is now possible to suggest some needed remedies.

1. The Validation of Traditional Catholicism

As asserted above, there are a surprisingly large number of pockets of healthy, thriving traditional Catholicism in the United States—parishes, religious communities, even whole dioceses. Such groups demonstrate that, contrary to what is so often declared publicly, genuine Catholicism is still viable in the last quarter of the twentieth century. In fact, rather than merely surviving, many such communities (especially those of religious women) are attracting new members and show no signs of decline or decay.

Yet for the most part, along with the even larger number of individuals who are profoundly steeped in traditional Catholicism, they have not been given encouragement or support in the postconciliar Church. Often Church leaders, including bishops and major religious superiors, have manifested coldness, hostility, or at best a forced tolerance towards such people and such communities. One of the many ironies of the age of renewal has been the fact that, although a gospel of love is proclaimed as normative, many progressive Catholics seem to feel exempt from manifesting love toward the conservatives. Religious superiors who bend every effort to placate discontented progressives in their charge often show scant patience with those who are deemed stubbornly backward.

What is at stake here is not merely the obligation to be tolerant, however. Rather the cavalier treatment often meted out to traditionalists, even by Church authorities, has done much to foster the common impression that the Church is turning its back on its past. Probably the majority of the laity harbor deeply conservative instincts in matters of religion (taken phenomenologically, religion is a deeply conservative thing, always concerned not to lose touch with its sacred traditions). However, many have also been embarrassed, intimidated, or cajoled into silence. In countless struggles which have gone on in schools, parishes, and dioceses, traditionalists have been effectively beaten down, a lesson not lost on the great silent majority.

Two unhealthy effects have resulted. One is a loss of morale and inner conviction on the part of many Catholics. Their faith has been damaged by the apparent experience of being told that everything they were raised to believe was somehow false. Without having been converted to the new, they have come to doubt the old, which leaves them in a spiritual no-man's land. Even their receptivity to new religious ideas and movements has been severely restricted by the instinctive caution they now feel towards all religious affirmations. They are, all too often, frozen in apathy and timidity.

The second unfortunate result is that the Church has been left without an effective bulwark against indiscriminate innovation. The resistant role which a naturally conservative laity would normally play has been severely eroded. Consequently, in the absence of effective opposition, ecclesiastical innovators have won too many easy victories, which have been good for neither the Church nor the innovators. Some Church leaders have unwittingly made themselves wholly vulnerable to pressures for innovation by effectively stifling all genuine traditionalism within their jurisdictions, an action they may have cause to regret.

The point is not that traditionalist Catholics have all right on their side or that they alone deserve to be listened to. The point is rather that a healthy and respected traditionalism is essential to a healthy Church both for the sake of balance and as a firm foundation on which other structures can be erected. The modern liberal churches are essentially perpetual-motion machines. They ceaselessly innovate, to the point where innovation no longer has any meaning, because it seems to occur in accordance with no firmly held principles. Catholicism, before it is too late, can insure the solidity of its social and intellectual base.

Just as there are many liberal Catholics whom the Church will find it impossible to placate, no matter what its policies, so there are traditionalists the validity of whose beliefs cannot be admitted without doing severe damage to the fabric of the Church. It is obvious, for example, that most of the members of the Catholic Traditionalist Movement, or the followers of the retired French Archbishop Marcel Lefevre, are schismatics at heart. They have rejected the Second Vatican Council, which for Catholics is an impossible stance. Their demand for a Latin liturgy is merely a symptom of much deeper grievances, the satisfaction of which would require that the Council be repealed. Even among nonschismatic traditionalists there is sometimes a rigidity of mind, often an angry hysteria, and an inability to discriminate which may well render reconciliation impossible. Such people, obviously, cannot be permitted to set the tone for Catholic life.

It remains to identify the major features of the responsible kind of traditionalism which is here being discussed.

A sacral liturgy. Most Catholics desire a liturgy which is dignified, restrained, solemn, and marked by "the beauty of holiness." To achieve this, certain changes are probably necessary in the present official English liturgy.[3] However, much could be achieved simply by a serious and thoughtful effort on the part of the clergy to celebrate the liturgy as the Council and the great classical modern liturgists envisioned its celebration. There is room in the Church for "small group" eucharists. But on Sundays and great feasts people should be encouraged to take part in the solemn, complete liturgy of the whole Church. The Latin Mass, encouraged by the Second Vatican Council and by the late Pope Paul VI, should be celebrated with sufficient frequency to become once again familiar to all Catholics, something they can participate in with meaning.

Orthodox catechetics. Next to liturgy, no area of contemporary Church life has stirred up more controversy, anger, dismay, and alienation than catechetics, in which many parents have discovered not only that their own religious beliefs are not being passed on to their children but that they are made to seem, in their children's eyes, benighted and backward. Often they are exhorted to take personal responsibility for their children's religious formation even as their attempts to do so are being systematically undermined in the schools. The point is not a return to the Baltimore Catechism, a book which did an admirable job of presenting Catholic doctrine in a concise, condensed, and comprehensible manner. The point is rather, no matter what textbooks are used or what methods of instruction employed, that the starting point be a solid grounding in doctrine. From that base many varieties of "enrichment" or personalized learning can occur.

Clarity of doctrine. In the popular mind virtually all the teachings of the Church are now in doubt, and it is a truism that, upon consulting ten priests on a given question, a lay person will obtain ten different opinions. Such a situation is fundamentally demoralizing and progressively undermines people's faith in the Church itself. Bishops and priests need to give firm and unambiguous guidance to their people concerning the distinction between official Church doctrine and mere opinion, as well as between opinions which are compatible with official teaching and those which are not. The Church's teaching function can once more be effective and respected.

Moral firmness. A category of the above, it is nonetheless a special case because of the high degree of sensitivity which it stimulates, and its practical implications. Many lay people find themselves living in an increasingly pagan culture, a culture whose paganism expresses itself especially through sexual behavior, and they find the Church of only slight support in their struggle to withstand this influence. Catholic doctrine on sex needs to be articulated with much greater firmness than has been the case in recent years. Equally importantly, the Church should attempt to articulate for modern man a strong and compelling vision of the beauty of chastity (understood in its full sense). If the Church once again makes its teachings coherent and credible with regard to sex, its moral witness in other areas (for example, social justice) will likewise gain in credibility.

2. The Continuity of Generations

It is now a commonplace that, while traditional Catholicism may still be viable for some older people, it has no meaning for the younger generation. Anyone now involved in teaching, especially at the college level, knows this is not true—there are a surprising number of young people (including a growing number of seminarians) who have a deep interest and belief in Catholicism in all its fullness and reject the various ploys which have been used to make religion "relevant" to youth.

In an age of religious searching, there are probably many more young people who would be receptive to such a faith if they had any real knowledge of it. However, the conditions of religious education and parish and campus life are now often such that many young people have not so much rejected Catholicism as simply never been taught what it is.

The ability to communicate Catholic teaching to the young obviously involves a revitalization of the Church at all levels. Liturgy and catechetics, as suggested above, are central. However, it must also be recognized that in matters of religion formal instruction is ultimately less important than the experience of a living faith. This does not mean, as it is often facilely taken to mean, that Catholicism will be credible only when all Catholics are saints. It rather means that Catholic beliefs must be encountered as rooted in believing communities—especially parishes and families—among people who sincerely try to live in accordance with them.

The importance of encouraging the remaining bases of traditional belief which exist in the Church is also obvious at this point. A generation gap has developed in the Church in part because children have often been allowed to think that their parents' faith was merely something quaint and eccentric, even as contrary to the mind of the Church. Once a viable traditionalism has been reinvigorated among adults, it will come to have plausibility among their children.

Church leaders have made a serious tactical error in the past fifteen years by the apparent decision, in many dioceses and religious communities, to assign troubled priests and religious (especially those troubled by doubts) to work with young people. Whatever has been gained in the short run in terms of "relevance" and empathy with the young has been more than lost by the long-term sapping of the foundations of youthful belief which has also resulted. Many young people have had little contact with priests and religious who were not themselves in the throes of doubt and even rebellion. On the other hand, campus chaplains with firm vocational identities and deeply held beliefs often have remarkable success in nurturing a strong Catholicism in the students under their care.

For the sake of both adults and children, the proclamation of Catholic teaching should emphasize its continuity with the past rather than its discontinuity. Amidst the sometimes frenetic changes of the conciliar era, the emphasis on newness was perhaps inevitable. But among some Catholics (and especially among some priests and religious) a reflex instinct has developed by which, at every point, they reach out for what is new and discard what is traditional. If the continuities of Catholic life were emphasized instead, and if a sincere effort were made to maintain those continuities, legitimate change would also become more credible in many people's eyes.

3. Responsible Innovation

Unyielding traditionalists are not the only people whose needs the Church must meet. Furthermore, the spirit of authentic Catholicism is not static but developmental. The Church takes history seriously, and tradition is not tradition unless it is developmental.

However, for the past twenty years it has not been necessary to emphasize these points (although many have emphasized them to the point of nausea). The spirit of the age has inexorably pushed the Church towards innovation and attenuated contacts with its past.

The time is now ripe for a systematic critical assessment of that change. Recognizing that much of what has occured since the Council has been frenetic and impulsive, motivated more by the *Zeitgeist* than by the Holy Spirit, the leaders of the Church should set in motion a systematic and carefully planned review of what occurred.

Crucial to such a review should be an *a priori* agreement on the criteria which would govern it: the authentic teachings of the Church, especially as they culminate in the decrees of the Second Vatican Council. These decrees remain among the great unread documents of modern times. Although practically everyone, Catholic and non-Catholic, has an impression of what the Council said and did, relatively few demonstrate an intimate familiarity with its actual statements. Even theologians have been known to censor some of its blunter passages, preferring to rely on the vaguer formulations which lend themselves to free interpretation.

Besides the essential doctrinal basis for evaluating change, certain more pragmatic criteria are also appropriate. For example, there has been much talk about "experimentation" but almost no real experimentation. For experimentation implies precisely the existence of controlled conditions, systematic review and evaluation, and established criteria for such review. In the many experiments carried out in liturgy, in catechetics, in religious life, and in countless other areas of the Church, few such processes have been implemented. Yet many of them have had the opposite effects from those intended—they have not made Catholicism more credible and attractive but less so (sometimes after a brief initial period of artificially induced euphoria).

The process of evaluation which must now be carried out will necessarily be a painful one, more painful by far than if there had been evaluative efforts at every stage of postconciliar development. The primarily negative, destructive, or unfruitful character of many experiments, some of them now of rather long standing, will have to be publicly admitted. There are groups of people, especially professionals in various fields, who are committed to such programs with unyielding bureaucratic tenacity.

If much of the debris of the postconciliar scene is cleared away, the alternative is not necessarily a return to preconciliar conditions. Many features of the preconciliar Church, especially in liturgical and devotional life, were thoughtlessly discarded and can be reclaimed. However, history is never simply repetition of the past, and it is true that certain features of the preconciliar Church needed to be discarded. Irresponsible innovators have, in a short period of time, accomplished the remarkable feat of almost making the "unrenewed" Church seem idyllic, which those who lived in it understand at least intellectually was not the case.

In principle it is correct to say that in each age God may be calling His people in radically new and unexpected directions, and the late twentieth century is no exception. New ministries are developing and new understandings of the world, to say nothing of new questions which the Church has never before had to face.

What is essential in all this is that the Church seriously ask itself the question when it is truly God who is summoning and when it is other, more seductive voices. No Catholic can finally believe that such discrimination is based on merely subjective and personal experiences. Final authority is given to the Church, speaking solemnly and objectively. In principle there are perhaps many "radical life-styles" open to modern Catholics. What is minimally required is that all such new paths be shown to lead not away from the Church and its truths but closer to them. (The historical example of Dorothy Day and her movement remains salient.)

The same principle obtains with regard to doctrine. Modern theologians are justified in saying that theological truth cannot be bound irrevocably to certain philosophical positions and that no doctrinal formulation is ever exhaustive. There is room in the modern Church for theologies which are genuinely daring, in the unfamiliar ways in which they look at eternal truths. What is required, however, is that these new theologies not be contradictory of authoritative past formulations and that they demonstrate proper concern for the fullness of Catholic truth.

4. Confident Self-definition

Modern culture is at its very root hostile to the act of definition and prefers an endlessly fluid reality, capable of being endlessly manipulated to serve the purposes of history. Historical Catholicism manifests precisely the opposite bias, and it is a measure of how deeply modern culture has taken its toll in the Church that so many people, even among the Church's leaders, appear now to recoil instinctively from the task of definition.

Put bluntly, that task is to state with some degree of precision who does and who does not belong in the Roman Catholic Church.

For this purpose it would be useful to delineate several categories of members: (a) Those who manifest a close congruence between the Church's teaching, in all its fullness, and their own lives—in other words, saints. (b) Those who believe in the Church's teachings, insofar as they know them, and struggle to live in accordance with them. In times past this was by far the largest category of Church membership, and probably still is. (c) Those who have sincere difficulties with certain of the Church's doctrines but accept its authority on the whole and attempt to cope with their difficulties in a genuine spirit of humility and docility. (It is highly instructive concerning the spirit of modern culture that the word *docile,* meaning "teachable," has gained an almost wholly negative meaning.)

Disproportionate attention, both inside and outside the Church, is now bestowed on a fourth category of members—those who pick and choose among doctrines at will and conceive for themselves a role of combative dissent in the Church.

Except in cases of blatant public scandal, the Church need not feel obliged to cut itself off from people in this category, although the effects of their continuing membership—both on themselves and on the Church at large—appear to be largely negative. However, it is fatal and unproductive to adopt a strategy of compromise in the hope that they will finally be won over by a show of "openness." As argued in Chapter Three, the right of dissent has become for some people the duty of dissent, and some know no other way of life.

There is, however, a crucial distinction to be made between the mass of the laity and its relationship to the Church and the relationship of priests, religious, teachers, ecclesiastical bureaucrats, and others who represent the Church in official capacities. The "right of dissent" accrues to the private person, not to those on whom the Church has conferred the privilege of leadership. Vast harm has been done by leaders who misused their authority, and perhaps the single most effective step towards authentic renewal in the Church would be for its leadership to insure that it present its people with coherent signals as to what is expected of them.

As stated earlier, the historical Catholic Church has always been very strict about what it will accept but not about whom it will accept. As the refuge of sinners, it welcomes all who come to it with good will, and even good will is defined generously.

But for better or for worse—by now it is an ineradicable historical fact—the Church takes belief very seriously. The unwillingness to be generous in accommodating beliefs, the insistance that there are true beliefs and false beliefs, is not a function of insecurity or rigidity. Among other things it reflects the Church's awareness that false belief, when tenaciously held to, cuts off even the possibility of repentance and reconciliation.

The Church now requires a pastoral style which combines sincere human kindness, a genuine personal openness and warmth, with firm conviction and the willingness to teach and, if necessary, rebuke.

In a poll taken especially for the Catholic Press Association, George Gallup proclaimed "good news"—although more and more Catholics might disagree with various Catholic doctrines, they were less inclined than formerly to leave the Church.[4] A survey by Father Andrew Greeley found that Irish-American Catholics under thirty were the "second most permissive group in the country" with regard to sexual morality, although their parents' generation was the least permissive.[5]

Faced with statistics indicating a general popular interest in religion, along with a willingness to discard specific doctrines almost at will, Catholic leaders might be tempted to follow the policies pursued by liberal Protestant leaders for many years—maintaining virtually no doctrinal conditions for church membership, discarding doctrines deemed unpopular or meaningless, and eagerly adapting the church to whatever social uses intrude themselves at any given moment. The pitfalls of such a procedure are obvious—for years the most liberal Protestant churches in America have been losing members steadily, while the more conservative (that is, more demanding, in terms of doctrine and discipline) have been gaining, some of them rather spectacularly. Membership in the Roman Catholic Church has continued to grow slightly, but not as noticeably as in the period before the advent of "reform."[6]

The objection will immediately be made, and properly, that it is not the task of the Church to accommodate itself to popular tastes and that statistics regarding church membership are ultimately irrelevant. This is true. However, much postconciliar reform has been justified on the grounds that without it the Church will cease to attract modern people. Reflection on the statistical pattern of American church membership in recent years may force a reassessment of the idea of what the real pastoral needs of the age are.

The question of authority and its exercise must be faced with courage. If it is true that the Church is not simply a papal monarchy, it is even more true that it is not a babble of competing voices, and the Second Vatican Council offers no grounds for negating either papal or episcopal authority.

A Church which seeks to define itself with the necessary precision will inevitably invite the change that it is authoritarian. In modern society, authoritarianism is permitted only in that area where dogmatic certitude is permitted, namely, politics. But a Catholicism without authority is not Catholicism.

An appropriate response to the charge of authoritarianism is simply to deflate the myth of the democratic Church. The Church is not now democratic and never could be. Those churches which claim to be democratic are not so in reality. As the anointed leaders of the Church surrender their authority, it does not evaporate but passes into other hands. The amazingly swift and pervasive innovation which has occurred in the past twenty years has not been due merely to the breath of the spirit. It has been planned and willed, imposed by fiat and implemented by manipulation, by people who have recognized a vacuum of authority and have gladly sought to fill it.

A word must be said about intellectual freedom in the Church, because the subject is greatly misunderstood. The Church permits free speculation which is precisely that—speculation. It does not permit the attempt to propagate speculation as though it were authoritative, and especially it does not permit the use of speculation to undermine established doctrine.

When speculation is purveyed to future priests and teachers as though it were truth, and when they in turn purvey it to the Church at large under the same guise, the Church is justified, and indeed obligated, to counter it forcefully. Among the rights of the laity which self-appointed champions of those rights have failed to notice is the right to be taught, and to have their children taught, authentic doctrine.

Modern conditions of communication may make it impossible for theological speculations to be confined to scholarly circles and thoroughly tested before being made public. However, the speculator who is truly Catholic does not actively seek public celebrity and does not make use of media eager to notice the smallest signs of dissension in the Church. The chosen style of operation of some contemporary theologians is not properly academic but involves the deliberate manipulation of public opinion to achieve political goals within the Church. As such it cannot claim the academic freedom which might accrue to a truly speculative thinker.

5. The Recovery of Zeal

As argued in earlier chapters, Catholicism, and indeed most of Christianity, apart from the evangelicals, now suffers from a severe demoralization, an inability and unwillingness to confront the world in vigorous and confident ways except in terms which secular society has already approved.

The root of this malaise is essentially intellectual or credal, stemming from severe doubts about the truths of Catholic doctrine.[7] As such there will be no significant improvement until some of the steps indicated above have been taken. A firm faith will inevitably result in a reawakened zeal.

It should be noted that this process of recovery is not primarily a matter of trying to whip up a religious frenzy in passive people. There is rather a natural dynamism in Catholicism which has been artificially restrained in the postconciliar era. Many Catholics sense that the Church has been signalling them, in a variety of ways, not to be aggressive and apostolic in their actions. A reversal of those signals would in time have the opposite effect.

Although not every Catholic will live an actively apostolic life, the choice between such a life and a diffident, passive Catholicism is not a valid one for the Church as a whole. Christianity by its very nature is a missionary religion, and when it ceases to be so it rapidly begins to lose its identity. And in modern pluralistic societies any movement which is passive and diffident soon loses all claim on public attention.

In this as in many other aspects of genuine renewal, change will have to come from the top down, in that the foundation of solid faith which exists at the bottom must first be activated and inspired from above. Too often Catholics have found examples of diffident passivity first among their clerical leaders and have simply followed that style. Even in the age of the laity, the Church will continue to depend very heavily on clerical and religious leadership.

On a very simple but crucial level what is now required is to instill in people a healthy pride in their Church. The process by which the real meaning of the Second Vatican Council was distorted is nowhere more bizarre than in the fact that a hopeful, joyous, and confident event was made the occasion for a sometimes compulsive orgy of breast-beating and self-recrimination, a process by no means over and one which has had severely demoralizing effects throughout the Church. In this as in every other area, the beginnings of authentic renewal would require a massive and comprehensive program of education in the true meaning of the Second Vatican Council.

6. The Revitalization of Institutions within the Church

After the period of romantic anti-institutionalization in the 1960s, the importance of institutions for any kind of sustained and effective life in the world is once again recognized. However, the Church finds itself at a severe disadvantage in this regard because the romanticism of the immediate postconciliar era did severe damage to many of its institutions.

The decline of Catholic institutions stems primarily from three causes: economic pressures, internal secularization, and the demoralization of personnel.

The first is part of the larger problem (discussed in Chapter Eight) by which the financial resources of the state are increasingly such that few private institutions can survive without state money. Simple inflation takes an enormous toll. Yet the price of such assistance is likely to be precisely the loss of religious independence.

The process of secularization has been severe, especially in Catholic institutions of higher education, and has come about partly as a result of the financial pressures referred to above and partly because of a simplistic idea of professionalism, in which firm and visible religious commitment has been understood as incompatible with "high standards."

The third cause of institutional decline has been partly a result of the first two but partly also a sharing in the general confusion which has spread through the Church. Many staff members of Catholic institutions—teachers, administrators, physicians, journalists, bureaucrats—simply do not know what is expected of them or their institutions and are unable to conceive a positive vision of what their institutions should be. The recovery of such a vision will have to await the recovery of vision for the entire Church.

There has occurred, willy-nilly, a winnowing of Catholic institutions in recent years—fewer schools, hospitals, charitable institutions, organizations, and journals than twenty years ago. Some such winnowing was necessary, and there must be even more of it. However, it has not been the right kind of winnowing. It has taken place largely as the result of financial pressures and the exigencies of local situations, not according to some overall vision of which institutions are necessary to the Church's mission and which are not.

The time has now come for the leaders of the Church to make some hard and often controversial decisions regarding institutions: which are to be kept and which allowed to die. Two criteria should govern: which institutions are serving purposes important to the Church's mission in the world, and which serve those purposes in a genuinely Catholic way.

To those which meet these tests the Church should offer financial and moral support adequate not only to their survival but also to their continued qualitative improvement. Every effort should be made to turn them into effective and respected agencies, which the world must take seriously.

As with the necessity of clear self-definition mentioned above, this process of institutional evaluation will be the occasion of much controversy, even of bitterness. However, the alternative is the present state of things—a declining number of Catholic institutions, most of them becoming less and less Catholic each year, most of them also becoming progressively weaker in terms of material support. It is clear, for example, that many Catholic colleges and universities have no future except the hazardous one of publicly proclaiming their secularity and hoping to survive on that basis, in competition with existing private schools and the vast public system.

In all areas of Catholic renewal, but especially in this one, the anointed leaders of the Church will have to confront the very serious problem of bureaucratic resistance—specialists and administrators in the various institutions who have learned to prefer the present amorphous state of affairs and whose policies and advice have to a great extent brought it about. The wholesale replacement of many of these bureaucrats may be a necessary prelude to effective institutional revitalization.

7. The Recovery of a Sense of the Social Order

Until now these proposals are open to the criticism that they seem to lay too much stress on orthodox belief and give little scope to what has come to be called "ortho-praxis."

The heightened awareness of social needs which is now present in the Church is perhaps the only area in which there has been a definite and measurable improvement of Catholic life in the postconciliar era. As argued in Chapter Eight, what is wrong about this awareness is not its substance or even its zeal but its fashionableness and its tendency to claim for itself exclusive validity in the contemporary Church.

Someone has pointed out that, while Catholic agencies concerned with social problems used to employ terms like *social order* in their titles, contemporary agencies are likely to employ words like *concern*. A firm, intellectual, and principled position has been exchanged for one that'borders on the sentimental and merely fashionable.

The dichotomy between other-worldly and this-worldly Catholicism is and always has been false, since real Catholicism requires both. There is in principle no restriction on the degree to which Catholics (including priests and religious) can be involved in social and political affairs, provided their involvement stems from a genuine religious commitment and a genuinely religious understanding of the world.

The vast upsurge of social awareness and "concern" which followed the Council now needs to be systematically evaluated, educated, and channelled. The study of authentic Catholic social doctrine is almost wholly neglected. Papal encyclicals, for example, are commonly ignored except for the occasional citation of a conveniently useful passage.

The question is not the familiar choice between being "liberal" or "conservative" in politics. The preconciliar temptation of many Catholics was to identify their religion with the status quo; the postconciliar tendency is to identify automatically with the forces of change. In reality an authentic Catholic social awareness would question the assumptions of both the right and the left and would come to see social problems in wholly new ways. Then the Church would begin to be truly prophetic.

8. New Ecumenical Directions

Although this work has dealt largely with Catholicism, and although it has argued for a self-confident and aggressive Catholicism, the modern Catholic is not free to ignore the ecumenical aspects of faith.

However, like most other things, ecumenism has suffered in the past twenty years from false and facile understandings. Too much has been made to depend on mere good will. Most seriously, the chief ecumenical efforts have been extended towards the liberal, mainstream Protestant churches.

This effort, although it has been superficially successful in terms of good will (whether this good will runs as deep as it appears is another question), has been misdirected for two reasons—the churches towards which it has been directed have weak doctrinal positions and thus "agreements" are too easily arrived at, and these same churches are infinitely flexible in their relationships with contemporary secular culture.

The real ecumenical task, which presents both the greatest difficulties and possibly the greatest rewards, is to begin explorations with the Protestant groups broadly called evangelical. The greatest difficulties are found here, because these groups take their own beliefs very seriously and will not compromise easily. However, the greatest rewards are also to be found here because by the end of the twentieth century the liberal denominations will probably have ceased to be Christian for all practical purposes and the future of Christianity will depend on Catholics, Orthodox, and evangelical Protestants.

Short of actual doctrinal agreements, this new kind of ecumenical dialogue can be especially fruitful in terms of a reinvigorated Christian influence over American culture—the insistence that Christian beliefs and Christian moral principles be treated with respect and given proper weight in the formulation of public policy.

* * *

Some conservative Catholics have all but despaired of the Church and fall into the temptation of regarding the Second Vatican Council as a disaster. But the Council drew to a close barely fifteen years ago. If its great promise remains unfulfilled, nonetheless the promise remains.

The "ghetto Catholicism" of the preconciliar era has been widely derided, and there was much in it which was silly, shallow, and distorting of true Catholicism. Yet, in the end, whether or not a particular people constitute a ghetto is not a decision they themselves can make. It is primarily imposed on them by their culture.

Catholicism cannot and should not return to the preconcilar ghetto, in part because the conditions of preconciliar Catholicism were, as the Church's present disarray demonstrates, inadequate for the needs of modern faith. Yet a modern faith, that is, one lived in the midst of modern culture, will not be a faith which simply allows itself to be shaped by that culture. To the degree that it insists on its independence, on its right to judge the culture in which it dwells, the Church will be condemned as a ghetto.

Many Catholics find this idea insupportable and hasten to make their separate peace with their culture. The Church of the year 2000 may be a significantly smaller body than the Church of the year 1960. Yet Catholicism, and any religion which takes its beliefs seriously, has no other alternative open to it. To be in the world but not of it will, in the year 2000 no less than in the year 200, be a command which requires no end of humility and courage.

Notes

For full bibliographical data on books cited in the Notes, see the Bibliography.

Chapter 1

1. See on this point James Hitchcock, *The Decline and Fall of Radical Catholicism,* especially Chapter 2.
2. Respectively: *Perfectae Caritatis,* art. 5 (*The Documents of Vatican II,* ed. Walter M. Abbott, p. 470); *Lumen Gentium,* art. 10 (Abbott, p. 27); *Optatam Totius,* art. 10 (Abbott, pp. 446–47).
3. Respectively: *Lumen Gentium,* art. 44 (Abbott, p. 75); *Gaudium et Spes,* arts. 18, 41, 51 (Abbott, pp. 215, 240, 256).
4. See *Gaudium et Spes,* art. 42 (Abbott, p. 242).
5. Kieran Quinn in *On the Run,* ed. Michael McCauley, pp. 173–75, 179–80, 183–84.
6. Eugene C. Kennedy, M. M., in *The National Catholic Reporter* (hereafter N.C.R.), 23 March 1973, p. 9.
7. Eric Voegelin, *The New Science of Politics,* pp. 123–24, 129, 131.
8. St. Theresa of Avila, *Interior Castle,* trans. and ed. E. Allison Peers, p. 120.
9. Gregory Baum, *Religion and Alienation,* pp. 270–73, 283.
10. Langdon Gilkey, *Catholicism Confronts Modernity: A Protestant View,* pp. 66–67.
11. Dennis J. Geaney, O.S.A., in N.C.R., 6 June 1975, p. 11.
12. Janet M. Bennett in N.C.R., 10 December 1976, p. 12.
13. James H. Ebner, *God Present as Mystery,* pp. 94, 99.
14. Don Brophy, "Why I Don't Pray Anymore," N.C.R., 1 March 1974, p. 9.
15. Rev. George Clements, N.C.R., 4 February 1977, p. 4.

Chapter 2

1. Respectively: *Lumen Gentium,* art. 20 (*The Documents of Vatican II,* ed. Walter M. Abbott, p. 39); *Dei Verbum,* art. 9 (Abbott, p. 117). Virtually every one of the Council's decrees pays respect to tradition.
2. For a discussion of this phenomenon in a liturgical context see Hitchcock, *The Recovery of the Sacred,* especially Chapter 4.
3. Quoted in Marcelle Bernstein, *The Nuns,* pp. 112, 121.

4. Bernard Besret, O.C.S.O., *Tomorrow a New Church*, trans. Matthew J. O'Connell, p. 29.

5. See for example Alec R. Vidler, *A Variety of Catholic Modernists*, pp. 49, 55, 82, and Bernard M. G. Reardon, *Roman Catholic Modernism*, p. 66.

6. Mark Schoof, O.P., *A Survey of Catholic Theology*, trans. N. D. Smith, especially pp. 45–71, 180–87, 210–64.

7. Frederick Heer in *The London Times History of Our Times*, ed. Marcus Cunliffe, pp. 184–90.

8. "New Intellectuals," *The Tablet*, 31 January 1976, p. 117.

9. John W. O'Malley, S.J., "Reform, Historical Consciousness, and Vatican II's Aggiornamento," *Theological Studies*, XXXII (1971), pp. 575, 590, 597, 600.

10. See *Lumen Gentium*, art. 8 (Abbott, p. 22).

11. T. S. Eliot, *Notes Toward a Definition of Culture*, p. 30.

12. N.C.R., 14 May 1976, p. 16.

13. *St. Louis Review*, 10 December 1976, p. 1.

14. *St. Louis Post-Dispatch*, 11 February 1977, p. 6D. *Commonweal*, 4 March 1977, pp. 131–32.

15. Walter J. Ong, S.J., "Catholic Theology Now," *Catholic Mind*, June 1977, p. 37.

16. Rev. Louis Evely in N.C.R., 4 December 1970, p. 3.

17. Quoted in Francine du Plessix Gray, *Divine Disobedience*, p. 201.

18. Daniel Berrigan and Robert Coles, *The Geography of Faith*, p. 79.

19. John D. Mulligan, S.M., quoted in the *St. Louis Review*, 25 July 1975, p. 1. For the early Marianists see Katherine Burton, *Chaminade, Apostle of Mary*, especially pp. 23, 26–28, 31, 33–41, 52, 86–87, 105, 108, 181–86. A number of Father Chaminade's associates were persecuted in the Revolution.

20. John P. Sisk, "Fanaticism and Survival," *Worldview*, November 1976, p. 14.

21. Robert A. Graham, S.J., in *The Wanderer*, 30 June 1977, pp. 1, 71.

22. Norman Ravitch in the *American Historical Review*, LXXX, 4 (October 1975), 961.

23. Rev. Richard P. McBrien, "Rahner—Our Ambiguous 'Best' Theologian," N.C.R., 26 April 1974, p. 13.

24. Raymond A. Schroth, S.J., in *Commonweal*, 10 August 1973, p. 433.

25. *Lumen Gentium*, arts. 14, 22, 25, 37 (Abbott, pp. 33, 43, 49, 64); Pope John XXIII, *Journal of a Soul*, trans. Dorothy White, p. 305.

26. David J. O'Brien in *Journeys*, ed. Gregory Baum, pp. 69, 73.

27. Daniel Bell, *The Cultural Contradictions of Capitalism*, p. 4.

28. George A. Lindbeck, "The Catholic Crisis," *Commonweal*, 13 February 1976, p. 108.

29. Quoted by Lewis Mumford in *The New Yorker*, 26 October 1970, p. 114.

30. Wayne J. Holman, III, "James A. Pike: Child of His Time," *New Oxford Review*, May 1977, p. 7.

Chapter 3

1. N.C.R., 3 June 1977, p. 20.

2. Rev. Donald Ranly, quoted in Paul Wilkes, *These Priests Stay*, pp. 109–10, 115, 123.

3. O'Malley, "Reform, Historical Consciousness, and Vatican II," *Theological Studies*, XXXII (1971), p. 575. Father O'Malley rejects this formulation as no longer valid.

4. T. S. Eliot, *Notes Toward a Definition of Culture,* pp. 12–13.

5. Dean M. Kelley, *Why Conservative Churches Are Growing,* p. x.

6. Brian Wicker, "More Civilized, Less Interesting," *Commonweal,* 9 March 1973, p. 8.

7. Philip Rieff, *The Triumph of the Therapeutic,* pp. 12, 19, 22, 25, 73–74.

8. Ibid., pp. 35, 78, 236.

9. N.C.R., 21 February 1975, p. 23.

10. Marcelle Bernstein, *The Nuns,* p. 299.

11. Anthony Padovano, "Needed: Theology of Fidelity," N.C.R., 19 March 1971, p. 13.

12. Rieff, *Triumph,* pp. 2–3, 10, 14–15, 54–55, 58, 62, 78, 239–40, 259; Philip Rieff, *Fellow Teachers,* pp. 22, 93.

13. See, for example, *Lumen Gentium,* arts. 25 and 45 (*The Documents of Vatican II,* ed. Walter M. Abbott, pp. 48–49, 76); *Dei Verbum,* art. 11 (Abbott, pp. 118–19); *Gaudium et Spes,* art. 12 (Abbott, p. 210); *Apostolicam Actuositatem* (on the laity), art. 24 (Abbott, p. 513–14).

14. Bernstein, *Nuns,* p. 267.

15. *A Canterbury Tale: Experience and Reflections, 1916–1976,* pp. 53, 101, 119, 125.

16. Eliot, *Notes Toward a Definition of Culture,* p. 146.

17. Donald T. Campbell, "On the Conflict between Biological and Social Evolution and between Psychology and Moral Tradition," *American Psychologist,* XXX, 12 (December, 1975), pp. 1103, 1120–21. For other perceptive psychological critiques of psychological dogmas see Paul C. Vitz, *Psychology as Religion,* and John N. Kotre, "Religion, Psychiatry, and the Sterile Self," *Commonweal,* 12 May 1978, pp. 295–300.

18. Harold J. Berman, *The Interaction of Law and Religion,* pp. 78, 88, 95.

19. Rieff, *Triumph,* pp. 49–50, 63, 76, 92–93, 99, 232, 254–55. Rieff, *Fellow Teachers,* p. 86.

20. Richard Dunn, quoted in *The Christian Century,* 20 September 1972, p. 934.

21. "Priest Uses TA to Present Gospel," N.C.R., 15 November 1974, p. 4.

22. Quoted in the *St. Louis Review,* 22 April 1977, p. 9.

23. *New York Times,* 24 October 1974, p. 50.

24. Msgr. Stephen J. Kelleher, "The Laity, Divorce, and Remarriage," *Commonweal,* 7 November 1975, p. 4.

25. Dennis J. Doherty, *Divorce and Remarriage: Resolving a Catholic Dilemma,* p. 75.

26. Rev. Jack Finnegan, quoted in N.C.R., 5 September 1975, p. 4.

27. Kelleher, "Catholic Annulment, a Dehumanizing Process," *Commonweal,* 10 June 1977, pp. 364–68.

28. " 'Fuzzies' Show Spirit of Love, Sharing," Green Bay (Wisconsin) *Spirit,* 8 March 1974, p. 8.

29. Rev. Anthony Kosnik, ed., *Human Sexuality: New Directions in American Catholic Thought.*

30. See *Dignitatis Humanae,* art. 8 (Abbott, p. 687); and *Gaudium et Spes,* art. 17 (Abbott, p. 214).

31. "Teaching Right from Wrong," N.C.R., 13 May 1977, p. 10.

32. "The Democratization of Culture; a Reappraisal," *Change,* Summer 1975, p. 22. "Technology Cripples Family," N.C.R., 11 February 1977, p. 12.

33. See the description in N.C.R., 13 May 1977, p. 1.

34. "Getting Rid of the Pain of Sin," *Worldview,* XX, 6 (June 1977), p. 6.

35. Langdon Gilkey, *Catholicism Confronts Modernity*, pp. 75–76.
36. Daniel Bell, *The Cultural Contradictions, of Capitalism*, p. 19.
37. Gregory Baum, Religion and Alienation, p. 98.
38 Ibid., pp. 69, 76, 78–79.
39. Ibid., p. 124.
40. See James Hitchcock, *The Recovery of the Sacred*, especially pp. 144–49.
41. Bernstein, *Nuns*, pp. 97–99, 314–16, 153, 208, 270.
42. Robert Y. O'Brien, "Good News in Gospel," *The (Peoria) Catholic Post*, 16 June 1974, p. 9.
43. "Reflections: The Uses of Enchantment," *The New Yorker*, 8 December, 1975, pp. 50–114.
44. Quentin Anderson, *The Imperial Self: An Essay in American Literary and Cultural History*, pp. 24, 56, 231; "Practical and Visionary Americans," *The American Scholar*, Summer 1976, p. 408.
45. John Lukacs, *The Passing of the Modern Age*, p. 169.
46. Rieff, *Triumph*, pp. 16, 18, 232; Rieff, *Fellow Teachers*, pp. 179–80.
47. Reported in the *St. Louis Review*, 1 December 1972, p. 2.
48. *New York Daily News*, 2 March 1972, p. 2.
49. *Documents*, pp. 949, 952.
50. Lionel Trilling, *The Liberal Imagination: Essays on Literature and Society*, p. 233.
51. Doherty, *Divorce and Remarriage*, pp. 34, 130, 139, 141.
52. Rev. Jack Dominian, *The Church and the Sexual Revolution*, p. 69.
53. Eugene C. Kennedy, M.M., in *Commonweal*, 18 December 1970, p. 293.
54. James J. DiGiacomo, S.J., in *U.S. Catholic*, August 1976, p. 16, and *Living Light*, Winter 1977, p. 619.
55. Rieff, *Fellow Teachers*, pp. 100, 115, 170.
56. James Carroll, in N.C.R., 13 April 1973, p. 16.
57. "An Open Letter to Joe O'Rourke," *Commonweal*, 18 October 1974, p. 65.
58. Robert Nisbet, *Twilight of Authority*, p. 119.
59. In *The New Yorker*, 30 August 1976, p. 21.
60. Rieff, *Triumph*, p. 13.
61. Henry Ten Kortenaar, "Divorce, Si—Papa, No," *Commonweal*, 28 June 1974, p. 357.
62. Urban G. Steinmetz, *The Sexual Christian*, p. 88.
63. Sister Marie Iglesias, quoted in N.C.R., 27 May 1977, p. 16.
64. Rev. John McKenzie, in *The Critic*, July-August 1971, p. 79.
65. Bell, *The Cultural Contradictions of Capitalism*, p. 157.
66. Rieff, *Triumph*, p. 8. Rieff, *Fellow Teachers*, pp. 152, 166.

Chapter 4

1. *Gaudium et Spes*, art. 17 (*The Documents of Vatican II*, ed. Walter M. Abbott, p. 214); *Dignitatis Humanae*, art. 8 (Abbott, p. 687).
2. Philip Rieff, *Triumph of the Therapeutic*, pp. 3, 5, 11, 41; Philip Rieff, *Fellow Teachers*, pp 52, 136.
3. Rev. Henry Fehren, "Parade of the Wooden Soldiers," *U.S. Catholic*, February 1975, p. 42.
4. Hugh Calkins, O.S.M., "A Fresh Look at Old Catholic Devotions," *U.S. Catholic*, June 1976, pp. 7, 8, 10, 13.
5. Dennis Doherty, *Divorce and Remarriage*, pp 147, 149.

6. Evelyn Waugh, *Put Out More Flags,* p. 273.

7. Doherty, *Divorce and Remarriage,* p 127.

8. Dorothy Donnelly, C.S.J., quoted by Patricia de Zutter, in N.C.R., 23 November 1973, pp. 7, 18.

9. Rev. Leonard F. Chrobot in N.C.R., 1 July 1977, p. 12.

10. *The Tablet,* 7 February 1976, p. 149.

11. Ronald Luka, C.M.F., "Blessed Are the Streakers," N.C.R., 26 April 1974, p. 4.

12. Sister Margaret Ellen Traxler, quoted in N.C.R., 11 February 1977, p. 16.

13. Quoted by James H. Ebner, *God Present as Mystery,* p. 126.

14. Ibid., p. 112: "To meet the demands of the age (or, if you prefer, to heed the call of the Spirit). . . ."

15. Quoted by Marcelle Bernstein, *The Nuns,* p. 269.

16. James Young, C.S.P., "Stabilizing Marriage by Permitting Divorce," N.C.R., 1 February 1974, p. 9; and "Divorce and Remarriage," *Commonweal,* 22 November 1974, pp. 187–88.

17. Jacques Ellul, *The New Demons,* pp. 35, 210.

18. Edmund J. Egan, "Keep Faith," N.C.R., 5 July 1974, p. 8.

19. Rev. Joseph M. Champlin, "Establishing the Parish Council," New Orleans *Clarion-Herald,* 16 September 1976, p. 9.

20. Most Rev. Andrew McDonald, N.C.R., 19 April 1974, p. 8.

21. Rosemary Fleming, O.S.F., N.C.R., 24 September 1976, p. 13.

22. See *Commonweal,* 16 September 1977, pp. 589–93, and 2 September 1977, pp. 556–62. The suggestion that Novak's essay should not have been allowed to be published came from Robert J. Egan, S.J., and an Episcopalian, Rev. Gardner H. Shattuck, Jr.

23. "Planned Obsolescence," *New York Review of Books,* 28 October 1976, pp. 7, 12.

24. Langdon Gilkey, *Catholicism Confronts Modernity,* pp. 113–14.

25. James Bisset Pratt, "Religion and the Younger Generation," in *College Readings in Contemporary Thought,* ed. Kendall B. Taft et al., pp. 329, 330, 332.

Chapter 5

1. *The Documents of Vatican II,* ed. Walter M. Abbott, pp. 319–31.

2. Rev. Charles Curran in *Journeys,* ed. Gregory Baum, pp. 104–05.

3. For instances of media distortions see Hitchcock, "Bigotry in the Press: the Example of Newsweek," *The Alternative,* October 1976, pp. 19–21.

4. Curran in *Journeys,* p. 106.

5. *New York Times,* 12 February 1976, p. 25.

6. Rosemary Ruether in N.C.R., 8 October 1971, pp. 10–11.

7. *St. Louis Review,* 9 September 1977, p. 6.

8. Rev. Edward Pfnausch and Rev. Donald Heintschel, quoted in N.C.R., 21 October 1977, p. 19.

9. Quoted in the St. Louis *Post-Dispatch,* 26 October 1977, p. 3H.

10. Patricia Scharber Lefevere, "Küng the Personality . . . as Writer," N.C.R., 21 October 1977, pp. 8, 16, 18.

11. Francine du Plessix Gray, *Divine Disobedience,* pp. 281, 173.

12. Reported in N.C.R., 21 April 1972. The *Times* editor was Rev. Edward Fiske.

13. Quoted in N.C.R., 11 April 1975, p. 5.

14. Fiske, quoted in N.C.R., 3 December 1971, p. 4.
15. St. Louis *Post-Dispatch,* 25 September 1977, p. 54E.
16. 2 October 1972, "Religion" section.
17. For a discussion of this process see Hitchcock, "The Dynamics of Popular Intellectual Change," *The American Scholar,* Autumn 1976, pp. 522–33.
18. See also Hitchcock, "Power to the Eloquent," *The Yale Review,* Spring 1977, pp. 374–87.
19. For an analysis of this phenomenon see Hitchcock, "Prophecy and Politics: Abortion in the Election of 1976," *Worldview,* March 1977, pp. 25–26, 35–37.
20. This was particularly the case with Pope Paul VI. See Hitchcock, "Bigotry in the Press."
21. See Hitchcock, "How Is a Catholic University Catholic in Practice?" *Delta Epsilon Sigma Bulletin,* May 1975, pp. 40–53.
22. Reported by Robert McClory in N.C.R., 24 March 1978, p. 5.
23. T. S. Eliot, *Notes Toward a Definition of Culture,* p. 18.
24. Peter Berger, *The Sacred Canopy,* pp 29–31, 49–50.
25. Peter Berger, *A Rumor of Angels,* pp. 6–10, 21, 24.
26. Barbara Chenicek, O.P., N.C.R., 30 August 1974, p. 11, and Teresa A. McGeady, S.F.C.C., N.C.R., 16 August 1974, p. 10. See Harold Rosenberg, *Art on the Edge,* chapters 19, 21, 23, 24, 26, 27.

Chapter 6

1. Thomas P. Sweetser, S. J., "No Clear View at Parish Level," N.C.R., 2 September 1977, p. 9.
2. "The Future of Historical Thinking," *Salmagundi,* Summer 1975, p. 104.
3. George F. Lundy, S.J., "Old Policy-Makers for a New Constituency?" N.C.R., 24 November 1972, p. 11.
4. Ann Marie Mongovan, O.P., quoted in N.C.R., 25 November 1977, p. 3.
5. See for example, Eugene Kennedy, M.M., "The Psychology of Religious Suppression," *The Critic,* February-March, 1969, pp. 69–72.
6. Philip Rieff, *Fellow Teachers,* p. 76.
7. Ibid., p. 127.
8. Walter Goddijn, *The Deferred Revolution,* pp. 46–49.
9. See Alfred Loisy, *The Gospel and the Church,* especially pp. 139–225.
10. *Religious Media Today* I, 1 (April 1976).
11. See the N.C.R., 27 May 1977; 3 June 1977; 1 July 1977.
12. Joseph O'Donoghue, quoted in N.C.R., 24 March 1972, p. 8.
13. See reports of the meeting in the New Orleans *Clarion-Herald,* 11 August 1977, pp. 3, 10, 11; N.C.R., 26 August 1977, pp. 8, 13.
14. Sharlene Shoemaker, "Parish Tries Family Approach to Religious Education," N.C.R., 2 August 1974, pp. 8, 13.
15. Rieff, *Fellow Teachers,* pp. 37, 57.
16. 11 April 1977, pp. 63–64, 67.
17. Marcelle Bernstein, *The Nuns,* pp. 207–8, 286–88.
18. James P. Leahy and Robert W. Lee, "What to Do with Unused Churches?" N.C.R., 3 June 1977, pp. 8–9.
19. Robert Harvey, *The Restless Heart,* pp. 53, 56, 73, 80, 86, 118, 133, 178–80, 193–94.
20. For varied accounts of the conference see the St. Louis *Review,* 29 October

1976, pp. 1, 8; *The Wanderer*, 11 November 1976, pp. 5, 7; and 4 November 1977, pp. 1, 5; *Worldview*, March 1977, pp. 15–19; N.C.R., November 5, 1976, pp. 1, 16. The various accounts do not seriously disagree as to the facts of the conference, although they differ considerably in their interpretation of those facts.

21. Rev. Richard McBrien, " 'Call to Action' Reflects 'People of God' Image," N.C.R., 12 November 1976, p. 20.

22. See for example Rev. Richard Creason and Msgr. George Casey in the St. Louis *Review*, 5 November 1976, pp. 10–11.

23. Reported in the N.C.R., 5 November 1976, p. 1.

24. The substance of these hearings was published in a series of booklets by the National Conference of Catholic Bishops.

25. Langdon Gilkey, *Catholicism Confronts Modernity*, p. 74.

26. John Cogley, *Canterbury Tale*, pp. 49, 89, 125.

27. Ibid., pp. 18–19, 28.

28. Quoted by Robert Coles, "The Old Church, the Spanish Church, the American Church," *Commonweal*, 21 September 1973, pp. 495–97.

29. T. S. Eliot, *Notes Toward a Definition of Culture*, p. 15.

30. Donnelly, "The Empress Has No Clothes," N.C.R., 24 May 1974, p. 7.

31. *America*, 27 June 1970, p. 685.

Chapter 7

1. Sidney Lens, "Carter 'Simplistic' on Human Rights," N.C.R., 29 April 1977, p. 14.

2. "Distrust of Church in Cuba Fades," N.C.R., 19 November 1971, pp. 3, 4.

3. James Higgins, "New Church in New Cuba," *Commonweal*, 28 July 1972, pp. 399–402.

4. Rev. Frederick McGuire, quoted in N.C.R., 1 March 1974, p. 16.

5. Thomas E. Quigley, " 'Miss Freedom' Awards Are, at Best, Irrelevant," *Worldview*, November 1974, pp. 39–40.

6. N.C.R., 7 January 1977, p. 16; 14 January 1977, p. 3.

7. Quoted in the St. Louis *Post-Dispatch*, 12 May 1977, p. 2A; N.C.R., 20 May 1977, pp. 1, 10.

8. Rev. Patrick O'Malley, quoted in N.C.R., 17 March 1978, p. 5.

9. Rev. Harry Bury, "Religion in Vietnam," N.C.R., 24 November 1972, p. 14.

10. Tissa Balasuriya, O.M.I., "Theological Reflections on Vietnam," *Commonweal*, 26 September 1975, pp. 426–32.

11. Ibid., pp. 429–32.

12. Rev. Bill Hogan, in N.C.R., 30 April 1976, p. 8, and 10 September 1976, p. 11; *Worldview*, July-August 1976, p. 59.

13. David P. Chandler, "Transformation in Cambodia," *Commonweal*, 1 April 1977, p. 210.

14. Quoted in *Worldview*, July-August 1976, p. 30.

15. Quoted by John Deedy in *Commonweal*, 26 May 1972, p. 274.

16. The ecumenical journal *Worldview* and the democratic socialist journal *Dissent* have consistently published critical material about life in "progressive" countries. See also *Commentary*, December 1976; the *New York Review of Books*, 17 March 1977; 26 May 1977; and 9 June 1977; and periodical reports in the *AFL-CIO Free Trade Union News*.

17. Rev. John Stitz, quoted in N.C.R., 13 August 1976, pp. 6, 8.

18. Maud Russell, N.C.R., p. 8.

19. Donald J. Thorman, "China Does What Christians Don't," N.C.R., 26 November 1976, p. 8.

20. Paul Clifford and Herbert Dargan, S.J., N.C.R., 20 June 1975, pp. 7–8.

21. "Strannik" (pseud.), "A Pilgrim's Journal," *The Clergy Review,* July 1978, pp. 262–64.

22. E. R. Norman, *Church and Society,* pp. 428, 473.

23. Ibid., pp. 8, 10, 232, 469–70, 474.

24. "Churches Do Not Follow Leaders on Viet War," *St. Louis Review,* 2 June 1972, p. 8.

25. Clifford Longley in *The Tablet,* 20 August 1977, p. 786.

26. Reported in N.C.R., 28 May 1976, p. 1.

27. Margaret Brennan, I.H.M., *New Visions: New Roles for Women in the Church,* p. 31. Cf. footnote 51.

28. Eric Voegelin, *New Science of Politics,* pp. 123, 129.

29. *National Jesuit News,* February 1972, pp. 7–8. The spokesman for the paper was Dennis Willigan, S.J.

30. Giovanni Franzoni, reported in N.C.R., 1 October 1976, p. 6.

31. Juan Luis Segundo, S.J., quoted in N.C.R., 10 September 1976, p. 4.

32. Most. Rev. Gilbert E. Chavez, N.C.R., 19 March 1976, p. 11.

33. Antonio M. Stevens-Arroyo, C.P., N.C.R., p. 8.

34. Gregory Baum, *Religion and Alienation,* pp. 190, 212, 283, 198, 209, 220–21, 285–86.

35. R. C. Zaehner, *Our Savage God: The Perverse Use of Eastern Thought,* pp. 20, 71, 143, 161, 164, 167, 189, 232, 245, 250, 254, 260–62, 269, 274, 288, 248–49.

36. *National Jesuit News,* February 1972, p. 7.

37. *National Jesuit News,* March 1972.

38. See the issues of Maryknoll especially for June and September 1972, and June 1974.

39. Victor Hummert, M.M., in N.C.R., 2 September 1976, p. 21.

40. Al Imfeld, *China as Model for Development,* trans. Matthew J. O'Connell.

41. See Francine du Plessix Gray, "Harrisburg: the Politics of Salvation," the *New York Review of Books,* 15 June 1972, p. 8; interview in *Commonweal,* 14 July 1972, pp. 377–79. Robert Coles, *Geography of Faith,* p. 119; Daniel Berrigan, *The Dark Night of Resistance,* pp. 75–78; Philip Berrigan, *Prison Journals,* pp. 78, 81, 107, 146, 161.

42. *The Christian Century,* 12 May 1976.

43. Sr. Janice Ann McLaughlin. For her opinions plus further information on the Rhodesian guerrillas see the N.C.R., 4 November 1977, pp. 5–6, and 23 September 1977, p. 4.

44. Daniel Berrigan and Robert Coles, *Geography of Faith,* pp. 61–63, 167–68.

45. *New York Times,* 12 September 1973, p. 53.

46. For the activities of the Symbionese Liberation Army see the left-wing journal *Ramparts* for May 1974. See also the St. Louis *Post-Dispatch,* 20 May 1974, p. 5A; N.C.R., 4 June 1974, p. 6, 24 June 1974, p. 7; *St. Louis Review,* 14 June 1974, p. 4; *Commonweal,* 7 November 1975, p. 516, and 7 May 1976, p. 290; *New York Review of Books,* 26 June 1975, pp. 8–12. The nun in question was Margaret Brennan, I.H.M., the priest-journalist John F. X. Harriott. For Sister Brennan cf. note 27.

47. See N.C.R., 21 February 1975, pp. 1, 4; 17 January 1975, pp. 1, 2; 28 February 1975, p. 2; 30 March 1973, p. 2; *St. Louis Review,* March 7, 1975, p. 4.

48. Paul Seabury in *Commentary,* April 1975, p. 74.

49. Sir Geoffrey Jackson, "Christianity and the Guerrilla," *The Clergy Review,* January 1976, pp. 2–8. See also his remarks in *The Tablet,* 16 July 1977, p. 681.

50. For a critique of the Christian-Marxist dialogue see Dale Vree, *On Synthesizing Marxism and Christianity.*

51. "Faith and Revolution," *Cross Currents,* Spring 1973, pp. 35–47.

52. Mary Kay Suhor, "Church and State in Fidel's Cuba," N.C.R., 24 December 1971, p. 18.

53. Bob Maxwell, "A Proposal to the U.S. Bishops," N.C.R., 13 December 1974, p. 14.

54. Edward Guinan, C.S.P., "Dressed in Wine, Searching for Bread," N.C.R., 3 May 1974, p. 9.

55. Hugo Assmann, *Theology for a Nomad Church,* trans. Paul Burns, pp. 76–77, 83, 124.

56. Segundo, *Liberation of Theology,* trans. John Drury, pp. 111, 170.

57. Michael Harrington, *Fragments of the Century* (New York, 1973), p. 29.

58. Berrigan and Coles, *Geography of Faith,* p. 127.

59. *New Times* (Toronto), 20 November 1977, p. 8.

60. See for example the comments of James P. Sinnott, M.M., in N.C.R., 30 July 1976, p. 18.

61. Gerald O'Collins, S.J., in *The New China: A Catholic Response,* ed. Michael Chu, S.J. pp. 127–33.

62. For citations in this paragraph, see *Gaudium et Spes,* arts. 41, 63, 65, 71, and 39 (*The Documents of Vatican II,* ed. Walter M. Abbott, pp. 241, 271, 273–74, 280–81, 237); and, for the decree on the priesthood, *Presbyterorum Ordinis,* art. 24 (Abbott, p. 546).

63. Grey, *Divine Disobedience,* p. 126. See also *Commonweal,* 15 June 1973, pp. 325–26, and N.C.R., 8 June 1973, pp. 3, 27.

Chapter 8

1. Rosemary Haughton, "A British Eye's View," *Commonweal,* 11 April 1975, pp. 41–43.

2. Dale Vree, "A Fascism in Our Future?" *Worldview,* November 1977, p. 22.

3. Robert Nisbet, *Twilight of Authority,* p. 90.

4. Carolyn Osiek, O.C.S.J., "Reflections on an American Spirituality," *Catholic Mind,* June 1977, p. 26.

5. Rev. Bryan Hehir, quoted in the *St. Louis Review,* 11 June 1976, and 23 December 1977, p. 4.

6. St. Louis *Post-Dispatch,* 30 November 1977, p. 7A.

7. "Church-Labor Ties Debated," N.C.R., 11 November 1977, pp. 1, 6.

8. Traxler, quoted in N.C.R., 26 March 1971, p. 1.

9. See especially John Courtney Murray, *We Hold These Truths.*

10. Gregory Baum, "Is This Trend a Withdrawal?" N.C.R., 8 December 1972, p. 14.

11. Sr. Margaret Rowe in *Commonweal,* 19 May 1972, p. 266.

12. Christopher Dawson, *The Movement of World Revolution,* p. 100.

13. Matthew Fox, O.P., *On Becoming a Musical, Mystical Bear,* pp. 21, 94.

14. "Religious Set Aim: Justice for Poor," N.C.R., 9 December 1977, p. 1.

15. T. S. Eliot, *Notes Toward a Definition of Culture,* p. 158.

16. Francis MacNutt, O.P., quoted in N.C.R., 13 January 1978, p. 3.

17. Gerald Grosh, S.J., "On Commitment to the Poor," *Review for Religious,* July 1977, pp. 540–48.

18. Muriel Spark, *The Abbess of Crewe,* p. 34.

19. Thomas McGowan, F.S.C., "American Theology," *Commonweal,* 30 June 1972, pp. 353–56.

20. Jacques Ellul, *The New Demons,* pp. 26, 199, 210.

21. Osiek, "Reflections," pp. 27–32.

22. See photograph in N.C.R., 9 September 1977, p. 13.

23. Michael True, "The Future of the Catholic Peace Movement," *Commonweal,* 8 March 1974, pp. 14–15.

24. Eugene Bianchi in N.C.R., 23 June 1972, p. 12; 4 August 1972, p. 8; 17 November 1972, p. 13.

25. Sr. Carolyn Field in N.C.R., 24 November 1972, p. 11.

26. Sr. Mary Jerome Johnson in N.C.R., p. 10.

27. See Hitchcock, "The Single-Issue Voter," *Our Sunday Visitor,* 26 September 1976, pp. 1, 4–5.

28. David J. Bowman, S.J., quoted in *St. Louis Review,* 27 October 1972, p. 10.

29. Cynthia Wedel and Herbert Rogers, S.J., quoted in N.C.R., 16 February 1973, p. 21.

30. "Abortion: an Ecumenical Dilemma," *Commonweal,* 30 November 1973, pp. 231–35.

31. Reported in N.C.R., 13 October 1972, p. 3. The McGovern staff member was Mathew Ahmann.

32. Francis X. Murphy, C.SS.R., "Washington Letter," *The Tablet,* 3 April 1976, pp. 333–34. See also Jim Castelli, "A Critical Look at Anti-Abortion Strategy," *The Catholic Virginian,* 14 November 1975.

33. Castelli in the *St. Louis Review,* 12 November 1976, p. 8, and *Commonweal,* 8 December 1976, pp. 780–82. See also Hitchcock, "Prophecy and Politics: Abortion in the Election of 1976," *Worldview,* March 1977, pp. 25–26, 35–37.

34. N.C.R., 30 July 1976, p. 17.

35. Mary Anne Krupsak, quoted in the St. Louis *Post-Dispatch,* 13 July 1976, p. 5A.

36. *Commonweal,* 30 July 1976, p. 484.

37. William Shannon, "Carter and the Bishops," reprinted in the St. Louis *Post-Dispatch,* 8 September 1976, p. 3E.

38. Rev. James Rattigan, quoted by James Deakin in the St. Louis *Post-Dispatch,* 16 September 1976, p. 3C.

39. See the N.C.R., 15 October 1976; *The Wanderer,* 28 October 1976, p. 1 (Religious News Service dispatch); Hitchcock, "Prophecy and Politics."

40. McBrien, quoted by Deakin in the St. Louis *Post-Dispatch,* 16 September 1976, p. 3C.

41. Reported by Thomas W. Ottenad, in the St. Louis *Post-Dispatch,* 7 September 1976, p. 1.

42. See N.C.R., 3 September 1976, p. 2; New Orleans *Clarion-Herald,* 26 August 1976, p. 5; *The Wanderer,* 9 September 1976, p. 7; Hitchcock, "Prophecy and Politics."

43. Rev. "Marty" Peter, New Orleans *Clarion-Herald*, 16 September 1976, p. 7.

44. Quoted in *The Communicator* (Indiana Right-to-Life), March 1977, p. 1.

45. Reported in N.C.R., 23, January 1976, p. 3.

46. St. Mary Paul Ege in N.C.R., 6 December 1974, p. 11.

47. See the New Orleans *Clarion-Herald*, 11 August 1977, pp. 3, 10–11, and 12 January 1978, p. 3; N.C.R., 26 August 1977, pp. 1, 6; *St. Louis Review*, 19 August 1977, p. 12.

48. Ibid.

49. *St. Louis Review*, 11 November 1977, p. 2.

50. *St. Louis Review*, 12 August 1977, p. 4; *The Tablet*, 3 September 1977, p. 853; St. Cloud (Minn.) *Visitor*, 3 November 1977, p. 6 (National Catholic News dispatch).

51. Traxler, quoted in N.C.R., 18 November 1977, p. 5; New Orleans *Clarion-Herald*, 22 December 1977, p. 12. See also N.C.R., 18 April 1975, p. 21.

52. *St. Louis Review*, 25 November 1977, p. 3; N.C.R., 2 December 1977, pp. 1, 2, 4; and 6 January 1978, p. 10; New Orleans *Clarion-Herald*, 3 November 1977, p. 2; St. Louis *Post-Dispatch*, 25 November 1977, p. 9F.

53. Elizabeth J. McCormack, *The Critic*, Summer 1977, pp. 35–36. See also the *New York Times*, 8 January 1973, p. 68, and 22 June 1973, p. 39. *The New Yorker*, 18 December 1971, pp. 121–23.

54. Theodore M. Hesburgh, C.S.C., *New York Times*, 15 January 1977, p. 4.

55. See for example John Hart Ely in *The Yale Law Journal*, April 1973, and Joseph W. Bishop, Jr. in *Commentary*, July 1974, p. 104.

56. Rev. Raymond Decker, "More Christian Than Its Critics," *Commonweal*, 14 February 1975, pp. 384–88.

57. N.C.R., 3 August 1973, p. 17; *St. Louis Review*, 13 June 1975, p. 4; *The Wanderer*, 5 May 1977, p. 1; *Commonweal*, 9 May 1975, pp. 1–2, 102–03. Castelli, "Priests, Nuns, Ministers in Politics," *Commonweal*, 24 June 1977, pp. 398–400. See also the St. Louis *Post-Dispatch*, 15 January 1978, p. 17A.

58. Rev. Charles Curran, "Civil Law and Christian Morality: Abortion and the Churches," *The Clergy Review*, June 1977, pp. 227–42, and April, 1978, pp. 150–52, and "Cooperation: Towards a Revision of the Concept and Its Application," *Linacre Quarterly*, August 1974, pp. 152–67. Cf. Donald J. Keefe, S.J., "Church, State, and Charles Curran," *Communio*, Summer 1977, pp. 114–36.

59. Robert Roger Lebel, S.J., "Cutting Edge for Catholics," N.C.R., 7 October 1977, p. 12. "Scholars Criticize Hospital Directives," N.C.R., 12 June 1973, pp. 3–4. On Knowles see *NCCB-USCC Report*, June 1978, and *Family Planning Perspectives*, Spring 1973.

60. N.C.R., 4 March 1977, p. 4, and 17 June 1977, p. 11.

61. Reported by Charles Horner in *Commentary*, January 1978, p. 68.

62. "Jean Moffatt" (pseud.), "Let's Be Realistic about Population," N.C.R., 24 May 1974, p. 8.

63. Gertrude Himmelfarb, *Lord Acton*, pp. 104–05, 117, 170. *The Correspondence of Lord Acton and Richard Simpson*, ed. Josef L. Altholz *et al.* Edmund Campion (ed.), *Lord Acton and the First Vatican Council*, especially Introduction.

64. Rt. Rev. Stephen Bayne, quoted in E. R. Norman, *Church and Society*, p. 454.

65. Mary Theresa Glynn, R.S.M. See *National Right to Life News*, August 1978, p. 14, and September 1978, p. 10.

66. See for example the N.C.R., 8 October 1976, p. 3, 20 January 1978, p. 2; and 10 February 1978, p. 3; and the *St. Louis Review,* 29 October 1976, p. 16. See editorial in *N.C.R.,* 1 September 1978, p. 14.

67. *St. Louis Review,* 21 October 1977, p. 10. The former priest was Thomas Hinsberg.

68. N.C.R., 14 October 1977, p. 1; 21 October 1977, p. 20; and 18 November 1977, pp. 10–11. A headline in the paper proclaimed "Catholics 'Scared' in Wake of Bishop's Anti-Gay Stand." A vicious personal attack on the bishop, David Maloney, was published by a priest, Justin H. Betzen. See also N.C.R., 5 May 1978, p. 24. The Wichita and St. Paul laws were later repealed by popular vote.

69. Camela G. Lacayo in N.C.R., 15 September 1978, p. 9.

70. Edward P. Hollingshead, reported in *The Register* (Orange, Ca.), 21 October 1977.

71. Leo Pfeffer, "Issues That Divide: the Triumph of Secular Humanism," *Journal of Church and State,* Spring 1977, pp. 203–215.

72. N.C.R., 24 March 1978, p. 5. See comments of James Schall, S.J., N.C.R., 5 May, 1978, p. 13.

73. Janet A. Fitzgerald, O.P., *President's Report, 1973–1974* (Molloy College, Rockville Center, N.Y.), pp. 19–33. The report includes guidelines issued by the State of New York.

74. Daniel Maguire, "Unequal but Fair," *Commonweal,* 14 October 1977, pp. 647–52.

75. St. Louis *Post-Dispatch,* 31 August 1977, p. 1A. *Washington Post,* 19 November 1976. *St. Louis Review,* 14 January 1977, p. 2. New Orleans *Clarion-Herald,* 9 December 1971, p. 1.

76. Rev. Mark Corrigan, reported in the N.C.R., 23 June 1972, p. 20, and 20 September 1974, p. 6.

77. Victoria Mojekwu, quoted in the St. Louis *Post-Dispatch,* 26 June 1975, p. 4C.

78. James Barber, "Mother Teresa's Lap—Good Place to Dump Guilt," N.C.R., 18 June 1976, p. 14.

79. Quoted by George P. Elliott, "The Way We Live Now," *The American Scholar,* Winter 1974–75, p. 132.

80. Reported in the *National Catholic Reporter,* 13 January 1976; 13 February 1976, p. 6; and *Parade,* 4 April 1976, p. 14.

81. Elliott, "The Way We Live Now," *The American Scholar,* Winter 1974–75, p. 132.

82. Christopher Lasch, *Haven in a Heartless World: the Family Besieged.*

83. Daniel Berrigan, Robert Coles, *Geography of Faith,* pp. 44–45, 51–52; N.C.R., 19 October 1973, p. 6.

84. *Liberty and Justice for All, Atlanta Hearing—"The Family"* (National Conference of Catholic Bishops, 1976), pp. 3–8. The dialogue was between Robert Staples and the Most Rev. Carroll Dozier.

85. Philip Rieff, *Triumph,* p. 55; Philip Rieff, *Fellow Teachers,* pp. 56, 113, 210.

Chapter 9

1. *Unitatis Redintegratio,* art. 3 (*The Documents of Vatican II,* ed. Walter M. Abbott, p. 346). For the rest of this paragraph, see also *Unitatis Redintegratio,* art.

22 (Abbott, p. 364); *Lumen Gentium,* arts. 13–14, 8, 17 (Abbott, pp. 32–33, 22–23, 36); the decree on missions, *Ad Gentes* (Abbott, pp. 584–630); and the declaration on religious freedom, *Dignitatis Humanae,* art. 1 (Abbott, pp. 676–77).

2. Rosemary Ruether, *Faith and Fratricide.*

3. John T. Pawlikowski, O.S.M., in *Commonweal,* 31 January 1975, pp. 364–66; N.C.R., 11 May 1975, pp. 11, 14; 21 April 1978, p. 11.

4. Henry Siegman, "Jews and Christians—Beyond Brotherhood Week," *Worldview,* December 1975, p. 35.

5. Michael Wyschogrod, "The Future of Jewish-Christian Relations," *Face to Face* (Anti-Defamation League of B'nai B'rith), Spring 1976, pp. 19–20.

6. Bede Griffiths, O.S.B., in *The Tablet,* 5 November 1977, pp. 1053–54; 28 May 1977, pp. 512–13; see also his *Return to the Center.*

7. David Steindl-Rast, O.S.B., in N.C.R., 11 November 1977, pp. 7, 12.

8. See *Gaudium et Spes,* arts. 10 and 22 (Abbott, pp. 208, 220).

9. Frank Wessling in *The Critic,* May–June, 1974, pp. 71–72, 74.

10. James H. Ebner, *God Present as Mystery,* pp. 64, 68, 147.

11. Matthew Fox, *On Becoming a Musical, Mystical Bear,* p. 115.

12. William Bausch, *Positioning—Belief in the Mid-Seventies,* pp. 63, 101.

13. Robley Edward Whitson, quoted in N.C.R., 30 March 1973, p. 4. See also his *The Coming Convergence of World Religions.*

14. Quoted in *Commonweal,* 15 October 1971, p. 65.

15. Quoted in N.C.R., 17 December 1971, p. 4.

16. Gregory Baum, ed., *Journeys,* pp. 41, 43, 45.

17. Gerard S. Sloyan, "The Religious Shape of the Twenty-first Century," *Face to Face* (Anti-Defamation League), Spring 1976, pp. 16–17.

18. Most Rev. Carroll T. Dozier, "My Vision," N.C.R., 17 March 1978, p. 10.

19. Ebner, *God Present,* pp. 26, 29.

20. David S. Toolan, S.J., in *Commonweal,* 15 November 1975, pp. 128, 130; 9 November 1973, pp. 138–39.

21. Harvey Cox, *The Seduction of the Spirit,* p. 242. This book is the most telling expression yet of the syncretist mentality.

22. Ibid. pp. 327–28.

23. Diane Kennedy Pike, quoted in the St. Louis *Post-Dispatch,* 15 November 1976, p. 2D.

24. Fox, *Musical,* pp. 125, 127–28. Cf. R. C. Zaehner, *Our Savage God,* pp. 10–11.

25. Philip Rieff, *Triumph of the Therapeutic,* pp. 21–22, 27, 120, 241; Philip Rieff, *Fellow Teachers,* pp. 49, 67, 135, 184–85.

26. Fox, "Self-Denial Can Make You Selfish," *U.S. Catholic,* February 1978, pp. 37–39.

27. See N.C.R., 18 June 1971, p. 4A; 12, November 1971, pp. 3–4; 19 October 1973, p. 7; 6 May 1977, p. 21. The priest was the Rev. William Nerin.

28. Michael True, "A People's Parish," *Commonweal,* 5 August 1977, pp. 496–98.

29. Assmann, *Theology for a Nomad Church,* p. 124.

30. " 'Godspell' Good Drama, Good Theology," *St. Louis Review,* 28 July 1972, p. 7.

31. Charles Norris Cochrane, *Christianity and Classical Culture,* p. 278.

32. Gray, *Divine Disobedience,* p. 96.

33. Robert Hovda, "Bravo for Bernstein," N.C.R., 24 September 1971, p. 16.

34. Jack Gottlieb, "Bernstein's 'Mass' is Jewish," St. Louis *Post-Dispatch*, 26 September 1971, p. 5C.

35. John J. Gallen, S.J., "The Mass—Successful Liturgy?" *America*, 2 October 1971, p. 229.

36. Frederick Franck, quoted in the N.C.R., 15 February 1974, p. 12.

37. Peter L. Berger and Richard John Neuhaus, eds., *Against the World, For the World*, p. 57.

38. See the *New Catholic Encyclopedia*, III, 339–40 ("Catholicity").

39. May Moriarty, "A New Face for Baptism," *Today's Parish*, 6 February 1975, pp. 6–7.

40. Virginia Sloyan, reported by Naomi Burton Stone in *The Critic*, Winter, 1976, p. 10.

41. Michael Warren, "Youth Makes Its Ministry," N.C.R., 13 August 1976, p. 11.

42. Dennis Geaney, quoted in N.C.R., 12 May 1978, p. 5.

43. Rev. Daniel Coughlin, quoted in the *St. Louis Review*, 26 November 1976, p. 4.

44. James Empereur, S.J., quoted in the N.C.R., 20 December 1974, p. 18.

45. Ebner's *God Present as Mystery* is a notable instance.

46. *Abbey Press Christian Family Catalogue* (St. Meinrad, Ind.), Winter 1977.

47. "The Dameans," in the New Orleans *Clarion-Herald*, 19 August 1976, p. 15.

48. Rev. Joseph T. Nolan, "A Proposal to Put Arts in Celebration," N.C.R., 6 July 1973, p. 9.

49. Fox, *Musical*, pp. 150–51.

50. Valerie Hendy, S.L., "Bob Dylan—A Prophet Returns," N.C.R., 26 April 1974, p. 9.

51. Patrick J. Quinn, quoted in N.C.R., 17 May 1974, p. 15.

52. Raymond Schroth, S.J., "Journalism and Integrity," *Commonweal*, 7 November 1975, p. 531.

53. John Deedy, quoted in *Worldview*, March, 1977.

54. Charles Sullivan, quoted in the St. Louis *Post-Dispatch*, 5 April 1972, p. 24E.

55. Murphy, "The Fifth Roman Synod," *The Tablet*, 22 October 1977, pp. 1022–23.

56. Clifford Longley, "Bridgehead," *The Tablet*, 6 August 1977, p. 738. Longley is religious correspondent for the prestigious London *Times*.

57. Langdon Gilkey, *Catholicism Confronts Modernity*, already discussed.

58. Report by Bill Kenkelen in the N.C.R., 24, March 1978, p. 20.

59. See for example a typical "Catholic" novel of the postconciliar period, Thomas Fleming's *The Sandbox Tree* pp. 404 and Epilogue.

60. Don Jardin, "Jerry Brown: 'Basically Catholic,' " N.C.R., 2 July 1976, p. 3. Also N.C.R., 4 March 1977, p. 1.

61. Murphy, "Washington Letter," *The Tablet*, 3 April 1976, p. 333.

62. Rev. Thomas D. Corrigan in *The Boston Pilot*, 11 April 1970, p. 11. Reprinted (as an advertisement) in the St. Louis *Post-Dispatch*, 1 November 1971, p. 8A.

63. John Grigg, "Poor White Fantasy Figure," *Spectator*, 27 August 1977, p. 2.

64. Christopher Derrick, "Confitebor Tibi in Guitarra?" *The Wanderer,* 15 July 1976.

65. Vree, "A Fascism in Our Future?" *Worldview,* November 1977, p. 21.

66. Reported in *The Tablet,* 17 September 1977, p. 899.

67. "Judge Not," *The Tablet,* 23 July 1977, p. 691.

68. See for example Vidal, "Art, Sex, and Isherwood," *New York Review of Books,* 9 December 1976, pp. 10, 12, 14, 16, 18.

69. See Hitchcock, "Dynamics of Popular Intellectual Change."

70. *Humanist Manifestoes I and II,* pp. 15–16.

71. Paul Kurtz, quoted in N.C.R., 11 January 1974, p. 6.

72. Manifestoes quoted in *Christian Order* (London), September 1976, pp. 553–56.

73. R. R. Palmer, *Catholics and Unbelievers in Eighteenth Century France,* pp. 8–10, 12–15, 21–22, 26–27, 47, 178, 204.

74. Kurtz in *The Alternative* (now *The American Spectator*), June–July 1977, pp. 33–34.

75. Quoted in *The Tablet,* 28 May 1977, p. 519.

76. Griffiths in *The Tablet,* 8 May 1976, pp. 449–50; 11 September 1976, pp. 880–81.

77. T. S. Eliot, *Notes Toward a Definition of Culture,* p. 10.

78. Leslie Dewart in *The Critic,* Winter, 1976, p. 30.

79. Ann Patrick Ware, S.L., quoted in the New Orleans *Clarion-Herald,* 15 December 1977, p. 3.

80. Philip Scharper, "Change within Change," *Commonweal,* 8 December 1972, pp. 223–25.

81. Padovano in *The Critic,* March–April 1974, pp. 13–19.

82. David Gourlay, quoted in Philip Rieff, *The Triumph of the Therapeutic,* p. 252.

83. *The New Yorker,* 24 October 1977, p. 181.

84. Daniel Bell, *The Cultural Contradictions of Capitalism,* pp. 13–14, 168.

85. *The Church and the Catholic and the Spirit of the Liturgy,* trans. Ada Lane, p. 205.

Chapter 10

1. Leigh Johrdahl in N.C.R., 21 January 1972, p. 10.

2. *New York Review of Books,* 25 January 1973, pp. 30, 32.

3. For a more detailed discussion of some of these needs see James Hitchcock, *Recovery of the Sacred.*

4. *The Catholic Journalist,* June 1978, pp. 4, 7.

5. *St. Louis Review,* 9 June 1978, p. 14.

6. See Dean M. Kelley, *Why the Conservative Churches Are Growing.*

7. See James Hitchcock, *On the Present Position of Catholics in America.*

Bibliography

Abbott, Walter M., S.J., ed. *The Documents of Vatican II.* New York: Herder and Herder/Association Press, 1966.

Altholz, Josef L. et al. *The Correspondence of Lord Acton and Richard Simpson.* Cambridge, England: Cambridge University Press, 1975.

Anderson, Quentin. *The Imperial Self: An Essay in American Literary and Cultural History.* New York: Knopf, 1971.

Assmann, Hugo. *Theology for a Nomad Church.* Translated by Paul Burns. Maryknoll, N.Y.: Orbis Books, 1976.

Baum, Gregory, ed. *Journeys: The Impact of Personal Experience on Religious Thought.* New York: Paulist Press, 1976.

————*Religion and Alienation.* New York: Paulist Press, 1976.

Bausch, William. *Positioning—Belief in the Mid-Seventies.* Notre Dame, Ind.: Fides Press, 1975.

Bell, Daniel. *The Cultural Contradictions of Capitalism.* New York: Basic Books, 1976.

Berger, Peter. *The Sacred Canopy.* Garden City, N.Y.: Doubleday, 1967.

————*A Rumor of Angels.* Garden City, N.Y.: Doubleday, 1969.

Berger, Peter L., and Neuhaus, Richard John, eds. *Against the World, For the World.* New York: Seabury Press, 1976.

Berman, Harold J. *The Interaction of Law and Religion.* Nashville: Abingdon Press, 1974.

Bernstein, Marcelle. *The Nuns.* Philadelphia: Lippincott, 1976.

Berrigan, Daniel. *The Dark Night of Resistance.* Garden City, N.Y.: Doubleday, 1971.

Berrigan, Daniel, and Coles, Robert. *The Geography of Faith.* Boston: Beacon Press, 1971.

Berrigan, Philip. *Prison Journals.* New York: Holt, Rinehart & Winston, 1970.

Besret, Bernard, O.C.S.O. *Tomorrow a New Church.* Translated by Matthew J. O'Connell. New York: Paulist Press, 1974.

Brennan, Margaret, I.H.M. *New Visions: New Roles for Women in the Church.* Washington: Leadership Conference of Women Religious of the United States, 1975.

Burton, Katherine. *Chaminade, Apostle of Mary.* Milwaukee: Bruce, 1949.

Campion, Edmund, ed. *Lord Acton and the First Vatican Council.* Sydney: Catholic Theological Faculty, 1975.

Chu, Michael, S.J., ed. *The New China: A Catholic Response.* New York: Paulist Press, 1977.

Cochrane, Charles Norris. *Christianity and Classical Culture.* London: Oxford University Press, 1944.

Cogley, John. *A Canterbury Tale: Experience and Reflections, 1916–1976.* New York: Seabury Press, 1976.

Cox, Harvey. *The Seduction of the Spirit.* New York: Simon and Schuster, 1973.

Dawson, Christopher. *The Movement of World Revolution.* New York: Sheed & Ward, 1959.

Doherty, Dennis, J. *Divorce and Remarriage: Resolving a Catholic Dilemma.* St. Meinrad, Ind.: Abbey Press, 1974.

Dominian, Jack. *The Church and the Sexual Revolution.* London: Darton, Longman and Todd, 1971.

Ebner, James H. *God Present as Mystery.* Winona, Minn.: St. Mary's College Press, 1976.

Eliot, T. S. *Notes Toward a Definition of Culture.* New York: Harcourt Brace, 1949.

Ellul, Jacques. *The New Demons.* New York: Seabury Press, 1975.

Fitzgerald, Janet A. *President's Report, 1973–1974.* Rockville Center, N.Y.: Molloy College.

Fleming, Thomas. *The Sandbox Tree.* New York: Morrow, 1970.

Fox, Matthew, O.P. *On Becoming a Musical, Mystical Bear.* New York: Harper & Row, 1972.

Gilkey, Langdon. *Catholicism Confronts Modernity: A Protestant View.* New York: Seabury Press, 1975.

Goddijn, Walter. *The Deferred Revolution.* New York: Elsvier, 1975.

Guardini, Romano. *The Church and the Catholic and The Spirit of the Liturgy.* Translated by Ada Lane. New York: Sheed & Ward, 1953.

Gray, Francine du Plessix. *Divine Disobedience.* New York: Knopf, 1970.

Griffiths, Bede. *Return to the Center.* Springfield, Ill.: Templegate, 1976.

Harrington, Michael. *Fragments of the Century.* New York: Saturday Review Press, 1974.

Harvey, Robert. *The Restless Heart.* Grand Rapids, Mich.: Eerdmans, 1973.

Heer, Frederick. *The London Times History of Our Times.* Edited by Marcus Cunliffe. New York: Norton, 1971.

Himmelfarb, Gertrude. *Lord Acton.* Chicago: University of Chicago Press, 1952.

Hitchcock, James. *The Decline and Fall of Radical Catholicism.* New York: Herder and Herder, 1971.

——*The Recovery of the Sacred.* New York: Seabury Press, 1974.

——*On the Present Position of Catholics in America.* New York: The National Committee of Catholic Laymen, 1978.

Humanist Manifestoes I and II. Buffalo, N.Y.: Prometheus, 1973.

Imfeld, Al. *China as Model for Development.* Translated by Matthew J. O'Connell. Maryknoll, N.Y.: Orbis Books, 1976.

Kelley, Dean M. *Why Conservative Churches Are Growing.* New York: Harper & Row, 1972.

Kosnik, Anthony, ed. *Human Sexuality: New Directions in American Catholic Thought.* New York: Paulist Press, 1977.

Lasch, Christopher. *Haven in a Heartless World: The Family Beseiged.* New York: Basic Books, 1977.

Loisy, Alfred. *The Gospel and the Church.* Philadelphia: Fortress Press, 1976; first printing, 1903.

Lukacs, John. *The Passing of the Modern Age.* New York: Harper & Row, 1970.

McCauley, Michael, ed. *On the Run.* Chicago: Thomas More, 1974.

Murray, John Courtney. *We Hold These Truths.* New York: Sheed & Ward, 1961.

New Catholic Encyclopedia. New York: McGraw, 1967.

Nisbet, Robert. *Twilight of Authority.* New York: Oxford University Press, 1975.

Norman, E. R. *Church and Society.* Oxford: Clarendon Press, 1976.

Palmer, R. R. *Catholics and Unbelievers in Eighteenth Century France.* Princeton, N.J.: Princeton University Press, 1939.

Pope John XXIII. *Journal of a Soul.* Translated by Dorothy White. New York: McGraw, 1965.

Reardon, Bernard M.G. *Roman Catholic Modernism.* Stanford, Calif.: Stanford University Press, 1970.

Ruether, Rosemary. *Faith and Fratricide.* New York: Seabury Press, 1974.

Rieff, Philip. *The Triumph of the Therapeutic.* New York: Harper Torchbooks, 1968.

————*Fellow Teachers.* New York: Harper & Row, 1973.

Rosenberg, Harold. *Art on the Edge.* New York: Macmillan, 1975.

Saint Theresa of Avila. *Interior Castle.* Translated and edited by E. Allison Peers. Garden City, N.Y.: Doubleday, 1961.

Schoof, Mark, O.P. *A Survey of Catholic Theology.* Translated by N. D. Smith. New York, Paulist Press, 1970.

Segundo, Juan Luis. *Liberation of Theology.* Translated by John Drury. Maryknoll, N.Y.: Orbis Books, 1976.

Spark, Muriel. *The Abbess of Crewe.* New York: Viking Press, 1974.

Steinmetz, Urban G. *The Sexual Christian.* St. Meinrad, Inc.; Abbey Press, 1972.

Taft, Kendall B., ed. *College Readings in Contemporary Thought.* Boston: Houghton Mifflin, 1929.

Trilling, Lionel. *The Liberal Imagination: Essays on Literature and Society.* Garden City, N.Y.: Doubleday, 1953.

Vidler, Alec R. *A Variety of Catholic Modernists.* Cambridge, England: Cambridge University Press, 1907.

Vitz, Paul C. *Psychology as Religion.* Grand Rapids, Mich.: Eerdmans, 1977.

Voegelin, Eric. *The New Science of Politics.* Chicago: University of Chicago Press, 1972.

Vree, Dale. *On Synthesizing Marxism and Christianity.* New York: Wiley-Interscience, 1976.

Waugh, Evelyn. *Put Out More Flags.* Boston: Little Brown, 1942.

Whitson, Robley Edward. *The Coming Convergence of World Religions.* New York: Paulist-Newman, 1971.

Wilkes, Paul. *These Priests Stay.* New York: Simon and Schuster, 1974.

Zaehner, R. C. *Our Savage God: The Perverse Use of Eastern Thought.* New York: Sheed & Ward, 1975.